At any rate, when a subject is highly controversial — and any question about sex is that — one cannot hope to tell the truth. One can only show how one came to hold the opinion one does hold. One can only give one's audience the chance of drawing their own conclusions as they observe the limitations, the prejudices, the idiosyncrasies of the speaker.

— Virginia Woolf, *A Room of One's Own*

The Ship That Sailed Into the Living Room

SONIA JOHNSON

The Ship That Sailed Into the Living Room

SEX AND INTIMACY RECONSIDERED

WILDFIRE BOOKS

Estancia, New Mexico 87016

Inquiries about speaking engagements, workshops, books, and tapes of speeches should be directed to: Wildfire Books, Star Route 1, Box 55, Estancia, NM 87016, (505) 384-2500.

Inquiries should be addressed to:
Wildfire Books, Star Route 1, Box 55, Estancia, NM 87016
(505) 384-2500.

Cover art and design: Rebecca Carpenter

Cover photograph: Pat Stroud

Printed in the United States of America

First Printing September, 1991

Library of Congress Cataloging-in-Publication Data

Johnson, Sonia.
    The ship that sailed into the living room: sex and intimacy
reconsidered / Sonia Johnson.
        p.   cm.
    Includes index.
    ISBN: 1-877617-07-5 $12.95
    1. Interpersonal relations. 2. Intimacy (Psychology) 3. Lesbian
couples — United States. 4. Sex customs — United States. I. Title
HM132.J643 1991   91-15337
306.76'63 — dc20   CIP

ISBN   1-877617-07-5 Hardcover
          1-877617-06-7 Softcover

THANKS

To Christine Champion for once again being intrepid enough to co-publish with me.

To my editor, Caissa Wilmer, for not matronizing me by mincing words.

To Sally Tatnall and Phyllis Balcerzak for courageously and unfalteringly pursuing their vision of women's power.

To the following women of Anchorage, Alaska, for their guidance in the first major overhaul of the manuscript:

Chris Blankenship	Rachel King
Ann Boudreaux	Susan Klein
Karen Carlisle	Rose Levno
Deb DeProspero	Ann Milton
Lucille Frey	Rena Mulcahy
Janna Gingras	Shari Olander
Mary Lu Harle	Mia Oxley
Patricia Hooper	Barbara Soule
Lisa Jamieson	Sandra Tetnowski

To all the women who have so generously given me their ideas about relation Ships at festivals, workshops, and speeches, and by letter and phone, over the last two years. The book is immeasurably better for their contributions.

To Chris, who, even if she lost both arms, both legs, her eyesight, and her hearing, would roll happily about on the floor shouting, "Seize the day!"

CONTENTS

Ship Ahoy

S ometime during the day that Susan and I decided to have a relationship, we heard a knock at the door. Rushing from different places in the house to answer it, we opened the door together. To our amazed delight, there on our doorstep rode a magnificent ship. No ordinary ocean-going vessel this but a luxury liner tiered with staterooms, looking for all the world like a great floating wedding cake. "Our relation Ship!"[1] we cried joyously in unison.

We could hardly believe our senses, but there it was on our front porch, its fresh white paint and miles of polished brass sparkling in the sunshine, its rows of spiffily uniformed crewmen standing at attention on its gleaming decks, and its regal flags triumphant against the sky.

Giddy with excitement, we stepped back and watched it sail through the hall and up the stairs into our living room where it put down its mighty anchor and came majestically to rest. We walked reverently around it, hand in hand, gazing up at it in awe from every angle. One fact was certain: Neither of us had ever before seen such a Ship, certainly not

---

[1] I've chosen to make relation Ship two words when I use it as a noun and one word—relationShip—when I use it as a verb, adjective, or adverb. I know this choice may be confusing to others but for some reason it satisfies me. This clarification is for those who would otherwise be annoyed at what they perceived as my carelessness and inconsistency.

in the living rooms of anyone we knew. Proudly we congratulated ourselves on having one of the grandest relation Ships in the world, a Ship so superior to everyone else's that we were flooded with pity for the rest of human kind. How disappointing it must be to enter one's drawing room every day to be confronted by a mere yacht. How humiliating to live—as so many of our friends did—with sooty tugboats chugging about their living rooms. How tragic that even more multitudes existed with lowly canoes moored to their lamps, or life preservers bobbing under their coffee tables. Surveying our glorious Ship, we were deeply grateful for our good fortune.

But unbeknownst to us, even as it was steaming up Second Street looking for our address, our Ship had known it would have the upper hand in our home. It was well aware that from birth both Susan and I had been profoundly socialized to believe that a relation Ship was the one acquisition absolutely essential to our happiness. It also knew that by the time it sailed at last into our lives we would be so saturated with this assumption that we would feel it as a fact of life: Natural, inevitable, unarguable. We would so passionately believe that we *must* have it that a Ship could do with us just about as it pleased.

And it did. The instant it dropped anchor in our living room it began bossing us around.

"Now hear this! Now hear this!" the officer on the bridge shouted at us through his megaphone. "Don't just stand there gawking. Get to work on your relation Ship!"

We had expected this, of course, knowing that serious responsibilities accompanied Ships. So I dutifully fell to and began scraping a stray barnacle off one side of the hull while

2

Susan ran way around to the other side and began polishing the brass.

I waved at her every once in a while, whenever I caught a glimpse of her—or at least when I thought it was her; there was so much Ship between us I could barely make her out—and sometimes I was sure I could see her waving back. So what if the huge hull of the Ship prevented us from communicating with each other? What if we weren't able to be close or alone together? We expected to have to make sacrifices for a good relation Ship, and we were prepared to do whatever was necessary to keep ours riding at anchor forever in our house.

As it turned out, we were never to be close or alone together again. Unbelievably plastic, our Ship changed shapes to stay between us from that moment on. Becoming short and stubby, it sat between us in the car, or flattening itself out, separated us on walks, issuing commands the while.

But stretched out long and thin and lying between us in bed it was particularly dictatorial. "Now hear this!" the officer on the bridge began shouting at us almost at once. "You two had better have sex tonight. Sex is your Ship's basic survival need. So if you don't want it to sail out of your lives, rip those clothes off and start moving!"

Thus terrorized, we made love. Without asking ourselves whether we really felt like it, to keep the Ship happy we made love.

Equally compliant about its hundreds of other demands, we lived together, slept together every night, spent most of our spare time together, compromised and negotiated. At its command, we ceased being individuals and became instead one entity all-too-significantly called "a couple."

We stopped asking ourselves what we really wanted, how we genuinely felt. Instead we asked what would be best for our Ship, how we could keep it happy and safe and permanently ours. Like so many others, we had fallen under the deep hypnotic spell of the voice from the bridge.

Though Susan and I were regarded as one entity by our relation Ship, I was of course always only me. Trapped in my own skin, I was never Susan for even a moment—never thought with her mind, never felt with her heart. So this is my story—as it must be—not Susan's.

Nevertheless, I never forget as line after line of my writing focuses on my experience that Susan was living her own story at the same time every bit as passionately and courageously as I felt I was living mine. I want to be very clear that though I cannot attempt to portray her point of view—except when I quote her directly—I accept its validity and respect it utterly. I think, however, that it would be both fair and useful to say that this was probably not the experiment she would have chosen at this time. She was examining other—to her more disturbing and urgent—areas of experience and facing other very difficult facts. Since her world was spinning anyway, I surmise that she may have wished for stability in her life with me.

But this is only a guess. Despite our discussions, I have little real notion how she currently views that time in any of its particulars. If she were to write her impressions, they might bear little or no resemblance to mine. But like witnesses to an accident whose accounts wildly diverge, both of us would be telling the truth.

For many reasons, both parties in a relation Ship rarely want to investigate the same possibilities at the same time. This spells pain, and there was pain aplenty at 3318 Second

Street South that year. It intensified each time I wrenched at the Ship's anchor and Susan strove to keep her equilibrium on the pitching deck.

Though we are each doing well now, in retrospect my heart aches for us both and blames neither. Above all, in writing the following account of my life and thought, I want to avoid the implication that the one in a relation Ship who chooses change in a way and at a moment that frightens the other is somehow smarter, righter, nobler, or more advanced than the one who, bravely confronting a dangerous and uncertain world every day, tries to salvage what happiness is at hand. But neither do I wish to suggest that the rebel is less sensitive or compassionate or loving. People are on their own individual paths, paths that are non-parallel and non-linear. Words such as "ahead" or "more advanced," and "behind" or "less advanced"—linear concepts—are meaningless on the infinite spiral that is our lives.

The most accurate judgment I can make, therefore, is that the time came when Susan and I chose different tasks. What task she chose is hers to name. As for me, after half a lifetime of stuporous loyalty to Ship dogma, I began to stir in my relationsleep. Some glimmering of my servitude began to filter through the blinds of my understanding, some budding suspicion that the Ship wasn't the Ark of the Covenant after all but just a big bossy boat. A big bossy *menacing* boat. Realizing this, I chose mutiny.

PART I

ROCKING THE BOAT

1

Love's Language Lost

B y the time I began to rebel against the Ship, Susan and I had loved each other and lived together under its auspices for five years. Despite the Ship's constant inter-ference, they had been rich productive years, years filled with feminist passion and activity. Of course, we had occasionally had problems, sometimes serious ones, but we had always come through them with our commitment to each other and our relation Ship intact. If I had been asked, I would have insisted that we were happy together and that everything was going fine—certainly better than with most other couples I knew.

It was during our fifth year together that I began to be aware that I was suffering on some deeper, less visible level than I'd noticed before, that I was in a subtler, more constant sort of pain than my usual "having relationship problems" discomfort.

In fact, I sensed that something was seriously awry in my inner life long before I was ready to confront it, articulate it, and do something about it. Resolutely elusive, this something seethed underground for months like a deep volcanic storm. In transforming my internal landscape, its tremors shook loose old habits of thought and behavior, thrusting them at odd moments up under my nose for inspection.

This debris began to break through the smooth surface of my life so frequently in fact that I was constantly being awakened from my relationsleep. In this uncomfortable waking state I had scary premonitions that whatever was seething at my center was destined to become my spiritual equivalent of the Pacific Ring of Fire. Still, it was nearly a year from the early shiftings of my continental plates to my first conscious clue that my relationShip assumptions were the deepest and most dangerous of all my programmed beliefs.

My inner Wise Woman once again played guide in this process, prodding me into the maze of my conditioning about love. Though in retrospect I often wished she hadn't had to lead me to understanding via such labyrinthine ways as she did, I always had to acknowledge that as usual she had known what she was doing.

At that point in my growing intimacy with my Wise Woman, I understood her modus operandi. Early on in my feminist life—that is, in my more wakeful state—she had responded to my wordless plea for a true mirror, some way to *see* who I was, to understand who I was becoming, what was happening to me.

Because more than anything I wanted to be free of all the nonsense that separated me from my Self, and because I had got such a late start, I pressed her to reveal it to me rapidly, even—and particularly—when I didn't want to know it. I promised her that if she would keep trying until she found some way to get through to me no matter what barriers I threw up to thwart her, I would take her hints seriously and listen until I got her message.

Taking me at my word, she had spent a decade devising more, and ever more cunning, ways of getting my attention. Her methods, in fact, had become more ingenious in direct proportion to the terror-quotient of what she had to reveal to me. Earlier in my life she had realized that if she confronted me head on with difficult facts, chances were good that out of fear I would deny and resist. So she had perfected ways of sidling unthreateningly right up to my mind's window before I noticed.

Now that I was determined above all else to be free, and the truths about the Ship that I was begging her to deliver up to me were the most frightening truths of all, my Wise Woman had an even more difficult task. For the past many months she had probably been unimaginably oblique with her hints and clues in an effort not to terrify me back into denial coma.

Finally, however, she prevailed upon me to take my first step into the complex puzzle of relation Ships. What I couldn't know as I did this was that I would never be able to turn back to my old beliefs for comfort and reassurance; that no matter how alien or lonely the uncharted territory before me appeared, it was now my home.

She often cracks my defenses with language, my Wise Woman, knowing that I'll pay attention to words when nothing else can reach me. Now she did it again, alerting me to the thorough distaste I had developed for the language of love. Soon, in nearly every variety of social interaction, I found myself listening greedily to love talk—at least to its simpler, less threatening details.

I had been an English teacher and was by this time a writer. I knew that language, as symbol, determines much of the nature and quality of our experience. I had been seriously

11

dissatisfied and frustrated with available language for a long time, for most of my life it seemed. As soon as feminist consciousness struck me, however, men's language fairly appalled me. Then as a Lesbian, I was even more confounded by the words we had to describe loved ones and loving. More than ever I longed for womanspeech, subtle, lusty, holy words for our ways of being together. And what stiff, angular, bureaucratic sounds did I have at my disposal? "Partners"—dry as a business deal, dusty as a round-up at the Flying Diamond corral; "*life* partner"—dull and heavy, an emotional thud;[1] "mate" or "life mate"—a reproductive necessity or a spouse (and isn't "spouse" a pain?) or a fellow sailor or convict; "sweetheart" and "honey"—dead from overuse; "roommate"—don't be alarmed, we're just sorority sisters; "significant other"—jargony and shallow; "particular friend"—only insiders know she isn't my *fussy* friend; "posslqu" (person of same sex living in same quarters)—the census' version of roommate; "companion"—a paid employee; "lovesharer" (from *A Door Into Ocean*)—too hard to say, and some of us can't say "share" any more for any reason.

I listened to the limited and uninspired ways we introduced one another to friends: This is my squeeze (or my special squeeze), for instance, or my yummycake—evidence of the lengths to which we were driven to try to convey the sweetness and playfulness of the experience. Evidence of the depth of our failure.

---

[1] Karen in my workshop at the Michigan Womyn's Music Festival in 1989 said: "I use the term 'life partner' to mean that we are partners only so long as there is life in the relationship."

A group of us were lamenting at dinner one night in Illinois that matters of the heart and spirit are almost inexpressible in men's language. As we were deploring that there seems no way to talk about ourselves that has any integrity, one of the women at the table offered "heartfriend" as a beginning in thinking and speaking of loved ones in a more authentic mode. Across from her another dinner guest chimed in, "Some Native Americans I know say, 'This is my heartsong.'" Lovely, I thought. But the "my" troubled me.

I was at the place in my life where I could no longer say "my" anybody—"my" children, "my" friend. Though I was to discover that it still maintained a firm position in my behavior, by this time the assumption of ownership was theoretically unacceptable to me. But that night, thinking about how to avoid possessiveness in love titles, I concluded that it would probably require more words than usual, probably longer names than are conventional in English, names that sound Indian or Eskimo, aboriginal.

"How about, 'This is Mary, the woman who makes my heart sing'"? I proposed. "Or better, because it omits 'makes': 'This is Mary to whom my heart sings'"?

"Imagine introducing a woman in that way to the president of this university!" we laughed.

But it was the designation "lover"—exclusively amorous and sexual—that I found most distasteful. I began to notice that in conversation I circumvented it in a dozen ways. In informal introductions to other Lesbians, for instance, instead of saying, "This is my lover, Susan," I might say, "This is Susan, the woman I love." I couldn't bring myself to say "lover" in *any* context.

At first I worried that this antipathy to "lover" might signal homophobia, that perhaps on some level I was ashamed of being a Lesbian. Maybe I didn't want to come right out and admit that I had made the choice to love women in every way.

So what did it matter that I was talking freely and publicly about my predilection for women, for their empathy and compassion, their emotional sophistication and availability, their integrated right/left brain thought and behavior, their softness and curves fashioned around a core as clear and melodic as crystal? I knew that homophobia—like all bigotry—reveals itself in sneaky ways. Not liking the word "lover" was sneaky enough to be one of those ways.

Still, that I was harboring much homophobia in my breast seemed unlikely when I began to look at my aversion to the word "lover" from other angles. As soon as I did, I recognized it for the prime propaganda purveyor that it is. Pretending to be about love, it is really about sex. When in introducing a woman friend, I announce, "This is my lover," all that others actually know is that I am having sex with her. The kind, amount, and quality of whatever feelings I might have for her are not only not communicated but are not meant to be. It is the sex part that is important.

Others—equating love and sex as the word programs them to—may assume that I feel mostly warm and happy about her, and that may be true. It is just as likely to be the case, however, that I am not feeling total delight about her or that I may be at the point of breakup and full of misery, confusion, bitterness, or anger, and feeling no love at all. Or my feelings about her might lie anywhere in between. But neither they nor I will be enlightened, and all of us will be confounded, by the word "lover."

Because "lover" can only tell what is happening between two people in bed (or at least what the world *thinks* is happening) but nothing of consequence about their feelings or perceptions or the rest of their behavior—all crucial to love—the word "lover" doesn't mean "lover" at all. It means, simply, "sexer."

I considered a two-faced word like "lover" as dangerous as any other double agent. Pretending to be committed to our happiness, it is actually bent upon preventing our well-being. It is an example of the doublespeak that menstream convention has made of language, preventing our communicating either with ourselves or others. A calculated misuse of terms that blanks out reason, obscuring our true condition and confusing us about what we are actually experiencing. Every time we say the word "lover" when we really mean "sexer," we reprogram ourselves to believe the nonsense that love *means* sex and that therefore sex, not love, is the core of a relation Ship.

I could see that perhaps one reason the officer on the bridge might want to confuse us so utterly was because otherwise we might start asking such hazardous questions as, "What is sex? What is love? What, for pity's sake, is a *relation Ship?* Could what we are experiencing right now on this planet be the *ultimate?* What is possible between and among us?"

While I knew that such questions were dangerous because they frightened me, I also had a hunch that these were the easy ones, that there were other questions about love and sex just over my mental horizon that were going to drop by one day and scare me a whole lot worse. Fortunately I didn't know then that they were going to scare me half to death.

I wondered often in those early days of meditating upon "lover" why heterosexual men had set up conventions that demanded that everyone specify who their sex partner was,

15

and why they were so earnest about adhering to them. I asked myself if just because men seemed to find this labelling so critical, women had necessarily to follow suit and announce who we were being sexual with, too. I doubted that we had many of the same reasons that men had for this puzzling behavior, and therefore wondered mightily why, man-like, we were proclaiming, "This is my lover," meaning, "This is the woman I'm having sex with. I may also love her—whatever that means—but that, as you know, is irrelevant."

As most women would agree despite society's massive propagandizing, I thought then that sexuality was far more inclusive and encompassing than mere genital manipulation and orgasm. I thought about it as the spring of our awe-inspiring creativity, our passion, our joy, our positive pulsing energy. It seemed to me to be the life stuff itself, the power stuff, surging like a great river through all the living of our days. I considered our touch-adoring vulvas only one small part of our sexuality repertoire, believing that we were sensual beings from brain to belly, from thigh to instep, from fingertip to nose. Every atom of our bodies filled with intelligence and wisdom, gloriously alive, avid to experience itself as a living thing—to me this and so much more was women's sexuality.

But, I theorized, sexuality viewed in this way is far too wild, too free and powerful to harness. And men have had not only to harness it, but to usurp it, to own it, because so far on Planet Earth, men as a class have had no success with their own internal personal power generators. So over the centuries, they have reduced and localized and debased women's immensely rich sexuality until it now officially resides in what they view as our reproductive organs, babies the only acceptable evidence that we have been left even a shred of our original creative power.

I thought how, having shrunk the goddess to a cunt, men could tame her, gaining access to her truly limitless creative power through women's sexuality. (Typical how, to make their dependency invisible, they then turned it around, making women believe that, instead, *men* had power and that women had to go through *them* to get it.) I suspected that men, having no power in themselves, have had to plug into women's power from the beginning of their sojourn on this planet.

But when they began to take control, they needed more—and more dependable—power supplies: Each man his own woman, his own goddess battery pack, his to control, his to plug into any time he needed a jolt of generative energy.

A goddess battery pack—"battery" being a highly appropriate word here—was so essential for individual men's success in the world that other men judged his potential as a man first by the very fact of his being plugged into a goddess battery pack at all—he was useless without at least one—and second by the power of the goddess(es) to whom he had unlimited access. (Another reversal. Women in patriarchy have always been judged by the control-potential of the men by whom they are owned.)

Small wonder, according to this scenario, that men have always found it necessary to affirm their ability to cope in the world by proclaiming certain women as their sexers—their vicarious sources of power—and by establishing ownership of particular women, particular taproots to the generative springs of the goddess—through marriage, if possible, but always through announcement of sexerShip.

Well, I thought to myself when this occurred to me, I *am* the goddess. I need neither the status nor the vicarious power that drives men to own a goddess battery pack. So why should I announce who I'm having sex with? I couldn't see any reason then why women were making such announcements other than to imitate men. But somewhere off in the distance lurked that wretched day when I would look squarely at the assumption of ownership in my own relation Ship.

Meanwhile, I was still thinking about "lover," how it would be a fine word if it really meant love (whatever "love" means). "It has such marvelous brio, this word," I thought to myself. I coveted its use for the dozens of women for whom I cared passionately but for whom there was no term. "Friend," than which in menstream society there are few words weaker or more lackluster, was unsatisfactory in all respects. If I were to say about a woman, "This is a friend," no one could tell if I knew her more than slightly, to say nothing of whether I even liked her.[2]

Having no intrinsic value or energy in menstream language, the word "friend" must always be supported and encouraged by enhancing modifiers. For instance: "This is Roberta, a very dear old friend," or "the best friend in the world," or "the most loyal and steadfast friend anyone could ask for."

"Lover," on the other hand, because of its function in patriarchy, is such an extraordinarily high-energy word that it

---

[2] I know that as feminists we are making serious efforts to return "friend" to its original and hallowed position. Though this is our direction, I believe we have some distance to go before "friend" is as consistently significant a word in our feelings and behavior as "lover."

not only does not require such augmentation but actively spurns it. It would be absurd to say in introductions, for example, "This is Frances, a very dear old lover from college days," or "my best and closest lover," or "the most steadfast and loyal lover." Though it will tolerate informational modifiers—"this is a former lover," or "a prospective lover"—"lover" needs no energy assistance. It is the ultimate just as it stands.

I wanted to use this powerful word for the many women in my life for whom "friend," even with strings of modifiers working diligently to boost its value, was a totally inadequate designation.[3] Wanting to interrupt the constant programming that sex was the most important element in my personal connections with women, I decided to bestow integrity upon the word "lover" by using it only to describe the women I loved, in this way making love, not sex, the core meaning of the word. I stopped saying "lover" when I meant "sexer" even though I loved my sexer.

Best of all, I decided that no one needed to know who my sexer was, that was not important to me. When I said that some woman was a lover, any person who still cared about such things was going to have to guess what was going on between us sexually. I refused to continue to play the game that seemed to me to elevate sex at the expense of love.

I began without explanation to sign my letters to the wonderful women I adored all over the country, "Your lover, Sonia," and was thrilled when they wrote back and signed themselves, for instance, "your red-headed lover in Kansas."

---

[3] Loraine Elms from Houston suggests that "compañera" expresses this better than "lover."

I noticed that by changing the meaning of "lover" in this way I began to free myself of my former feelings around it. I had, after all, never *had* feelings about the word "lover" as signifying anyone and everyone in my life that I loved. In this way, I subverted another conditioned response, came a little further out of my patriarchally-induced trance and woke up for a moment.

Though I tried at that time to figure out other reasons that the word "lover" (meaning "sexer") has such high status in our language whereas "friend" lives on the other side of the tracks, it took many more insights gained over many difficult months to clarify this in my mind.

My aversion to the word "lover" began to extend to the sentence, "I love you." I noticed that saying it threw me immediately back into non-think robotitude, and wondered what I might say in its stead. But though I had suffered the clumsiness of men's language acutely, I had so far only suffered. I hadn't thought of ways out of it, of modes of speaking that were not hopelessly club-tongued.

But I knew that I couldn't use society's sleepwalker phrases and hope to stay awake. So for nearly a year I stopped saying "I love you," first in romantic situations, and then, after I had recognized the great value of this exercise, in all others. I thought to myself that even if it weren't the great hypnotizer, the phallocratic mantra, that it is, it was still too generic a message—like a greeting card or horoscope: Appropriate for anybody, any time, any place. What had it to do specifically with me? What had it to do specifically with anyone?

What I noticed from *not* saying it was that when I got to the place where I would ordinarily say it, where, in fact, I was *dying* to say it, where I thought I *had* to say it or burst

. . . but then *didn't*, it was as if someone threw a bucket of ice water in my face. I was shaken wide awake, tingling in every neuron, consciously and frantically searching among my lexic souvenirs for some way to convey to someone that I was overwhelmed by the wonder of them, bursting with gratitude for the good fortune that had brought me within their sane and holy ken.

Then, of course, there was no phrase that even began to accomplish this feat and so I was mute, speechless, a seething mass of unexpelled energy. But incredibly alive, more awake than I had been for a long time, more aware of myself and therefore more aware of others.

I had suspected as much for a long time but having to try to find another way to express myself persuaded me that saying anything at such a time was reductionist, that it let energy escape from me like air from a punctured balloon.

Whereas, if I would simply be still and experience the feelings, they expanded and filled me with vigor and passion. Perhaps, I thought, "expressing our feelings" is a way of avoiding feeling. Perhaps it can sometimes be a way of externalizing our energy and power and dissipating it. Perhaps we are trained to respond because response gives our power away.

Whatever the case, certainly—being a world-class talker—I knew I could suffer no harm from, could only learn from, keeping my mouth shut awhile.

So I tolerated the discomfort and distress I sustained during those experiments in silence. Resting in my feelings rather than constantly struggling to express them was alien to me. I felt as we all feel when we step out of the model—ungrounded, wrong in some basic sense.

In the past, this uneasiness had been my first evidence that I had stumbled upon some useful stratagem for breaking out of the prison of my conditioning. In fact, because the extent of my uneasiness had so often been directly proportional to the usefulness, I assumed that this was now also the case, and continued to reject the clichés that popped into my mind when I looked at, talked with, and touched the lovable people in my life.

Then I would switch experiments and for awhile try to tell them, without resorting to any of these clichés, how dear they were to me. Running headlong into the solid wall of the fathers' dead language, this was nearly as difficult as holding my tongue. It reaffirmed my belief that someday we would communicate directly from heart to heart, bypassing language altogether.

It was while I was still focusing on society's woeful dearth of love language that I realized one day how thoroughly I loathed the word "relationship." Every time anyone said it, I winced. "Well, it's because it's jargon," I assumed, "as well as such an ugly word." It seemed to me an example of yet another way in which masculinist language lacked integrity. A word with integrity would not only mean what it said, its sound would be congruent with its sense.

In a language that emerged from a whole, healthy, truthful inner place, such ugly constructs as hatred, violence, and scarcity—if they still existed—would be cacophonous. Their jangling, jarring sound would reinforce their moral discordance.

The reverse would also be true. I thought that to describe women's connections we needed mellifluous words that in their harmony reflected the loveliness of our ways together. I imagined having at my tonguetip noble words that erased the spirit's boundaries at their hearing, words that themselves were as intrinsically complex and beautiful as I perceived our bonds to be.

I thought how, if we were speaking womanstongue, we would have access to hundreds, perhaps thousands, of the most expressive, most discriminating words for these ties, for all the degrees and kinds and qualities of loves, for the infinite variety of lovers. Ravenous for this richness of expression, I nearly strangled on that dry lump, "relationship."

"Relationship," an add-on, afterthought sort of word, little bits of noise strung clumsily along the tongue: re- plus la- plus tion- plus -ship. Such an insipid, pedestrian ditty could convey none of the grace or sweetness or delight I experienced in my connection with Susan.[4]

Until then I had thought that my passionate yearning of the past months was primarily for a language spacious enough, gorgeous enough, complex enough to reflect my experience in loving women. As time went on, however, I realized that my concern was not so much for beautiful language to express beautiful feelings. It was feeling itself—the rich, limitless possibilities of feeling—I hungered for. Not only was I becoming more numb by the day but I must also have sensed that even at my most perceptive I was very far from experiencing my potential range and depth of emotion. Like the one-tenth of our brain that we currently use, I think now that most if not all of us have access to about one-tenth of our possible feelings.

---

[4] Kerry Wohlrei in my workshop at the Michigan Womyn's Music Festival in 1989 suggested "creationship" instead. Though a considerable improvement, it is, alas, still a Ship.

For some time I didn't realize that this sudden super-concern about our lumpish love language was my Wise Woman adroitly inducing me to challenge my most cherished misconceptions about love and intimacy. But somewhere in the midst of it all I recognized, by the atmosphere surrounding it, that it was indeed she who was directing my informal study and that it was therefore significant in a way I hadn't yet imagined. Though I was becoming impatient to know what she had in mind, early on I had learned that it was futile to try to push her for insights. That archaic, wild part of me would entrust information to me only as I was ready for it.

So I had to be content with the knowledge that since my dissatisfaction was clearly significant, more insights would follow and that gradually the puzzle would come together in my mind. All the signs said that my Wise Woman was priming me for some major modification of thought.

But as wary as I was, I could not possibly have known then how formidable a breakthrough she was requiring of me, how cataclysmic, how excruciating—and, ultimately, how happy—a change in my perception of relation Ships and in all my subsequent behavior.

Still in fembotic[5] innocence, I put this realization, along with many other bits of information that had come forward in the past year to tantalize me, in the back of my mind. But I was alert now, waiting to see if there were to be further communications on this matter from the goddess, my Self.

---

[5] Mary Daly's happy construct, a combination of "feminine" and "robot."

2

"I Could Live There"

I n this state of semi-awareness, disquietude, and standing
by, I set out one fall morning in 1987 to do my usual
race-walking around my neighborhood in Arlington, Virginia.
Though I felt no different that day from any other day and
had no premonition that I would never return "home" from
that walk, knowledge of the imminent collapse of my life's
entire substructure was nevertheless pounding on the gate of
my consciousness as I dashed out my front door.
The breakthrough occurred as I passed a house that was
for sale. Suddenly I heard myself thinking, "I could live
there" and realized to my amazement that for several weeks
during my walks I had been measuring all "For Sale" houses
with an eye to whether or not I would want to buy and live
in them.
I was astonished—for two reasons. First, only a few
years before this with the dowry from my twenty-year
marriage I had bought a brand-new townhouse in an excellent
location, and I adored it. Second, I lived there with the first
woman I had ever loved in a romantic, sexual way. My
experience with her had been so indescribably sweet that to

have found myself thinking "I" instead of "we" and imagining living apart from her, distressed me acutely. The revelation broke my stride in more ways than one. Shaken, I sat down on the curb to sort things out. I recognized my Wise Woman's indirect style and was absolutely certain that she had just handed me another clue, an unmistakably clear one this time. Putting together the bits and pieces that had been accumulating in the back of my mind, I faced with dismay the suddenly indisputable fact that if I wanted to be free I had to look honestly at my relation Ship with Susan.

But I was afraid to apply my hard-won and considerable deprogramming skills to my relation Ship. On some level, I knew that if I did, Susan and I would have to "break up," and I loved her. The thought of not having her in my life made me feel sick. Besides, I believed I *had* been honest with myself and Susan all along. I didn't know how to be more truthful, how to look deeper.

Though I was frightened and confused, the necessity to be free of my mind bindings was full upon me, and I knew I had no choice but to begin. So once again with difficulty I put aside my conditioned qualms about botching things up and causing myself and others pain, took a deep albeit shaky breath, and plunged in.

3

The Kiss in Bed

At the time, the decision to look with courage at my
relation Ship was not as super-conscious as I've made it
sound. There was, however, a definite moment when I
relented internally and agreed to face what felt frighteningly
unfaceable. As usual, the moment I honored my deepest
wisdom, I began to see beneath the smooth surface of my life
to its disquieting realities.

I began gently, recognizing first the least frightening of
these—the many small rituals that gave shape to my daily life
with Susan. Though some of these were more like habits
carried over from previous relation Ships, some we created
purposefully. "The Kiss in Bed" was one of our favorite
creations.

All day while we worked together we talked
nonstop—about the women's movement, feminist theory, our
families, speaking engagements, our relation Ship, book
promotion, our financial situation, our friends. We crawled
into bed at night still talking. Finally, when one or the other
of us judged that talk time was over for the day and it was
time for sleep, she would say, "It's time for The Kiss in
Bed." At this point we would kiss, arrange ourselves like a

soft, warm spoon set (that is, until my hot flashes intervened and for a few years prevented my assuming that most delicious of all positions), and go to sleep.

One night we went to bed, talked for a while as usual, until as usual one of us said, "Well, it's time for The Kiss in Bed." But as I dutifully puckered up, even as my lips were sticking out in the air awaiting hers, I had the unwelcome thought, "I wonder if I really want to do this." While we kissed, I argued with myself. "What kind of silly question is that? Of *course* I want to. I love kissing her!" After the kiss, though, lying there wide awake and solitary on my menopausal side of the bed, I pondered it.

Having learned from experience that unusual clarity attends messages from my Self, I knew from its distinctness and lucidity that my wonderment about The Kiss in Bed was significant. So I circled the situation in my mind, around and around in ever-decreasing arcs, trying to pinpoint the source of my discomfort. Was it that I really didn't want to kiss Susan that night? Or was there something about the ritual itself that I disliked? What *was* The Kiss in Bed, anyway?

Trying to characterize it, I remembered that The Kiss in Bed was usually not a passionate or even a thoughtful kiss, that in fact sometimes during The Kiss we almost forgot to kiss at all. Though no one could always feel like kissing, especially when they were exhausted or sick, I thought how even if Susan or I were dropping in our tracks or really ill, we never omitted that Kiss. From this and other evidence, I concluded that The Kiss in Bed was not functioning as a kiss, that it did not seem to be about kissing at all, but about something else altogether.

I wanted to make that "something else," whatever it was, visible. In addition, my curiosity was piqued: What was I *really* doing when I thought I was kissing?

Focusing my thoughts firmly on this question, I soon discovered that what I had been doing was making The Kiss carry burdensome responsibilities that kisses were not intended to bear. I was making it tell Susan that as far as I was concerned everything was all right: I still loved her, our relation Ship was still okay, I still wanted to sleep with her, I was not interested in being sexual with anyone else, she was still safe and secure here in our little nest, I would not change.

What heavy metaphysical communication jobs for a mere kiss! Moonlighting on so many other jobs, no wonder it stopped being able to function well at its only legitimate task, that of expressing affection and closeness as well as exciting and expressing physical desire.

Of course The Kiss was not a "mere kiss." In fact, my original hunch had been right: The Kiss wasn't a kiss at all; the fact that our lips touched was irrelevant. The Kiss was a re-sealing of some pact, a re-making of commitments, a reassurance that we were still married.

If this is true, my Self argued, is there ever such a thing as a kiss that is *only* a kiss? Is there such a thing as a genuine kiss? Just what *is* a real kiss? Is it a purely physical experience? I thought it over and answered myself—with a great deal of uncertainty—that a real kiss, a kiss with integrity, an honest kiss, was mouths touching because—*at least*—bodies desired it. Mere acquiescence was not sufficient. They had to wish eagerly for it.

My assumption was that when a person is whole, her body desires such an experience in concordance with the rest of her perceptions and senses. So, though the physical response represents the total person, I thought then that ultimately whenever feelings were being expressed through the body honesty would mean above all *physical* honesty. An honest kiss would therefore be a kiss the *body* wanted.

Had my body wanted to kiss Susan tonight, I wondered? I didn't know, I couldn't tell. The atmosphere surrounding The Kiss was confounded by too many elusive feelings, a shadowy assemblage of desires all whispering insistently at once. But I promised myself closer, more thoughtful scrutiny of the subject in the coming days.

In addition, I realized that my rebelliousness at Kiss time was occasioned in part by the fact that The Kiss in Bed had come somehow to feel compulsory, an institution, as if I no longer had any choice in the matter. I felt that if I were to refuse to participate, I would be breaking some sort of unspoken contract, and that some unspecified but fearsome consequences would befall the relation Ship.

I knew I had to hold firmly to my insight that if I kissed for any reason other than that I genuinely felt like kissing—my body as well as my psyche—I would become more and more detached from my feelings. I determined that I would do my best from then on to kiss honestly, without compulsion or duplicity. That settled, I fell into a satisfied sleep, with no idea that I had sketched out for myself a nearly impossible task.

The next day was miserable. Having perceived the ghostly multitude of meanings, intents, and desires pushing at me from beneath The Kiss in Bed, I began now to sense similar phantasms lurking under every act. Everything we did was The Kiss in Bed. I felt as defenseless in this vast and unfamiliar complexity as if I had strayed into the Twilight

Zone. Nothing could be trusted to be as clear and simple as it seemed. Everything was quite frighteningly other; was, in fact, many other things. Wherever we were in the house, whatever we were doing, shades of meaning lay stratified in the air between us, almost palpable. I felt as if I were wading through them, blundering into them, without catching more than the merest glimpse of them, without gleaning a clue about what they were. Weren't our hugs really hugs? Our smiles really smiles? What was this strange shadow under my going to the post office? Under making a sandwich? I concentrated my attention upon our relation Ship for more than a year before I began to discern those ghosts on the undersides well enough to name them.

In the meantime, after The Kiss in Bed episode, clues about my way of having a relation Ship seemed to fly at me in flocks from all sides. I realized from my own life that it was emotional dependency, not physical desire, that undergirded kisses-and-sex-as-symbols, and that this dependency, masquerading as "love," was a most sinister saboteur of intimacy. I saw that it was everywhere, in a thousand guises.

I remember an afternoon I spent with members of a professional women's club in Texas. At the head table after my speech, the subject swung around to co-dependency, a theory I was seriously critiquing by then. Perhaps because I had been boasting a little about doing just what I wanted to do, one of the officers remarked that she envied how independent I was.

At first I was pleased and probably preened a little. But after a moment or two I remembered myself and replied, "Perhaps I *am* sometimes independent. But it's likely that more of the time I edit my desires before I even become aware of them, long before I act on them. I think most of us do this to some extent. I've had many women say to me, for instance, 'What do you mean, women are oppressed? *I've* never felt oppressed!' And I respond, 'Not *feeling* oppressed is not evidence of not *being* oppressed.' In the same way, my feeling independent may not be true evidence that I *am* independent, but could instead simply be evidence of successful programming."

It had been clear to me for some time that there isn't a feeling in my own or others' repertoire named "dependence." We don't say to ourselves or one another, "I'm feeling wretchedly dependent today." Instead, we say, "I'm feeling restless, smothered, resentful, angry, guilty, depressed, hopeless, sorry for myself, victimized, afraid, or suicidal"—everything *but* dependent, though any of these is likely dependence in disguise. We are assiduously trained not to see readily the problem beneath the symptoms, because if we recognize our dependence in our personal lives, we are more likely to recognize it in our public, political, extrapersonal lives—an act so radical that it would be fatal to the status quo.

Early on in my life as a feminist I had decided that to keep awake I would, at least for some time, have to accept that my *genuine* feelings wouldn't be the first ones I identified in myself at any given moment, the first ones I thought I was feeling. Now, a decade later, however, my real desires had finally struggled up very close to the surface and were confronting me one by one.

An important one of these struck me in the shower. There I was, happily loofahing away before going to bed, thinking about nothing much in particular, when a question swept into my mind with great vigor and settled there: "Are you sure you want to sleep with Susan tonight?"

"Oh, no!" I groaned aloud, though I knew that, having thought it, there was no pretending I hadn't, no going back to happy mindless loofahing. I would have to confront myself again. So, sighing, I began. It seemed easy at the outset All I needed to do, I reasoned, was to find the place inside me where the feeling "want to" lived and examine whether I wanted to sleep with Susan that night. I was sure I did—I *loved* sleeping with Susan (didn't I?), it was one of the most pleasurable parts of living with her. But it wouldn't hurt to check it out just to quiet the voice inside me.

Standing there in the shower, I searched for my want spot(s). Where in the body does one feel desire that isn't sexual, I wondered? Concentrating on one area after another inside my torso, I checked for signs of "want to." But it was as if nobody that might know its whereabouts was home in there. All was silence and emptiness. I backtracked and, turning my eyes and mind inward, scoured my entire internal terrain again. Not a twinge of a "want to" sensation turned up anywhere.

I was bemused but not yet alarmed. Surely it was just a matter of time and practice. I would continue the search, exercise my "want organ"—wherever it was—a little more every day, until finally one day soon by a definite tingle it would announce itself. Then, knowing how it felt and where to find it in the future, I could easily check in with it from that time forward on all matters of desire.

But though I asked myself every night thereafter if I wanted to sleep with Susan, listening intently for some internal response, weeks passed without the faintest quiver from within. My mild worry progressed to something like panic. Perhaps having ignored it for fifty years, almost never exercising it, I had allowed my want organ to atrophy. Maybe it had long since died and been assimilated into my bones and tissues, or as a tiny hard mummy of itself, passed out of my body.

Even while I was laughing at these absurd images, I was frightened. Who was I but how I felt, what I perceived and thought, what I valued, what I *wanted?* If I couldn't tell how I felt and what I wanted, how could I know my Self, how could I learn to be my Self? Did individual Self even exist without conscious feelings and desires upon which to base choices?

I decided to back up out of this fruitless turn in the labyrinth and approach the mystery from another direction. Starting from the beginning, only this time with the left instead of the right side of my brain, I asked myself, "What is the probability that any person would want to sleep with another person—*any* other person—every night of her life?" My left-brain computer cranked out the answer on the spot: The probability is very small.

This was important information. I hadn't been at all sure that, despite the implications of the question in the shower, I *didn't* want to sleep with Susan every night. Now I knew that chances were very good that some nights I would rather sleep alone. All I had to do was figure out which nights those were.

But I was still back where I started, not able to tell what I wanted at any given moment. So I decided to try another avenue for finding out.

In the days following my "I could live in that house" shock, I had concluded that my problem was simply that I needed more space in my relation Ship. (Does that sound familiar?) So I had reclaimed one of the rooms in my house and had industriously made it over into "my room." I had intended to spend time alone there, sleep there on occasion when in the mood (if I could ever tell when I was in the mood), have a sanctuary. I had bought new blinds for it, a fold-out couch, and a little antique desk, and put all my clothes in its closets. It was a lovely room, full of sun and flowers—and I almost never went into it.

But now it suited my purposes. I thought that if I slept in my own room alone three nights of the week I might gradually be able to tell whether I wanted to sleep alone or together. Methodically, I chose Monday, Wednesday, and Friday and solemnly set about the experiment.

As I lay in my own room in my own bed every Monday, Wednesday, and Friday night I asked myself, "How does this feel? Do you like this?" And I would answer myself truthfully, "It feels great. I like it a lot!" The next night, lying close to Susan in our former bed, now hers, I would ask myself the same questions—and get the same answers. No matter how hard I tried, I couldn't discriminate. I liked them both and I still couldn't tell which I'd prefer at any particular time.

After several months of musical beds, I had to declare the experiment a failure. I was no closer than before to tracking down any real feeling of "wanting"—either to sleep with Susan or not to sleep with her, or to discovering in myself feelings of wanting and not wanting in other areas of our life together. In fact, my relationShip investigation had bogged down on several fronts, and in some, such as this, was at a standstill. I was beginning to feel a sort of desperation about this as well as about dozens of other relationShip matters.

But I had reached one clear conclusion. I had decided that the act of sleeping together, loaded as it is with assumptions, was among the most symbolic—and hence least amenable to conscious choice—of all relationShip acts. It was no accident, I realized, that we didn't say, "I'd like to *wake* with you"[1] instead of, "I'd like to sleep with you." Also, like The Kiss in Bed, only infinitely more so, this behavior stood for much more than itself. It had been transmogrified into a short-cut communication system that had inevitably short-circuited. I had hoped that sleeping alone now and then would redefine and clarify it, help me see it for what it intrinsically was. I had wanted to devitalize the issue of where I slept, to make sleeping alone now and then appear as natural and loving as sleeping together, both just something I did, something neither affirming nor threatening to the relation Ship, of no great significance one way or the other.

But I had not succeeded. I judged the depth of my failure in a couple of ways. To begin with, my thinking was still dichotomously either/or. Closely linked with this was the fact that sleep was still as relational as it had ever been, as relational as everything else I did in my life: I never merely slept; I slept either *with* Susan or *without* Susan.

Finally I told her that, though science informed us that linear space was an illusion and it therefore didn't make any sense to ask this of her, I felt that if she were some distance away in her own house in her own bed, and I was here in my

---

[1] One of Sarah David's contributions to my workshop in Victoria, British Columbia, 1989. She hypothesized that we may also be trained to perceive ourselves as wanting to "sleep with" instead of to "wake with" because, unlike in wakefulness, in sleep we are all very vulnerable.

own house in my own bed, I would be able to tell better whether or not I wanted to sleep with her. I thought that if I were alone I would be able to tell how I felt about much else in my life as well. Knowing, for instance, that "having sex" was an even more significant barometer of the health of a relation Ship in menstream society than sleeping together was—which made it very portentous stuff indeed—I was beginning to worry seriously about my inability to tell whether or not at any given moment I really wanted to have sex. My desire to keep the relation Ship in good repair had been programmed into me so deeply that I wasn't able to distinguish between the feelings of wanting to "make Susan (and the Ship) happy" and really wanting to be sexual.

During neither of my marriages—to Rick and then to Susan—had I needed to ask myself whether I felt sexually excited, because I thought I was sure that I was—or that if I wasn't, I could become so in plenty of time to join in honestly. I was conditioned over the years to believe that to have a relation Ship I essentially had no choice but to "want" to—at least some of the time. In this way "wanting" to preserve the Ship and "wanting" to be sexual had come dangerously close to being synonymous.[2]

Finally, now I felt a fierce desire to discriminate between my conditioning and my own true feelings. I was even ready to face what I felt then to be the sad possibility that my long years of betrayal and renunciation of Self had left me with no sexual passion at all, even that I might find sex distasteful.

---

[2] Though the fad is to believe that sex can be addictive, I remain adamantly unconvinced. In my book, *Wildfire: Igniting the She/Volution*, I discuss the critical distinction between addiction and brainwashing.

(I am intrigued now in looking back on that time by my assumption that sexual excitation was a necessity for happiness. Even more interesting is why I accepted so unquestioningly in the first place that it was a given in human life.)

Women are born free, and though we are gradually inured to slavery we never stop longing for the wild wind in our faces and the salt of the lawless sea on our tongues. Because freedom is our nature, the rule of our Ships taxes our souls beyond bearing. My soul was sick of slavery, and I redoubled my search for freedom, for ways to discover and change my deepest, most shackling core beliefs about love and sex and intimacy.

Never again, I vowed, would I allow a despot Ship to anchor in my living room; never again would I genuflect before one.

4

Born to Merge

I n one of the very first of our hundreds of Shipwreck
discussions in the difficult and awe-filled year of 1988, I
remember telling Susan—with only a vague idea of how trite
these words had become: "I don't know any longer where you
leave off and I begin, or I leave off and you begin. I feel
submerged, drowning in 'us.'"

I didn't know that there was already a name for this
syndrome and many words describing it, that there had
already been pioneers, that countless women had already said
to one another exactly what I said to Susan, and that countless
others needed to and would. Until I learned that, I felt as
alone in my confusion as if I were the sole explorer of a new
planet.

Even in my isolation, I began uncovering and measuring
the astonishing dimensions not only of my own dependence
on those around me for my identity but the profoundest
conditioning of women in general to have no Self separate
from parents, lovers, or children; to judge our success as
persons by how happy we made others, how fully we met
their needs, how much they loved or respected us; to feel as

if we had to be all things to our lovers, assessing our value by how indispensable we were to them; to believe that we were not worthy of love simply by being ourselves, but that we had to "earn" it.

Then co-dependence jargon suddenly started tripping off every tongue, and I pounced on parts of that theory to explain what was going on between Susan and me and how to change it. For an exciting few weeks I thought it would clarify everything, and I felt enormously hopeful and relieved to have a path of investigation to follow through the jungle of love.

It could be said of me that I was born to merge, taught assiduously from the moment my head crowned between my mother's legs to give myself away, to dissolve into others. Groomed from birth to marry, I never viewed myself as whole in myself, but always as half of some future twosome that would be called *his* name. So for those twenty-three years before he came along, I had no idea who I was, waiting in emotional limbo for him to come and claim me so that I—and everyone else—would finally know.

Since then I had been part of someone else every moment of my life: For twenty years the second half of Rickandsonia, for twenty-five years "Mommy" to four children, for five years half of Susanandsonia.

Though through some magic I had separated myself from my parents early on, my relation Ship with my husband had been another story altogether. When he left me, I suddenly found out how many steely cords of dependency had bound me to him all those years, dependency that mensmachine[1] had taught me to call love.

---

[1] Courtesy of Rose Levno, Anchorage, Alaska.

After months of grief mixed with panic, I emerged into the sunlight of knowing that what I had thought was love had probably for much of the marriage really been fear, the absolute conviction that I had to have Rick in order to have Sonia, in order to be allowed to live. Though I had been forced to confront this absurd belief when Rick left, and though I had successfully broken similar patterns in my interactions with most of my children by then, I had failed somehow to generalize the learning. Because I hadn't understood the dynamics of internalized oppression, which is self-hatred, I slipped back into it easily with Susan.

So now she and I had to disentangle the skein of our entwined lives. The labor of unraveling two such interwoven lives was daunting, made all the more so by our having merged everything for five years, including our businesses. Susan arranged the speeches, I gave them. I wrote the books, she publicized them. In addition to my deep emotional dependency, I had also built my economic security upon her. When I tried to imagine how I would do my passionately loved work without her, a fist of fear squeezed my innards, and the image of me as a little old bag lady flashed before my eyes.

But knowing that fear was the sure way back into the Ship's brig, I was now more afraid of being afraid than I was of being a bag lady. I had finally reached the point where working with Susan had to be a free choice or I could no longer do it, no matter the financial consequences.

So when I had to face the real possibility that we might not choose to work together if we no longer lived together, I decided that somehow—goddess knew how!—I would be all right.

I remember saying to her, "When I choose to be with you—if I do—after I realize that I don't need you for either emotional or economic survival, I will know that, at last, I am making an authentic choice." I wanted to be unafraid, constantly in my power. I wanted to know, and I wanted all my lovers to know, that I chose to be around them not out of any lack in myself or fear or desperation or some other manifestation of powerlessness, but entirely because I found them lovable and delightful to be with. I wanted my behavior to speak honestly for my motives. This, I decided, would be an essential part of my developing definition of integrity.

Though even at that early time I was confronting phantoms in our predicament that had nothing to do with codependence, I reasoned that Susan's moving to her own place would at least help us sort out our co-stuff: Physical closeness had contributed to our fusion, *ergo* physical separation might be an ally in our *un*fusion.

In breaking free of my bondage to menShip, I had to recognize another tightly woven thread of my enmeshment. I had been taught by my culture that taking care of others, rescuing them, was behavior of the highest moral caliber. I was given an imprimatur to take unrightful responsibility for others' lives and feelings, to invade their most private territory and rule there, benevolently—or so it was made to appear, though we are all learning that such violation of boundaries is never benign.

The covert underside of this training was that I took care of others as a way of controlling them. As repositories of me, for example, *my children* must be all right in order for *me* to be all right. I had learned mistakenly that controlling them by usurping responsibility for their lives—responsibility that they needed to take for themselves—was necessary to my survival. I had learned first hand that rescuing necessitates assuming unethical obligation for others' feelings and behavior, a pattern for which I could have posed as the archetype.

From my own experience I also came to understand that rescue not only requires victims, it breeds them. Painfully I had to recognize that at least a part of my defining myself as a person who cared about and helped others was a way of proving that I was stronger, wiser, and better than they. As a rescuer, my message to myself was, "I am a superior person because I am helping people who are not okay become okay."

But those of us depending on this kind of thinking and behavior for feelings of self-worth must face the fact that deep down we *can't* want everyone to become okay because if they did, there wouldn't be anyone left for us to feel superior to.

In addition, if we didn't need to rescue others to maintain our self-esteem, we would soon realize that, in fact, people in general neither need to be nor can be rescued.[2] The assumption that they do and can is not only demeaning and inaccurate; it also perpetuates phallocracy's deadly hierarchical worldview.

---

[2] I am as aware as anyone that there are situations that require literal rescue—saving a child from drowning or from abuse, for instance. I am talking here about the rescue we do that does not need to be done, that we do for dishonest reasons and out of a lack of respect for ourselves and others, and that is harmful to everyone concerned. Though the distinction is not always easy to make, it will become increasingly easier as more of us realize that the necessity, rights, and responsibilities of self-determination apply to politics as rigorously as they do to our personal lives.

I recognized that, true to form, patriarchy has reversed the truth and that what it styles self*less*ness is actually self*ish*ness. For at least two flawed reasons, then, we selfishly take care of others: In the attempt to have happiness through them, second-hand, and to experience the thrill of pleasure that derives in a sadistic system from being "on top."

My recognition that this pattern flourishes on every hand, that it is the foundation of liberal politics and its fundamental weakness—this might be thought to have comforted me. In fact it made me very glum; the rescuer/victim model, because it is not merely endemic to patriarchy but, being sadomasochism, *is* patriarchy,[3] was ultimately to prove the most difficult of all patterns for me to admit to and to change aboard my own Ship.

Publicly I had been for many years too busy saving the planet to save my own life, blind to the perfect positive correlation between the two. At home I was too busy worrying about how my behavior would affect Susan and my children to notice the price I was paying. More focused on and interested in their emotional conditions than in my own, trying not to hurt their feelings or upset them by telling them how I really felt or what I wanted, believing wrongheadedly that being dishonest was being kind (though of course it never

---

[3] Any "-archy" (except for *an*archy which is *no*-archy)—matriarchy, oligarchy, monarchy, patriarchy—is a hierarchical, and hence, a sadomasochistic, system. By "sadomasochistic" I mean that one person or group controls another person or group by physical and/or psychological force. Central to this one-up/one-down paradigm is that pleasure is primarily derived from being in either top or bottom position—the oppressor or oppressed, the pain-giving or pain-receiving role. The word "patriarchy," denoting that men own and rule women, is the current form of sadomasochism on Planet Earth. I therefore consider the words "patriarchy" and "sadomasochism" to be synonymous. I also use "sadism" and "sadomasochism" interchangeably.

occurred to me that I was being dishonest), I lost track of truth and honor, of my own feelings and desires and perceptions and, consequently, of my Self and my power.

Having learned thus to oppress and to be oppressed, I lived in constant fear that I might not be able to manipulate the lives of my dear ones enough to keep them happy or successful and that their unhappiness would ruin my life. Once in the middle of my struggle for clarity about all this I confessed to Susan in tears, "I hate the woman I am when I'm around you." The woman I hated was the rescuer. I recognized all too painfully my superior, rescuer/controller stance in nearly every interaction with her.

For example, I was afraid that because of what I perceived—rather, projected—as her need for the assurance and safety of the relation Ship, she might not realize at any given moment how she really felt, what she really wanted. So I took it upon myself, in what I must have felt was my greater wisdom and understanding, to save her from confusion and bungling by disregarding her perceptions of herself and insisting on mine.

On some level, of course, I knew how very matronizing and disrespectful—and, yes, how thoroughly unethical—this behavior was, and just under the surface of consciousness despised myself for it.

Such need to leap over others' boundaries to save them from themselves stems from a serious lack of self-centeredness. Because such a lack is painful, I lived in constant pain, but pain so deeply buried that I wasn't sure it was there, could not have told anyone so. Like many women, I have an incredibly high pain threshold. It took me over a half century of self-denial to reach my limit. What is marvelous to me is that when I finally chose freedom and autonomy, my Self was still there waiting for me even after all those years of neglect and of outright abuse.

Waiting for me, perhaps, but mad as hell! I soon learned that anger was the alarm that went off when I was not being true to my Self, when I was renouncing me, as I was so in the habit of doing.

A most useful corollary of this was the recognition that my increasing fury, as I struggled to extricate myself from my conditioning about love, was not intended for Susan but for me. I was furious at myself, for instance, not only for violating her right to self-determination but now also for not acting as if I had a right to my own, a right, for instance, to keep anything—from information to good things to eat—to myself, for feeling as if my wanting privacy was somehow devious and deceitful. I demanded aloud of myself one day why I felt compelled to tell Susan everything, why I didn't feel that I had a right to my own internal space, a right to privacy, a right to set up uncrossable boundaries *with anyone* whenever I wished.

I realized that day that my sudden revulsion against telling her everything—who I talked with on the telephone, where I had been, where I was going—was evidence, not of duplicity, but of my separateness coming into being, my growing intent if not my ability to feel good about keeping my Self to myself, a sense of having the prerogative to have no one know what I thought, how I felt, what I said to others, what was going on in my life, *unless I chose to.* The novel feeling, that is, that I had a right to own and govern myself.

That was the real beginning of breaking free from my lifelong fusion habit, the morning of my belief that a certain kind of distance is essential to intimacy. I began to think then that closeness was only possible if I enforced all my No Trespassing signs and trusted others to be answerable for enforcing theirs.

Zoe Nicholson,[4] whom after several years I chanced to meet again one day on a coast-to-coast flight, gave me a memorable glimpse into her handling of co-dependency. Somehow we got talking about relationships and the old idea that familiarity breeds contempt. She told me that she had learned the necessity in her close connections of being formal, of granting permission to have her borders breached. She used an example from her study of Aikido. At first she had thought that because it required a lot of touching, Aikido would be very intrusive. But she discovered that the formal rules that were always obeyed about entering and leaving someone else's personal space prevented the kind of violation she had feared.

"I have had both a husband and a wife at different times in my life," she concluded, "and now, in my present connection, I want no more marriage." No more assumption of rights to trespass upon another's domain, I took her to mean. She told me a little story to illustrate: "The other day I said I wanted a hamburger, and my lover said, 'Aren't you having too many hamburgers?' I replied, 'You have only two choices when I say that: Either to say nothing while I go get a hamburger or to go get me one yourself. It is not an option to try to edit my behavior.'"

Having given the necessity of appropriate boundaries a great deal of thought since that day, and having also experienced my own power more fully and for longer periods, I think at this moment that when any one of us is in her

---

[4] Formerly Zoe Ananda, one of the seven women with whom I fasted for ratification of the ERA in Springfield, Illinois in the summer of 1982.

power, she will find both the word and the concept "boundaries" to be not only irrelevant but totally meaningless. I am persuaded more firmly every day that predetermined boundaries of any sort are interim measures, necessary to protect us only so long as we are caught in sadomasochistic thought and behavior.[5]

But back then, still trying to understand boundaries and thinking about familiarity breeding contempt, it occurred to me that the habit of merging was what made it impossible for anyone else's declarations of love ever to make us feel loved, or lovable, or to help us love ourselves. When we lose our boundaries, we feel as if we *are* the other person, and since we loathe ourselves (for renouncing our Selves and a possible thousand other reasons), we assume that anyone who can love us must be loathsome, too—the "birds of a feather" syndrome. Because they have now also become us, we extend our feelings of personal worthlessness to include them.

That reminded me of Groucho Marx's saying that he wouldn't belong to any club that would accept him as a member. This is why it is futile to believe that our loving someone with a poor self-image—and the poorer our self-images, the faster and tighter we fuse—will help them feel better about themselves. It may make them feel temporarily safe—though I doubt that it really does—but it cannot make them love themselves. Instead of raising *them* in their own estimation it only lowers *us*.

I grew to respect and fear the complexity of fusion: What a yawning chasm of robotitude, of misconstrued and misplaced loyalties, of passivity, and of mutual distrust it

---

[5] Clarified—at least to this point—in conversation with Sara McIntosh on the way to Freedom, New Mexico, February 25, 1991.

was! So when one day another lover and sexer walked into my kitchen and grabbed my crotch, I sat her down immediately and told her what I had learned about control and oppression, about overstepping and violating boundaries. I thought I understood it so well that I would never fall into it again.

But, of course, I was wrong. No conditioning is deeper or more thorough in phallocracy than women's conditioning to give up our personal power. The habit continued to crop up.

I woke up one morning, for instance, feeling that something was amiss somewhere, and poked around in my mind until I found it. On the phone the day before, a lover had made plans for my life, and I had acquiesced in them.

As I lay there in embarrassment recognizing what I had done, I remembered how on the morning of her phone call I had also talked with Susan and had with great firmness told her that from that day forward I was going to make my own plans, even if they weren't as brilliant as the ones she might make for me. I insisted to her that I was going to take full responsibility for the course of my days from then on. And not eight hours later I was listening to another woman plan my entire resettlement, step by step, from Virginia to New Mexico and nodding my head as I wrote it all down. "Damn it!" I fumed. "I've done it again! How many times do I need to relearn this lesson before I get it?"

But being negative and hard on myself never got me anywhere, so I reviewed the situation, this time looking for something, anything, I might have done right. It occurred to me that it was pretty remarkable that I had awakened with a sense of danger. It meant that I could finally *feel* violations of my freedom, not just intellectualize about them. *Hurrah* that my intuition had joined the fray and that my very inadequate left brain was no longer my only safeguard against fusion! *Yippee* that I had finally internalized some checkpoints! *Brava*, Sonia, let's hear it for you! Lying there rejoicing in my quickened sensibilities, I said aloud to impress it upon myself: I can learn from other women best by watching them use their skills for their own lives, not by watching them do my work for me. So I called the "helpful" lover back and told her thanks but I would take care of my move myself. I explained that my acceptance the day before of her Rescue Sonia Operation—her one/up stance—had forced me to occupy the only other position available in patriarchy's dichotomous and hierarchical system—the one/down, victim position—and that this dynamic was unacceptable to me.

"So I want you to mind your own business," I continued. "Unasked, don't propose plans to me, don't think up ideas for me. Regard me as capable of managing my own life, because of course I am. If I want suggestions or help, I'll ask for them. When I'm doing something you're willing to help me with, I want you to ask if and how I'd like your help. I want to decide what advice and help I need, and I want the choice of getting it or not; I don't want it thrust upon me. Unless I ask for them, keep your opinions to yourself.

"Now having said this, the truth is that your behavior isn't the problem, because no matter what *you* do, the onus is on me to feel the way I want to feel. So relax and be yourself and enjoy me and I'll take care of myself."

I was reminded of that conversation a few weeks later when another lover said something sarcastic to me, apologized, and asked me to help her not to do it anymore. Almost instantly, however, before I could expostulate, she corrected herself. "No," she said. "It doesn't feel right to ask you to monitor me. It feels as if I'm handing over my power, giving up responsibility for doing my own sentry duty. So please *don't* help me recognize and stop my sarcasm. I'll do it myself."

Once I understood this pattern in my own life, of course, I saw it everywhere. During the time I was most focused on it, I became acquainted with a Lesbian couple who thought they had worked the co-dependence out of their interactions. One of the ways they perceived themselves as having accomplished this was by giving each other "permission" to take over certain specifically designated responsibilities in each other's life.

For instance, one of them wanted to overcome her habit of procrastination but was finding it very difficult. So she gave her partner permission to call her attention to instances of it as well as to any unwise uses she seemed to be making of her time. "Unwise" turned out to mean anything her partner thought that the procrastinator probably wouldn't do if she were thinking clearly about it. This required not only a superabundance of mind reading and of projection, but of feelings of one/up-womanship.

There is a deep lack of respect in merging, in the belief that we know what others need better than they know themselves, and that they can't live their own lives adequately.

When we take responsibility for other people in any way, we encourage them to doubt their own competence. So instead of helping them, we insult, limit, and disable them. If it were clear to us all that no one's purpose on the planet is to be responsible for anyone's feelings but her own or for meeting anyone else's needs, and that any attempt to usurp another's accountability is unethical and coercive, we could begin to think in earnest about freedom.

But of course we can only pretend to carry others' burdens or to make others answerable for any part of our lives, because the truth is that whether we want it or not we have complete responsibility for ourselves every moment and cannot get rid of it no matter how hard we try. We can't even delegate, not the minutest fraction. How we feel, what we perceive—these are our own decisions from the moment we're born.

I don't pretend that they are totally free decisions. We are continuously pushed around by the Ship's brutal brain-washing bullies. Nevertheless, each of us decides what to make of and what to do with their lies, their manipulation, and their violence. There is always choice and we are to this degree free agents whether we will or no. It is our nature to be free.

Since I have seen how deeply ingrained my habit of fusing is, on occasion I've been tempted not to do *anything* with a lover for fear of participating unwittingly in this particularly virulent brand of non-freedom. I said as much to Sara McIntosh one Thanksgiving when I was visiting her in Wisconsin, lamenting the difficulty of recognizing manunkind's co-inculcated patterns of powerlessness and domination.

While we were pondering together how we might be sure we weren't merging with anyone, what criteria we could use, we realized that though we could understand it rationally, merging itself is an irrational process. Trying to figure out intellectually beforehand whether some behavior amounts to fusion or not was likely to induce paralysis and render us unable to act at all. After a certain point of awareness, thinking alone didn't seem likely to get us any farther in overcoming our conditioned reflex to abandon ourselves in relation Ships.

From this, we thought of a tentative plan for marshalling all our resources, not just our brains, to help keep us awake and free.

On the assumption that we have access to many sources of information within ourselves that we don't often use, and assuming a certain necessary level of understanding of the mechanics of merging, we decided that instead of getting stuck in intellectual agony over whether or not certain behavior constituted enmeshment, we would just *do* it. Then as we were doing it, we would take frequent checks of our feelings to see if and how they were changing, pay attention to our body's responses, and notice how the dynamics between us and others were affected—how the mood changed, for instance, and what happened to the general balance and tone or aura of our interactions.

Thus, relying on our intuition in combination with the rest of our organism's moral compasses, perhaps one of these days we would wake up and find ourselves unable to merge; find our Selves become so inalienable, in fact, that nothing and no one could shift us off our own calm, sure centers and out of our freedom and power.[6]

But we both admitted to being leery of relying on feelings alone to guide us in connecting closely with others. The danger of being unable to discriminate between conditioned responses and genuine choices was still all too real, and more threatening in relation Ships than in any other area of our

---

[6] Since then she and I have discovered that never thinking or saying "we" helps prevents merging.

lives. Searching for a more definite yardstick, some way to measure when we were about to lapse into relationship cocoma, we agreed that "comfort" would do for the moment. Conditioned responses feel deceptively "natural," comfortable, safe, and "right." Because they still often felt so comfortable and right to us both, we agreed that a worthy short-term accomplishment would be to feel—naturally and automatically—most uncomfortable about feeling comfortable.

I am glad to report that my conditioned responses have been feeling less and less pleasant since that day over two years ago when Sara and I talked. In fact, many of them now feel distinctly wrong and *un*pleasant, even repulsive, and can scarcely tempt me to give them any credence. My knowledge that this seachange has taken place also in the souls of hundreds of thousands of other women makes me want to leap wildly about and whirl and shout. I know that when the feeling of freedom becomes as congenial to us as our chains once were, mensgame[7] will be finished.

Though on a certain level co-dependency theory offered an explanation for much I was experiencing in my love life and cleared up some superficial confusion, I needed to learn hard truths about myself, and I needed a way of thinking about my experience that filled in the large gaps that remained in my understanding of relation Ships in phallocracy.

I needed a perspective that paralleled my radical feminist worldview. But as my mother always wisely told us kids, "If you want something done so that it suits you, you'll have to do it yourself." The reality became increasingly clear: If I

---

[7] Courtesy of Caissa Wilmer, Cortland, New York.

wanted any feeling of resolution, I would have to figure out my love life *my* way. That's how I thought of it then: *My* love life. For a long time I thought that my Wise Woman's alert was personal and private only, that it was about Susan and me, about our "patterns," our personalities, our idiosyncratic dynamic. Slowly, however, it dawned upon me that my Wise Woman was requiring that I look at the *essence* of the relation Ship, at how manunkind insists that love looks. And why.

5

"Do You Know How Miserable You Are?"

A few months after my race-walking revelation, during my first tentative gropings and sloggings about in the foggy swamp underneath my relation Ship, I got a phone call from a woman who had recently visited us but whom I knew only slightly.

"I'm aware that you hardly know me," she began, "and that what I want to say is impertinent and really none of my business. But even if you're outraged and never speak to me again, I'm going to say it: You're miserable. Do you know that? Do you know how much pain you're in?"

It is a measure of the depth of my deadening despair that until the moment she asked those questions, I actually did *not* know that I was miserable or in pain. I knew I was confused but I didn't realize that to escape the fear of facing what I had to do with Susan I had become emotionally almost comatose. I hadn't been joking when I'd assured my caller during her brief visit the week before that I could hardly tell how I felt any more; that if she had asked me what I wanted for myself more than anything in the world, I wouldn't have known what to answer. It seemed natural that a woman I scarcely knew would say to me, "You're suffering. Why don't you stop?" Perhaps I was so desperate to understand myself that I never thought to find her familiarity obnoxious, or to question her invasion of my privacy. At the time of her call, I hadn't yet decided to say no to kindly "helpers," and though it seems contradictory now to say it, I'm glad I hadn't. She proved to be such a catalyst for change that instead I thank whatever powers gave her the courage to call and encourage me so boldly to confront in myself what I was feeling, to acknowledge and begin to observe the great continental plate that was shifting in my internal world. Clearly there are times when it is salutary to grab the metaphorical boat hook when it is extended, and I can only trust that my Wise Woman will help me distinguish those times from instances of dependence and fusion.

My caller kept at me to think and talk about what might be wrong, kept at me to pin down my errant feelings, refused to let me off the hook. I writhed on it inarticulately for hours that week, her on the other end of the line with pitiless kindness and patience cutting through my denial, my absurd justifications.

At some point during those pivotal conversations when I reverted to worrying about my relation Ship—trying aloud to think what it needed, how to navigate a return to the buoyant ocean—my caller said something that totally and permanently redirected my thinking:

"Why would you think of doing anything for something called a 'relation Ship'—some idea that has no real life, no real existence—when there are two real, live, suffering women involved here? Can you see that you're so focused on this figment that you're giving it more importance, more credibility, more power in your life than you're giving either Susan or yourself? It seems to me that it has indeed become a Ship, a vehicle that's driving you, that drove you places you never chose to go even before you knew you were on a journey. Look where it's brought you, to this place where you can't see either yourself or Susan, but only *it*. You know, Sonia, there are really only the two of you. There is no such thing as 'the relation Ship.'"

(The irony is that, months later, this woman discovered herself in exactly the same fix, and I got to ask wickedly, "Well, isn't it time for you to stop worrying about this abstraction that you refer to with such great deference as 'your relation Ship' and start being concerned with the two real suffering women involved here? In a word, hadn't you better get your *own* relationshit together?")

She was right about relation Ships, of course, how they are objectifications of us, perpetual performances of patriarchal patterns. But I shouldn't have had to hear it from her; I should have known it from the word itself. A fundamental feature of the Ship is that it always requires us to be relational[1] instead of centered in Self, to concentrate our attention outside ourselves. It forces us always to externalize and so to neglect our most crucial obligation to create and nurture happiness in our own breasts. And it does this precisely because otherwise we would find our Selves,

---

[1] Some women insist that women's great contribution is our relationality, by which they mean our connection to one another and other life forms. As I use it in this book, relationality is not synonymous with connection or with concern for the continuance of life. It means using others as one's prime reference points in making decisions and choices instead of oneself, a habit that *prevents* connection.

discover our power, and using it for our own benefit, cut off the Ship's power supply.

Her mini-lecture helped me understand that when we create a relation Ship, we put ourselves on board a vessel with its own voracious imperatives, a vessel with a code of discipline that supersedes individuality and seeks to mold both crew and passengers into a single obedient unit. From this perspective, I didn't find either surprising or accidental that we therefore very often lose track of ourselves in our fervor to meet its needs, to "save" it. We know that in order to have it at all we have to put it first in our lives, obeying all its commandments, particularly the one that says: Thou shalt keep thy beloved happy.

We talked that day about how a relation Ship instantly establishes a hierarchy of needs: Those of the Ship first, confused and enmeshed with those of the beloved, and finally, far, far down the line—if they are in line at all—our own. The most significant demand of relation Ships, we realized, is that we *do not* take care of our own needs, because if we were to do so, we wouldn't need to create a Ship. We create *it* out of need, we create *it* to take care of us, to make us feel safe and loved, "supported"—a therapy buzz-word intended to make us feel weak, staggering, falling down, and needing to be held up by others.[2]

We talked about how we had each created our relation Ships out of a refusal to take responsibility for making *ourselves* feel safe and upheld, loved and cared for. We had created them out of refusal to pay attention to ourselves, to know and get what we wanted for ourselves, out of ignorance

---

[2] Bonnie Mann, "Working with Battered Women: Radical Education or Therapy?" Unpublished paper, p. 108.

that anything we "needed" we could provide for ourselves and that what others did or did not give us was incidental—the proverbial frosting on the cake. We agreed that in establishing our Ships we had invented and then depended upon something external and "not-us" to do it for us and to make us happy—tasks at which it can't succeed. We realized that we created this illusion just as people invent and depend upon and are ultimately disappointed by government, the church, and AA. As Sara says, "Relation Ships go to therapy, people don't."[3]

Knowing that the woman on the other end of the phone line was right about my not having a life of my own and suspecting that Susan didn't either but that we were being subsumed by the life of the relation Ship, I resolved that if I ever disentangled myself I would never again allow anything or anyone to come between me and my Self, or between me and the women I loved.

My phone caller was a wise young woman. But like all intuitive wisdom at this point, hers continued to prove slippery. Not many months after her "relation-Ship-is-a-vehicle-that-is-driving-you" insight, I asserted forcefully to her during another phone call, "I'll never have another relation Ship in my life!" To my astonishment she replied in soothing tones, "Now Sonia, of *course* you will. When it's painful like this we all think we'll never do it again, but then—well, look at me. You'll change your mind like the rest of us."

"You don't understand," I explained patiently, suppressing my surprise. (Could this be the same woman who such a

---

[3] Conversation with Sara McIntosh, Arena, Wisconsin, November 26, 1988.

short time ago lectured me about the inescapably malign nature of Ships?) "I'm not saying what you think I'm saying—that I've been so hurt that I won't open myself again to the possibility of intimacy. I'm acknowledging the most important insight I've had over the last few months which is that relation Ships are designed deliberately to *prevent* intimacy. So because I desire intimacy, I don't want a Ship."

She finally got it: I'd never again enter into an unspoken agreement to subvert my own best interests, I'd never put the welfare of an abstraction before my own, I'd never again agree to behave according to the assumptions and expectations that are part and parcel of life aboard a relation Ship.

But how would I have affection and closeness in my life? I had no idea, but I did have a strong hunch that the closeness and affection available in relation Ship mode, no matter how wonderful it was perceived to be, offered little more than a glimpse of the intimacy that was really possible between and among us. *That* was what I craved, and I wasn't willing to settle for menstream society's pitiful substitute any longer.

I'd like to be able to report that, knowing all this, I extricated myself from my patterns at once and went briskly on with my life. But I was floundering in Shipness, stuck up to my eyes in it. I remember shouting at Susan one day: "Who the hell are you being loyal to, yourself or this damned Ship? Would you really want to keep this relation Ship if it extinguished *you*? Because that's what it's doing, dammit!"

This was purest projection. I was shouting at her to get myself to hear what was happening to *me*.

Perhaps I hadn't noticed earlier that my feelings, needs, and desires were so blurred because, contradictory as it may seem, though robotitude was paralyzing my relational life, in most of the other areas of my thinking and being, clarity and spiritual strength were increasing at breakneck speed. I may not have been able to tell whether I felt like kissing Susan or sleeping with her, but I was absolutely certain that I would, for instance, never again vote, lobby, or demonstrate. I also felt daily more beautiful, more serene, and more powerful—more like the goddess I in truth was. This may be why my inner Wise Woman chose this time to lead me to the hardest work of my life.

Talking to the woman on the phone, I became uncomfortably aware of the pattern that had dominated both my public and my private lives. In both I had so often submerged my own desires in the interest of fulfilling the needs of others that I had lost the ability to know and to enunciate what I wanted for myself. I had lost—if I had ever found—my own shape. I'd got the message that the personal is political, all right, and had set about madly rescuing others on both the home and the public fronts—out to save my children from the many possible miseries of their lives, out to save Susan from unhappiness, out to save the women of the world from rape, incest, poverty, and powerlessness. At least I had integrity of a sort: I was living the same wrong principle on all levels of my life!

As so many of us have had to do in the last few years, I knew I had to begin to figure *myself* into the center of my life's equation. I was surprised at how difficult this turned out to be. I didn't even know my own rhythms: What time I would get up in the morning if no one else were in the house or had a claim on me, what time I would feel like going to bed, when and what I would eat, what I would do for entertainment if no one else were voicing a choice.

I was suddenly avid for news of myself, as curious as a lover to learn about me. Who would I be if I were alone for months? And not only physically alone: Who would I be if I were living in my deepest places, living in relation only to myself? Who would I be when I was alone with my soul? Far from being afraid of solitude, I realized suddenly that I was as afraid now of *not* having it as a woman marooned on a desert island fears not having water. In over half a century I had never lived alone, never had myself to myself. It was high time.

I also knew that until I could be happily alone, until my love and company were enough for me, I couldn't be healthily together with anyone. *Needing* someone else in order to feel loved and secure—I wanted to jump that ship and jump it forever. I had written a book about this kind of relationality,[4] after all, affirming that women are not free, can't be free, as long as we do what we do *in relation* to men, in reaction to them, for them, with them, *needing* them or their institutions for whatever reason, even to fight against. I recognized that we had been conditioned to ignore ourselves and to focus on men as long as they were anywhere in actual or psychic sight.

Now I understood that until I applied this principle in my closest relation Ships, it didn't matter how radical I was in a publicly political way; I would be wallowing in the paradigm I was determined to transcend. I could no longer live *in relation* to anyone but myself.

To have integrity—by now I had added freedom to my definition of this condition—I knew I had to get to the bottom of my dependencies and fears and to learn to live, moment by moment, in genuine knowledge of who I was, how I felt,

---

[4] *Going Out of Our Minds: The Metaphysics of Liberation.* The Crossing Press: Freedom, CA, 1987.

what I wanted. Not only to know, but to act as if I mattered as much as the homeless, as much as those dying of AIDS, as much as the oppressed of all nations. And to be brave enough to care for myself as much as I had been caring for everyone else. I began to become more and more greedy for intimacy with Sonia. I longed to cherish and adore myself, to prove that I could trust me to take care of myself emotionally and in every other way, that I could trust me to give myself generously of my time and attention, that I didn't need to look outside myself any more.

As I ask myself now what brought me at last to the point in my life where after a life-time of self-sacrifice I was ready to look steadily at the most painful facts, I see that of course this resolve hadn't just come out of nowhere; it hadn't even just come out of finally being fed up with being miserable and denying it; as we know, women can endure endless misery with scarcely a whimper.

What I think was occurring with me was that I felt as if I were philosophically, spiritually, professionally, and creatively bursting out of my chains and soaring away into the stars.[5] Experiencing the ecstasy of freedom in some areas of my life, I longed to feel it in them all.

I also knew that I couldn't ultimately be free just here and there in myself, that if I didn't extend freedom to all parts of my life, if I didn't free every captive in my internal prison colony, I would lose the possibility for liberty for any. We

---

[5] I have recounted the last dozen eventful years of my life and thought in my first three books: *From Housewife to Heretic, Going Out of Our Minds: The Metaphysics of Liberation,* and *Wildfire: Igniting the She/Volution,* all available from Wildfire Books, Star Route 1, Box 55, Estancia, NM 87016.

often say that as long as any of us is oppressed, we are all oppressed. I think the same is true in the microcosm of each of our individual lives: As long as any part of us isn't free, no part of us can remain free for long.

The reverse, of course, is equally true. Since all aspects of our Selves are intimately connected, when one finds the way to freedom, the others begin rapidly to follow, having been shown the way, coveting, in a sense, desiring for themselves, the bliss of liberation. I saw how being free in one area began a chain reaction—all other chains began to fall off. One prison door being flung open modeled for others how to swing free.

There I was in the winter of 1987, talking to a near-stranger on the phone, in tears and frightened but by this time thoroughly fed up with the game, eager to quit it no matter what it took. This time I was intent on having a life of my own. This time, though I had taken action only when faced with the choice either to flourish or to wither away, I was choosing to flourish, opting for my own growth, for an expanded life. I was becoming *my* ally, my own true and trustworthy friend and this time I meant to find Sonia and take her home to my heart once and for all.

Among other things, that meant heeding the movement of my tectonic plates that were by now no longer merely shaking politely but were ominously pitching: Danger! Watch out! I knew I was too befuddled still to make sense of it all, to find my lost self, in the presence of others' strong needs. I knew I might not be able to resist the lure of the old patterns, might fall again into the coercion and subtle abuse I hated in myself. Also, I knew I had to get me alone and find—become acquainted with and honor—the boundaries of my Self. I had to be alone.

So Susan moved out.

We both recognized at this point that for reasons we didn't understand, our eventual living apart had been inevitable from the first. But since this had meant "breaking up," we hadn't thought we could bear it. Separating from her finally was excruciating for me. Not only had I so *become* her that it was like parting from myself, but for herself alone she was dear to me.

Nevertheless, I knew absolutely that I couldn't drag the corpse of society's deadly dream of intimacy around with me any more, that I wanted out of relationShipness as designed by the fathers forever. I wanted to dream another kind of love into reality.

When Susan moved into her condo a few blocks away, miraculously—or so it seemed—I could tell at once how I felt about sleeping with her. Suddenly I could also see the Ship more clearly and was able to differentiate between it and me, between its needs and desires and my own. This was gratifying and exciting, but greatly mystifying as well. I hadn't actually believed that Susan's moving out would make it easier for me to tell what I felt; there simply hadn't been anything else left to try.

Why it had worked puzzled me for a long time. Obviously, when she wasn't around her needs weren't psychically competing with mine, her wants weren't clamoring for attention and drowning mine out. But I felt certain that there was more to it than that, and found myself coming back to it again and again, wondering.

6

Farewell to Self Blame

But Susan didn't move until almost the end of this story. In the meantime, the surprising thing is that we each did our very different and separate work so well, particularly since the other was always trying to head us away from it. Susan's response to my growing rebelliousness against the Ship was to try to pull me back to the safety of the known world. Mine was to try to pull her over to the edge of the abyss and make her look into it with me, force her to *leap* into it with me.

"Force" is the pivotal word here. I tried every coercive trick I knew. After six months or so of this, I realized that my attempts to make her accompany me on my journey instead of accepting her autonomy and leaving her in peace to continue her own, my haranguing and tormenting her to care passionately about what I cared passionately about—this was the stuff of abuse.

In this way, I had sped from rescuer to persecutor, shouting at her and cutting her off when she tried to talk, feeling annoyed and impatient when her face crumpled and she began to cry. It took my acting this vile to wake me up, right in the middle of the tempest, to my abusiveness. Sick at heart, I understood in that moment the connection between powerlessness and violence.

My hurtful behavior came out of my fallacious belief that I had to get Susan to change, that I was responsible for motivating her, for getting her to understand. I was frantic to convince her because I thought she had to be where I was in order for me to change in the way I wanted to. I thought I couldn't grow unless she grew right alongside me in exactly the same way—evidence that I still couldn't tell where I left off and she began, evidence that I thought she had to be *me*. I was afraid, afraid, afraid. Afraid that if she wouldn't come with me I couldn't make this most important trip of my life. At the time, the irony of my fear that I couldn't un-couple without her was quite lost on me.

But rejecting my violent role in our relation Ship, I gave up trying to make Susan, or anyone else—except me—be me, and finally leapt into the abyss alone.

My direct verbal assaults were only the most obvious abusiveness in our relation Ship. Others were more subtle and difficult to recognize. Whereas I tried to control by bluster, Susan, in the role of victim, ruled by indirectness. I remember the night we stumbled onto another abusive pattern. Susan describes it:

> I was the mistress of the art of covert manipula-tion. One of my manipulative methods of trying to change and control Sonia, for instance, was to cite theory to her, or to quote someone else's opinion. We discovered this integral part of my passive Victim role in a long expensive long-distance telephone conversa-tion one night.

I stealthily inserted the subject of kindness into the conversation. Sonia was definitely abandoning the variety of kindness I was accustomed to in her, the rescuer variety—always being nice, trying not to hurt my feelings, avoiding fraught subjects—and the starkness of her new direct manner sometimes hurt me. I wanted my feelings taken care of again, I wanted the old Sonia back, so without saying any of this, I quoted a friend who had told me that she believed that no matter what, one can and should always behave in a kind way. I reminded Sonia that the means are the ends.[1]

That night on the phone I realized for the first time what an enormous burden Susan's speaking in such riddles put on me. Since she didn't come right out and say that I hurt her with my bluntness and that she wanted me to be kinder, I had to guess why she was bringing up the subject of her friend's kindness at all.

To do this, I had to sort out all the possible reasons: Did she want to talk about this woman at more length because she had been working on unmerging, too? Was she implying that this woman was wiser than I, doing the unmerging work better? Was she telling me that she wanted me to believe what the woman had said about kindness so I would begin being kinder? What part of this did she want me to respond to? What response was she after?

As was usual with us, I then accepted the onus of ascertaining what she was driving at by asking her a dozen questions: Was she saying that she thought I wasn't kind? In

---

[1] Unpublished manuscript, 1988.

what ways had I not been kind? How had that made her feel? What would she like me to do instead? And so on. Then when I had figured it out, my job in our relation Ship was to *say* it for her, to relieve her of the risky business of having to express it herself.

I pointed out to Susan that night that the pattern we were in right then was part of our classic rescuer/victim pattern—my taking wrongful and her relinquishing rightful responsibility. I became furious as I realized how much effort both of us had always expected me to make, how much energy we had both assumed I would expend to communicate with her, how much of the communication work of two people I had "nobly" taken upon myself to do alone, how much energy it had taken me to rescue in this way, and how such behavior disempowered Susan. I was livid at myself not only for agreeing to this but for assisting in setting myself up in this role. It takes two people working hard side by side, obeying the Ship's commands, to create such confusion and misery.

The Ship (in the guise of therapists and well-meaning friends backed up by the system's continuous belchings forth of propaganda) temporarily deflected my rebellion from itself, adroitly turning my anger—though only for a little while—in quite the wrong direction. The problem, it informed me authoritatively, was simple: I had picked the wrong Shipmate. Susan wasn't for me. Forget that I loved her completely. Something was wrong with her, or I'd be happy. All I had to do was to work on a Ship with a candidate more qualified for my affections.

Somehow, though, I actually knew better than to find fault with Susan even as I did it. While I acknowledged that I could no doubt get along better with some women than with others, I was becoming increasingly certain that no matter who I picked there was no way on earth that I could successfully maintain a relation Ship with any one of them. This wasn't because I thought there was something terribly wrong with me or all other women, but because I strongly suspected by this time that the problem was systemic, not personal; not about me or other women, but about patriarchy. Though I knew that neither Susan nor I was perfect—I believe I could see us each with reasonable clarity—I was also increasingly aware that it was the Ship itself—the imperatives of all present relation Ships: Couple, family, friend, etc.—that was at fault.

The indescribable relief of this reminded me of the sense of liberation I felt when as a budding feminist I understood that the reason I had been treated disrespectfully all my life had little or nothing to do with me personally. It was not because of lack of individual merit that I wasn't taken seriously but because I was a member of an underclass that was routinely and intentionally disparaged. I would never forget the relief of realizing that society's undervaluation was not of my particular *Sonia-ness* but of my general *woman-ness*.

Now, seeing that this applied also to relation Ships, I felt similar excitement and relief. I realized that we do not fail at them because we are co-dependent, or afraid of intimacy, or wounded by incest, or fraught with patterns picked up in families that by definition do not function, or addicted to this and that. Though these problems don't make the Ship's path smoother, the reasons we fail are ultimately not personal at all. We fail because failure is built deliberately into menstream patterns of relating.

Some protest that not all relation Ships fail, and hold theirs up as evidence. But in my experience, their protests and efforts to prove me wrong succeed only in revealing their fear. They are afraid because if they dared lift the veils society has so carefully draped over their eyes and look at themselves starkly, honestly, they would have to agree that their relation Ship has been neither what they dreamed it could be nor what they fondly imagine it to be at that moment.

If they remembered what they believed was possible between them at first and then systematically traced how over time they adapted to the many large and small disappointments, limitations, and disillusionments, lowering and revising their expectations, redesigning and smallening their dream because they thought they had no choice, their hearts would break.

It is also too frightening to think of letting the lid off the pent-up rage and despair generated by the innumerable and inevitable compromises of integrity, grievous deprivations, feelings of loss and loneliness, the unavoidable curtailment of freedom and erosion of personal power. On some level, they believe they cannot survive such an explosion of feeling, that they will be blown apart by it personally and as a couple. The longer they have been together, the more built-up pressure there is, the more terrified they are of breakup, and therefore the more resistance they have to seeing themselves truthfully.

So they insist that their relation Ship is a success. But I have yet to see one that is not a failure by my standards. My criterion for success is choice made freely out of clear-eyed and pure desire, where each person's only commitment is to being her own best and happiest self. Everything I value is indissolubly linked with this. Freedom is necessary for honesty, honesty for integrity, integrity for power, power for creativity, and all of them for intimacy. Because my desire for these attributes of character—wholeness, power, creativity, and genuine connection with myself, the universe, and all other living things—is fierce and foremost in my life, freedom is the basis of all that is desirable to me.

It seems to me that what most people perceive as success in a relation Ship is lack of obvious misery or outright failure. But since to keep a Ship anchored in their lives, everyone must ignore certain feelings and tamp down certain others, what is left is at best a sort of deadness that might be called contentment. Since this state is touted as the most that is possible in conventional relation Ships after the first rosy glow has dimmed, women who have attained this level of numbness and fear perceive themselves as happily coupled.

They stay together because they care about each other and believe that this is the best they can do, because it's the best yet, because it's better than being alone or trying again, because they can't believe anyone else will ever love them and they are afraid of not being loved, because they cannot imagine that every single aspect of their lives could be altogether different and more wonderful if they banished Ships from their lives, because they believe they will have to lose each other as heart friends if they break up, because they are afraid to look at the monsters swimming beneath the surface of things, because they no longer believe in the possibility of freedom and have ceased to long for it, because they are in despair.

Though I generalize as usual from my own, better-known-to-me and more-thoroughly-understood sample of one, I have heard countless tales of woe and watched innumerable bitterly painful breakups in my fifty-five years, breakups that often had nothing to do with lack of caring. From all this experience, I have also learned where to look for manifestations of non-free perceptions and feelings in others' relation Ships. And regardless of protestations to the contrary—and though it took me a long time to figure out why—non-freedom has been obvious if not blatant in every relation Ship I've ever observed for more than a few minutes.

I asked myself often in those days, why, in the face of the absolutely overwhelming evidence on every hand that relation Ships do *not* make people happy, that they are *never* what we dreamed they would be, that they must *always* disappoint us, and that they inevitably cause either a deadening of feelings into "contentment" or incalculable grief—why do we continue to believe that they are the best possible way to be close to others? The pure irrationality of it proclaimed to me that this belief was the offspring of brainwashing.

Criss-crossing this country repeatedly during the previous decade, I had come to the conclusion that the single greatest grief among women was the grief of relation Ships. Whatever ranked second was so far below it on the misery-scale that a telescope was necessary to locate it. I had arrived at the juncture where if all I disliked about relation Ships was the anguish they caused—and that was just the beginning of my list—that would have been reason enough for me to jettison them from my emotional repertoire. It seemed to me that how we connected most closely with others had to change radically or we would all die of heartbreak.

In addition, if, as I believed, life was by definition joyful and glorious, something highly unnatural was happening in relation Ships, and happening on a huge scale.

Despite menstream propaganda to the contrary, I did not believe that pain and grief were "natural" human conditions or that we needed them in order to learn. Emotional pain, like physical pain, I knew to be evidence that something was wrong. It was a warning to us that we had to change something quickly, do something differently at once, or risk seriously undermining our health and well-being. I wondered why, despite conclusive proof that they cause such an inordinate amount of emotional pain—pain that signals emotional illness—I had continued to believe that relation Ships were "normal."

I saw, of course, that misery was inherent in men's world, but I knew that men's world was only one possible reality, and real only so long as we focused on it and lived in it. I believed that a world in which joy was the norm and pain an aberration was also a reality—a reality even more powerful. I believed because, whenever I had caught glimpses of this world or only-too-fleetingly dwelt in it, it had been wonderfully congruent with everything I valued, completely harmonious with the very stuff of my woman's spirit.

As to the necessity of suffering for learning, from my own experience and from watching my four children's lives, I was certain that human beings learn more in one minute of happiness than it is possible for us to learn in weeks—perhaps months—of misery. When I or any of my children had been wretched, we almost *couldn't* learn. It was only when the suffering lightened for a moment that we had access to any insight at all.

I understood that mensmachine has trained us to accept our oppression passively by programming us to believe that in human life suffering is a given. I knew that we had learned not only to accept the inevitability of it, but even to value it as if it were some great treasure. But gradually, I realized that any "lesson" that could be learned through suffering and negativity could be learned one hundred times faster and more thoroughly through positiveness and joy. I also discovered that I could reject unpleasant, painful situations as educational moments because I knew there would always be opportunities to learn the same things in gentle, pleasant ways.

Getting this far in my thinking and finally refusing to view either Susan or myself as culprits, I began an open, full-out rebellion against the oppressive authority of the Ship itself. In effect, I swung into my second adolescence.

7

A Kid Again

Though reverting to teen-age was necessary and ultimately very beneficial, it was also a humiliating development. I had just managed somehow to survive the long-drawn-out emotional sieges of three adolescent freedom fighters and was girding up my loins grimly for the fourth when, suddenly, at age fifty-two, I found myself defecting to their camp.

As I railed and ranted and threw myself about and cried and sulked and swore and raged and was, all in all, splendidly dramatic in a juvenescent sort of way, I kept pausing long enough to apologize to Susan—and anyone else who happened to have strayed into the maelstrom: "This is terribly embarrassing. I'm appalled at myself, but the crazy reason that I'm acting like a teenager is that I'm feeling like a teenager. I don't understand it yet myself. But please pay no attention to me. I trust I'll get it out of my system eventually like we teenagers do."

"But, damn it," and I took up the tirade against tyranny where I'd left it, "who said I have to leave a note telling everyone where I've gone every time I leave the house? Well, listen, whoever said it can just forget it! This middle-aged woman has earned the right to go where she wants when she wants without telling a soul. You got that, world? You hear that, universe? Don't go expecting any more sweet, compliant little messages from me because the answer is no!"

NO! NO! NO!

Like my two- and fifteen-year-olds, my favorite word became no. No matter what the question, the answer was no. No, I wouldn't go to the co-op planning meeting. No, I wouldn't bring the refreshments for the soccer team—this week or ever. No, I wouldn't eat what Susan had fixed for lunch. No, I wouldn't share my carrot juice. No, I wouldn't return that phone call. No, I didn't want to know where she was going. No, I wouldn't wash and deflea the dog. No, Noel couldn't wear my sweater. No, I wouldn't see a therapist with Susan.

I wouldn't do this, I refused to do that.

Like my teenagers, I said no to prove to myself that I had a right to say no, that I could no longer be forced to do anything I didn't damned well choose to do. I said no to things I might in reality have wanted to say yes to but out of principle—and an inability to tell where or what the oppressor was at any given moment—stuck to non-cooperation. Like my kids, I dug in my heels against the subtle coercion of belief.

I rebelled against, I wrestled with mocking shadows, fought against the terror of refusing to give in. Sometimes I was very brave, holding out against society's dictum to prove myself a loving, caring woman by apologizing for upsetting everyone, for instance, only to fold in the next instant and, denying my desire for privacy, leave the door of my room open so that I wouldn't appear inaccessible.

I acted big and strong and fierce because, sensing that I could never knowingly participate in another relation Ship, I was scared to death. I wasn't at all sure that I was capable of being a whole person, an independent adult, a woman in her power responsible for her own life. I was also frightened because I wasn't convinced that there was any other way to love, and I wanted love in my life. I threw relation Ships out wholesale and roared so that I wouldn't whimper at the size of the hole that left in my heart. Each programmed belief about relation Ships that I shed left me more frightened than the last. Finally, I had to face that what I was feeling was not simply fear, but terror, as if the ground had opened up under my feet and I was falling without hope of rescue out of the known and knowable world.

From the beginning—and more so as I probed steadily deeper into the inner workings of the relationShip mind—I was unpleasantly surprised by the intensity of the fear that the investigation was stirring up in me. I managed somehow for long stretches of time to deny it, ignore it, tuck it out of sight. But now the terror and panic were washing over me in such giant waves that I could no longer pretend that I wasn't going to be killed for my insubordination, for seeing through the fathers' tender love myth to the malevolence beneath.

The immensity of the fear catapulted me back to other times in my feminist life when I had suffered similarly intense dread. From remembering those experiences, I knew what the present fear was all about. I knew that its intensity was directly correlated with the importance to male rule of the dogma in question. The fact that I was experiencing such terror was proof to me that I was mucking about in the deepest strata of my conditioning. I had got down to the very foundations. I had reached the level of taboo.

Taboos govern life and death. All patriarchal cultures control through taboo, but in some groups—non-industrialized, non-intellectualized tribes, for instance—this material is overt, openly discussed among the people. In others, like our own, it is covert and largely unconscious, seldom called by its real name.

When I lived in Western Samoa in the late '50s, I learned from those more "primitive" people how profoundly taboos affect their behavior. The Samoans remembered a time not too far distant when if a person violated a taboo, they did not have to be punished by others. Knowing that life was now no longer possible, they simply lay down under a tree and died.

Behavior absolutely necessary to the maintenance of a system is governed by taboo. That we keep one another enslaved through relation Ships is of incalculable importance to the success of the reign of the phallus. Relation Ships are therefore governed by taboo. On a deep level, every one of us comprehends the taboos of our culture precisely and knows absolutely that violating any one of them makes life no longer possible.

As women we have broken—or have at least toyed with breaking—the principle taboos of menstream culture. One of the chief taboos—that women not focus on our own values but on men's—has frightened more women into more "safe," male-centered reformist activities than any other single prohibition.

Now in repudiating male-invented relationShipness, I was not only violating that taboo but others even more powerful.

Though I could only guess then that I was in great and valorous company—because I am never the first, having always so far been in the middle of the wave—that, in fact, proved to be the case. By the hundreds of thousands, each feeling alone and isolated in it, women were repudiating patriarchy's relationShip enslavement program all over the United States and Canada.[1] No wonder women were so afraid.

I went into mourning for the loss of the sweet dream of love manunkind had so perniciously implanted in my heart. I despaired of creating any way of connecting that was truer or more beautiful, of ever being able to rediscover and reconstruct women's ways of loving.

To bring me relief as well as clarity, my left brain reminded me of some of the facts I had learned previously about patriarchy: 1) it always lies; 2) its lies are exact reversals of the truth; 3) so whatever it says is the healthiest way to do things is always the most destructive; and 4) whenever it insists that there is only one right way, there are always hundreds of other, better, ways. Willing to take any comfort and reassurance at hand, I looked at relation Ships through those four lenses.

The realization that menstream society lies about relation Ships as about everything else was unavoidable by this time, and that it lies not just a little, not just now and then, but totally and always. I also knew it was true that it not only teaches us falsehoods but that it specializes in lies that are reversals of truth, in ironies.

It was the terrible ironies that hurt and disoriented me most. I could hardly bear the knowledge that everything I had believed would make me happy—living with a person I loved, sleeping with her, having sex only with her, process-

---

[1] Since I began thinking about relation Ships, I haven't traveled to any other countries and so do not know from my own experience how widespread this phenomenon is.

ing, compromising and negotiating with her, meeting her needs as well as I could, having her meet mine—that all this had instead made me wretched. Indeed, I wept at my realization that what I had been taught as the healthiest mode of life was in fact the most destructive. The first three facts I was looking to for comfort—1) that patriarchy lies, 2) that its lies are reversals of the truth, so 3) that what it says is best is always worst—had so far succeeded only in depressing me further. But the fourth—that there is never only one right way—gave me solace. Though I had been so well drilled by the system in the tenets of relationShipping that I couldn't imagine even one other way of being close and loving, let alone dozens, I knew such ways had to be possible. For years, the Wise Old Woman inside me had often and with great authority assured me that this was so.

Believing her, throughout my years of floundering through the relationShip swamp I clung to my conviction that women could re-create love, that out of our deepest Selves we would re-vision connection, that we were destined to rewrite, completely and gloriously, the story of the heart.

PART II

EXPOSING THE OFFICER
ON THE BRIDGE

8

Ship Shape, or OurBS

T hen one day, as I was trying to make some philosophical sense of the amazing fact that Susan's moving out had caused me to be more visible to myself, an image leapt onto my mental screen. As clearly as if it had been that morning instead of a decade earlier, I saw myself standing before a college English class delivering what had become a standard lecture, one I repeated each term without fail. The subject was the intimate bond between form and content, particularly in poetry.

I realized with excitement that my Wise Old Woman was using this memory to point out that the principles I had explained so many times in poetry classes were still useful, that they were applicable *now*, to this very situation with Susan. Galvanized, I began to reconstruct that lecture, searching for illumination into the mystery of why my living alone clarified my feelings, helped me know what I genuinely desired.

I recalled immediately that I was giving that particular lecture because once again some student had just said something like, "If this guy wants to communicate, why does he write in such a weird way that nobody can understand it? Why doesn't he just come right out and *say* it?"

I remembered that what I had explained to this exasperated student was that a poem communicates not only by *what* it says but just as much by *how* it says. And that because these two elements—the content and the form it takes—co-develop, determining each other as the poem comes into being, they are indissolubly bonded. In effect, they *are* each other and therefore cannot be separated without loss of the original intent; in fact, without loss of the poem itself.

This means that what we speak of as the poem exists only as it is laid down on the paper before us—those words with that rhythm, that sound, in that shape. The words do not carry the meaning alone. In fact, the form they are in dictates what they can mean at any given point. When we talk about the poem's meaning and how the poet achieved it, this is *talking about* the poem, it is not the poem. The poem is the experience—the emotions and thoughts—we have as we read the words on the page, or hear them read, with all their internal relationships and within their peculiar context and structure.

Recalling the thesis of this lecture, my understanding cleared at once and all the weeks of confusion fell away. Of course. Like poetry, most aspects of life, *including relation Ships*, are also fusions of structure and content.

I whooped with elation and relief. Having come to the end of the possibilities of co-dependency analysis, I hadn't yet found another theoretical path out of the relationShip fog. Now, magically, the poetry analogy sprang up to guide me. It was as if the mists parted and the North Star shone steadily through: *A relation Ship is a marriage of form and content.*

On solid ground now, my frustration blissfully forgotten, I began at once to make use of this idea.

My first step was to find the superstructure, the form, of what society calls a "romantic relationship." I knew that when I had done that, because the form and content are co-entities, the content might also reveal itself.

This was the sort of puzzle I most enjoyed. Settling down to the task, I began by asking myself, "How can I make the form apparent?" I answered at once, "That's easy. Pretend that two women walk into this room with their arms around each other and, gazing soulfully into each other's eyes, announce in unison, 'We are having a relation Ship!' From that declaration, what can be known about them?"

I made a list of what seemed to me at the time to be the most important bits of information that one sentence could yield about two people's lives:

They are having sex.

Because they are having sex, this is their most important relation Ship.

They are being sexually exclusive, or "true to each other."

That is, they have made a commitment to each other.

They believe that a good relation Ship requires negotiation and compromise.

They are either presently living together or planning to (your place or mine or should we get a different place together?).

They have a bedroom called "our bedroom" and a bed named "our bed" and they are sleeping there together every night unless one of them is sick or has a very good excuse.

They perceive of themselves as no longer "single" but as a couple, and are so perceived by others.

They spend most of their free time together.

Because they are a closed system, their outside friendships change.

They try to meet each other's needs and to make each other happy.

They think they will never break up but they almost certainly will.

This seemed to be the form of patriarchy's relationShip poem. I knew that within it abounded hundreds of conditioned expectations and assumptions that comprised the content. Though couples may deviate from the twelve-point form somewhat, it is nevertheless the form that we are all programmed to follow in this culture. The marriage model is the only model we have for relation Ships, and we all follow it with more or less devotion. At breakfast on Thanksgiving morning in 1988, Sara and her daughter Rachel and my son Noel and I took fifteen minutes and listed a few relationShip expectations and assumptions—not necessarily the most important, just those that came to mind. We entitled our list, "If You Really Loved Me, You Would."

IF YOU REALLY LOVED ME, YOU WOULD: Accept and share my family; tell me your secrets and ask my advice about your important problems; be my confidante, listening to whatever I have to say for as long as it takes me to say it; be responsive to my feelings; share my dreams; agree with me; need me; want me to have what I want; be sensitive to my moods, such as when I want to be left alone (i.e., read my mind); remember what I said two weeks ago; put me first in your life, even before your children; avoid hurting me, particularly by being honest; want to do things for me; eat what I eat, and eat with me if I am around; pool your money with mine; wear my clothes and let me wear yours if we are the same size; care as little about modesty as I do, allowing me into the bathroom while you are having a bath, for instance, or letting me talk to you while you are on the toilet; do anything to save our relation Ship; be willing to sacrifice for me; try harder to please me; trust me; remember our anniversaries, little rituals, and important facts—my birthstone, ring size, how much sugar and cream I take; forgive me; share my religious and political beliefs as much as possible; support me in anything I choose to do; tend my children; love my pets; avoid painful subjects and confrontations; take care of me; wait for me; help me carry my burdens; have a child with me.

In short, if you really loved me, you'd marry me.

Gradually, out of manunkind's mind-control swamp I unmired the putrescent program for which I used Sara's label: Patriarchy's RelationShip Belief System. At first I called it PRBS for short, but soon changed it to a more accurately descriptive nickname: "OurBS."

I knew, as all radical feminists know, that none of menstream's many and massive brainwashing programs is spawned to bring joy and freedom to women. Instead, each is devised to hurt and defeat us. The relationShip belief program was causing so much pain in so many women's lives that I knew it was no exception.

In fact, the more I studied it, the more unavoidable the conclusion became that OurBS was the archetype of mind-control programs in phallocracy. On no other subject could there be found such truly monumental barrages of propaganda so widely, so persuasively, and so incessantly fired off. In billions of ads, millions of songs, books, magazine articles, pictures, and films, and in most of the lives around us, the basic assumption of our lives is portrayed: That two by two, in loving couples who live, sleep, and rear children together, we can most safely, most successfully, and most happily experience the world.

The first question that springs into my mind when I stumble upon such a ubiquitous and effective brainwashing program is, "Why this? What's in it for mensystem?" Now with the shape of OurBS before me—the Ship's shape—I wondered why the men who control the world care so much about how we relate to one another in our private lives, why it is so important for them to convert us to their religion of love that they have kept their propaganda machine spewing out its doctrines around the clock for centuries.

But mostly I marveled at their gargantuan push to persuade us to do something that they themselves insist just comes naturally. It didn't make any sense to me that they would squander such vast resources of time and effort and money in a mad effort to get us to do what we would do anyway, without their intervention.

This confirmed my hunch that relationShip behavior is learned behavior, and that the incredible machine set up to teach and perpetuate it is necessary precisely *because* relationShipping is so contrary to anything we would do in our wild, uncontaminated state.

Since my most passionate desire for many years had been to be my original, powerful, untamed Self, my work had been to strip myself of layer after layer of disfiguring, sapping indoctrination. Now, acting upon my newly-reinforced belief that everything men have conditioned me to accept as true is instead profoundly false, particularly what they have taught me is "natural," I was ready to deprogram myself of their pernicious relationShip poem.

Having identified its form—at least in part—I began to search its embedded content for answers to "What's in it for the guys on top?"

9

Naked Together in Bed

T wo people who have just become a couple don't have to announce that they are having sex; everyone automatically knows it. Even if, out of embarrassment that their most private behavior is public knowledge, the couple should act decorous in public to throw people off the scent, all subterfuge would prove vain. In their presence, friends and acquaintances are acutely conscious that they have just risen from or will shortly be returning to each other's naked arms.

It is an open secret because nowadays the fact that two people are having sex[1] is the central condition around which the relationShip form is built. Because of this, the advent of sexual activity between them signals the launching of their relation Ship. This is why we know what two people are up to in bed as soon as a relation Ship is announced or becomes evident. It is the one essential ingredient, the core of the Ship's definition.

Even though along the way—and sometimes surprisingly soon—sexual interest may wane and a couple may stop being

---

[1] In my youth, the engagement—the announcement of the *intent* to have sex—signaled the Ship's official birth.

95

sexual altogether, no matter how this cessation is rationalized and glossed over, it is felt as deviant and as a loss. A relation Ship without sex is automatically not kosher and is therefore almost without exception a source of anxiety and stress, either consciously or on a less aware level.

Such concern is not foolish. Since the basic assumption in mensgame is that genital sex defines a relation Ship, fear haunts the one in a Ship who wants to be less sexual or not sexual at all. She knows that her failure to meet her partner's sexual needs puts the Ship in jeopardy. Her socialization assures her that since she is not holding up her end of the bargain, sooner or later her partner will probably—and justifiably—seek sexual satisfaction elsewhere, and they will break up.

Over many months I questioned why patriarchy makes sex the foundation of a relation Ship. As it has to many women, for years the menstream concept of sexuality had seemed to me fundamentally wrong-headed. But it took me a long, long time to figure out even sketchily how and why.

When I first began to think about this in earnest it seemed so fraught with connotations, suggestions, implications, arcane significances and dangers, that I felt unequal to any analysis. I was fond of saying with a laugh, "Thank goodness it isn't *my* mission to make sense of sex. I'm delighted to leave that to others!" The frequency with which I made that protest should have told me that I was resisting the strong impulse to figure it out for myself. Fortunately, when I was ready to take sex on, radical feminism gave me at least a starting point.

Since control in every race and class and major nation on earth is gender-based, gender is the most important fact of every person's life, determining as it does whether they will be master or slave. The fact that our gender is determined by our genitals confuses the issues of gender, sexuality, and control almost beyond sorting out. It renders sexuality the least understood, most contaminated, most compromised aspect of most lives, and therefore among the most hurtful.

In addition to this basic theory, I pondered as well the significance of women as the generators of the human life form. We not only have the unique power to create new human beings, but we have the power to create them ourselves without the assistance of men. Although knowledge that this is true is lost to conscious memory, I think that parthenogenesis still happens on occasion—by choice as well as by accident—and that we bore children parthenogenetically for hundreds of thousands of years at the beginning of human history. I also believe that long after the advent of male energy onto this planet, the memory of women as deity in and of themselves persisted in the human psyche. Men have always known that women do not need them for anything, and women have always known that men need them for everything.

In the meantime, men, having no such claim to godhood, have been hugely envious of our divine generativity. In order to establish patriarchy—which necessitated not merely control but usurpation of this ultimate power—they had to institute the concept of ownership.

I feel certain that in goddess times ownership—of *anything*—was not even a concept. Most of the women I know agree that to believe that land or trees or animals or children or even hunks of metal can be owned is truly bizarre. When applied to anything—but oneself, perhaps—what does the word "own" even mean?

Even though the belief that people can be owned is now implanted deeply in our unconscious minds and even though women are owned by men worldwide, hardly anyone would admit to believing that owning other human beings—i.e., slavery—is morally acceptable. But it is only ownership of *people*, not ownership per se, that is understood to be evil. Objects are assumed to be morally possessable. Therefore, in order for women to continue as owned persons they must be considered objects. To the degree that we insist on sexual fidelity/ownership, we must view others not as themselves but as objects. In this way, sexual exclusivity makes its substantial contribution to the objectification of women.

The concept of possession is as ontologically absurd as it is necessary to male control. So absurd, in fact, that it probably took several dozen centuries of both physical and psychic violence to force us to concede that human bodies can rightfully be owned by others, that men could and should own women's. But this understanding is now part of the core of belief of every person born on this phallocentric planet.

Since creative power has such indissoluble integrity—wholeness and intactness—female sexuality could not be separated out from it; hence the continuing necessity for men to control women's bodies in order to have access to creative energy, the centrality to patriarchy of the idea that people can be owned, and the enforcement of ownership through sexual domination.

The evidence that having sex means ownership is blatant and ubiquitous. When Jeannette tells me, "This is my lover, Allie," the word "lover" announces that she's having sex with Allie, and loverdom is monogamous by definition if not in fact. The "my" underscores the warning to the rest of us (potential owners all) that Allie is already owned by Jeannette so we must look elsewhere for chattel.

If, in a movie or book—B grade, of course—the man says, "I can't wait until you're mine," we all know he means he can't wait to get his penis into her vagina. When we hear lyrics such as, "I'm yours, heart and soul I am yours," we know that the singer is really saying, "I'm ready for sex with you."

Patriarchy's form or pattern—its paradigm—is sadomasochism: Someone ruling someone else, overtly with (often sexual) violence and pain and humiliation or covertly with fear of loss of approval or of sex or of association or of other sorts of support. All relation Ships in phallocracy exist along this master-slave continuum and partake of its corruption, marriage being the ultimate in patriarchy's panoply of ownership contracts.

This explains why my hypothetical couple consider their union their most important relation Ship. It is marriage, the confluence of sex and slavery. In patriarchy/sadomasochism, the chief value is control over others. Therefore, marriage—i.e., bondage through sexuality—has high status because it is in this form that control over another is most possible; in fact, it is in this form that control over another is at this moment in human history almost inescapable.

Because in OurBS women have least freedom, we are constantly and feverishly encouraged to adhere to it. To the degree that each of our personal lives is centered around keeping someone else enslaved, the system can focus its attention and energy on institutional oppression of the public kind, and menmachine's goal of non-freedom can be furthered expeditiously on many fronts at once.

Understanding marriage as *the* relationShip/owner-ship/sexual model helps explain why incest is endemic to male societies: Ownership began with and means marriage, and marriage means domination through sex. So owning children, as we are taught to do, is fraught with sexual peril for them.

As much as I wished to believe it, I saw little evidence that Lesbians relationShipped differently in any important respect from the rest of society. The more I looked for proof of genuine departures from the norm, the more heartsick I became. On the whole, we seemed to have embraced the marriage myth every bit as enthusiastically and unconditionally as heterosexuals.

Perhaps even more so. After all, we not only had the system's usual love/romance tapes washing our brains every minute, but also its homophobia tapes. These told us that there was no place for us in society if we weren't married, and that, in addition, we were bad/worthless/sick not to want to marry. (Though they mean marry a man, perhaps we feel that we can mitigate the situation a little by at least marrying *someone* and conforming to society's nuclear family pattern.)

I saw that many of us, while as feminists denouncing marriage and denigrating heterosexual women for entering into it, were essentially married ourselves. We "married," i.e., did what we were deeply programmed to believe was normal, not only because we wanted to feel a legitimate and acceptable part of the society in which we lived, but also because we believed the propaganda that relation Ships were the surest road to intimacy.

But like many others, I was rapidly coming to believe that having relation Ships was in itself unacceptable participation in gynocidal culture, to say nothing of heaping the mountains of honor, reverence, time, and attention upon them that we did. I knew there had to be other modes of connecting, other more alive and fervid, more stimulating and absorbing, fresher, more joyous ways of being together than even Lesbian society acknowledged or presently allowed.

And I intuited that patriarchal reversal prevailed on the subject of intimacy. That is, since menstream society insists that relation Ships generate intimacy, clearly the truth is that relation Ships kill all possibility of intimacy and are the last place to look for it.

While I was busily critiquing Lesbian relation Ships in general, I was also critiquing my own in particular. I had clung as long as I could to the belief that my Ship was different and better than those of my Lesbian friends, and certainly not of the same ilk as odious heterosexual marriages. But the fact had loomed more and more inescapably that I was indeed married, even more married to Susan than I had been to Rick; that I was, in fact, *doubly* married.

Marriage, as every feminist knows, was instituted to give men title to women's bodies, loyalty, time, energy, passion, talents, and attention, and not only to legitimize but to sanctify this enslavement of women to men. Though society goes to considerable lengths to persuade marriageable women that the marriage contract gives equal ownership rights to both men and women, in fact, however laws may change, it is part of our deep cultural understanding that the possession prerogative applies to men only. Women do not have society's imprimatur to own men.

It is women who can be and who are owned. Though marriage gives a woman a live-in master, every woman is first the chattel of the patriarchal state (meaning all men) whether she is married or not. When Lesbians marry, we join our heterosexual sisters in becoming both publicly and privately owned.

But even more than this. Human beings learn what they live, and because women have lived profoundest oppression, oppression is what we have learned best—how to be oppressed and how to oppress others. The more we have been oppressed, the more difficulty we have overcoming our education in how to oppress. The result is a dynamic that not only makes the women's movement potentially the least safe place for women but renders Lesbian liaisons even more hazardous than official marriages—which is saying a great deal.

Whereas in heterosexual marriage there is only one person with a slave consciousness, in Lesbian coupling there are twice that number, twice the amount of internalized oppression, twice the difficulty imagining loving out of captivity, twice the propensity to project self-hatred onto another like ourselves.

No wonder difficulty and pain are almost inevitable in our present relation Ships. Women are born to be free; this is our nature. That we[2] unwittingly imprison one another in cage within cage in the name of love and liberty is an intolerable irony.

---

[2] I'm trying to say "I" more and "we" less. But when I do generalize from a sample of one, it is perhaps not as lacking in political consciousness as it may at first appear. Experience has taught me that I am never the only woman or even one of only a small number of women to have been successfully brainwashed in a certain direction on any given subject; that, in fact, my conditioning is remarkably like that of most other women in my society. I know there are exceptions, but I believe these are few and that they are, at least at this moment, exceptional only in limited respects. From my wide first-hand observation of the women of the United States, I admit to judging myself a reliable barometer. I also trust my readers to exempt themselves when generalizations *genuinely* don't fit.

I remember how appalled I was when I discovered that I owned Susan, not metaphorically or figuratively but *literally* owned her. Thinking about marriage-style possession one winter afternoon and feeling very detached from it all, the realization struck me that if Susan wished to be sexual with someone else while still in our relation Ship, she would have to make sure it was all right with me; in effect she would have to *get my permission* or risk losing me.

That I, not she, was the ultimate governor of what she did with her body was proof that I owned her body. And of course she owned mine. Having automatically assumed proprietorship over each other's bodies, she had as much or more say about what I did with mine than I did.

Like all truth obscured by brainwashing, this seemed so blatant once I'd spotted it that I couldn't imagine why I hadn't noticed it sooner. I'm sure I had kept my eyes closed to it for so long because in some dim corner of my mind lay awareness of the enormous pain and confusion that would follow its discovery. And I was right. After all, my entire life, all my passion, was about freedom for women. And here I was, Susan's prison guard.

But after I had assimilated the very difficult reality that I owned Susan's body and she mine, it was easier to face the further hard fact that our rights of possession were not limited to each other's bodies. We owned all of each other—time, attention, talents, energy, loyalty. In every sense our relation Ship, like the marriage it was, had made her mine and me hers.

I began to understand how this fact played itself out in our daily affairs, and that it was this that accounted for much of the murk that underlay our interactions.

Many couples agree tacitly that each can use eight to ten hours of her allotted daily time at an outside job somewhere, leaving only about fourteen hours to be negotiated. But Susan and I worked together in our home. This gave each of us twenty-four hours worth of the other's time every day, which meant that to get any back for ourselves took almost constant negotiation.

One day, for instance, I caught myself in a covert negotiation with Susan for some of my own time that she was holding hostage. I knew as I observed it that unconsciously making such deals was a common occurrence with us, totally accepted and taken-for-granted behavior. On the surface, it looked something like this:

I get up from my desk, stretch, look at my watch, and picking up the outgoing mail, say, "I think I'll run to the post office with this before it closes."

"Great," Susan says from behind *Publishers Weekly*.

So far so good. She didn't say, "Why don't you finish designing the ad for *The Women's Review of Books*? There's nothing in the mail that can't wait," or "I need a stretch. I'll go with you." Having successfully negotiated with her for about a half hour of my own unmonitored time, I try for more.

"While I'm out, I'll go past the typesetter's and see if our work's done. Then I might check for organic carrots at the co-op. On the way home I think I'll stop by the nursery and visit the flowers. I should be home by, oh let's see, 6 or 6:30."

Then I wait for the verdict. Have I won or do I have to compromise somewhere?

Negotiation of this sort is risky for several reasons and requires considerable finesse. With every activity I propose, for instance, I increase the chances that I will overreach my quota and create resistance; the longer I propose to be away, (i.e., the more freedom from surveillance I request), the more discomfort she is likely to experience. Because she has been conditioned to feel that it is necessary to her well-being to prevent me from taking too large draughts of freedom—would I continue to opt for the bridle if I were allowed to experience the elation of wildness?—she is likely to curtail my plans in some covert way.

One of these ways is to accompany me. If she joins me, my negotiation for time is not all that fails. Every negotiation for time becomes secondarily a negotiation for attention. Now I will have to continue to give her much of my attention when what I had hoped for was to have it all for myself for awhile.

The scenario is similar for a negotiation in which attention rights are primary. Susan hangs up the phone from talking to her friend. "That was Bobbie," she informs me. "The papers from the trustees of her father's estate just arrived and she wants me to look them over with her tonight. Since it's an hour's drive, I won't be able to get there until after eight so I think I'll just stay overnight and come home in the morning."

"Fine," I say, allowing her not only access to her time over which I am keeping guard but also to her fund of attention. Magnanimously I am *letting* her pay full attention to Bobbie that night, and if you can *let* someone, you own them.

It might be argued that my saying "fine" is *not* about giving her permission or letting her. But evidence that it *is* is that I could just as easily say, "Suse, can't this wait until tomorrow night? We have so much to do tomorrow." Or

"You're busier than Bobbie. Why doesn't she come here?" Or "I wish you'd come home tonight. I've got to do that newspaper interview early tomorrow morning."

If I were to say any of these, she would have several choices. One, she could capitulate and quietly call Bobbie with proposed changes in the plan. Two, she could try to persuade me to go along with the original plan. Three, she could insist on doing what she wanted regardless of my wishes.

If she is interested in keeping our relation Ship securely anchored in the living room, however, she will probably avoid taking the third option very often. She really must keep in mind that there will be future negotiations when she will want my cooperation and that by rocking the boat now she might jeopardize her chances of getting at least some of her attention and time back for other occasions and other friends at some later time.

I'm sure many couples will swear and truly believe that they do not do this. I would have sworn that Susan and I did not. We cared deeply about each other, worked and played happily together, and were grateful every day for the other's presence in our world. Such negotiations as I describe were very gentle and very subtle, certainly never conscious or deliberate. It could be said that we kept the reins loose. Nevertheless without knowing it we did after all hold and manipulate the reins.

Negotiations for time and attention may be subtle and unwitting, but they seem to me to be dismally common—the rule not the exception—between any partners. I've watched every couple I know or have spent some time with participate in similar possessive behavior.

Until the fateful day that I identified these subtle instances of coercion as the shadows and mists that I had sensed swirling beneath our interactions, I would also have insisted that Susan and I were both perfectly free to do as we wished, that we were dealing totally up front with each other, and that we knew and approved of what was going on all the time. But none of this was the case, at least with me. All the while that I believed I was steering my relation Ship differently, I was fembotically following patriarchy's set course.

Though this was hard to look at, I wanted to understand OurBS more than I wanted comfort. So I laid aside my initial notes about why having sex—and thereby establishing rights of ownership—was the first, most basic, and most important element of the Ship's structure, and with trepidation—what difficult truth might I uncover next about myself?—turned my attention to the second.

10

The Phallacy of Numbers: Monogamy vs. Non-Monogamy

S ince sexual exclusivity was part of this owner-ship/marriage model, the probability was very good that the relationShipped couple standing in my study were being genitally sexual only with each other, and that they perceived their Ship as healthy as long as one of them didn't break loose and have sex with someone else.

I therefore turned my attention to monogamy and non-monogamy and the perennial feminist debate about which was less patriarchal and therefore more desirable. Right away I found myself in a thought-loop, going around and around and getting nowhere.

By this time in my feminist experience I understood thought-loops very well, having got trapped in them often enough along the way. To me a thought-loop is any concept that will not develop beyond its present form, that will not yield further insights, despite the great and concentrated effort of many women. A concept that is therefore powerless to change behavior. Thought-loops are the menstream's red herrings, those concepts that are deliberately designed and strewn across our path to distract us from ideas that generate behavior dangerous to the status quo. As an example, one of the system's most important thought-wheels—the one I had spun futilely around and around on for years—is that to change the world, women must change men's behavior.

As long as I was kept focusing on what men were doing—the red herring—I was prevented from noticing several facts that I saw as soon as I finally took my eyes off the guys and looked at the situation from an angle that did not include them at all. First, that since focusing on men was for women the very essence of slavery, trying to change men could not and had not worked to destroy but only to strengthen and perpetuate our oppression. And second, that the nature of freedom is that no one can give it to anyone else. It is always taken, and always on one's own terms, totally independently of the oppressor's institutions, beliefs, or behavior. Freedom means independence, and independence means *not in relation*.

As long as we keep dutifully looping-the-loop in our thoughts, going over and over the same ground without noticing that we are actually getting nowhere, the seditious ideas that can potentially fling open our prison doors don't occur to us. The monogamy/non-monogamy debate seemed to me to be a classic thought-loop. The evidence for this was that for at least the last quarter century the argument over which is more patriarchal has raged in the women's movement. But if we were to compare a recording of the first feminist discussion of it with a recording of feminists debating it this morning, we would find that they were idea-for-idea, almost word-for-word, the same.

What this tells me absolutely is that if, being as brilliant as we are, in twenty-five years we haven't been able to make any headway in our thinking about it, it has been the wrong debate to be having all along.

That it has been such a successful red herring notifies us that there is something *else*, something phallocracy has deliberately distracted us from noticing that is the truly significant, life- and world-changing mystery.

Given this, I decided to refocus my attention and look at something else altogether. Knowing how important quantifying everything is to the masculinist mind, I tried to figure out ways to approach sexuality from other angles. At once, I was able to discard the false and dangerous assumption that physical desire motivates people to climb aboard relation Ships. I knew that relation Ship (marriage), like rape, is not about sexual desire per se but pre-eminently about gaining possession and maintaining it through sex.

This helped me move rapidly beyond the relevance of numbers. The thought of continuing to own and be owned by any number of other women was intolerable, equally so if by one or two or a hundred of them, for any length of time, separately or all at once. Quantity large or small obviously had nothing to do with what mattered to me. What *did* matter was liberty, liberty and all that attends it. So I didn't hear an affirming "Yes!" in my soul when in various ways I questioned my intuition about the validity of either monogamy or non-monogamy.

In addition, I had by this time developed a large and healthy disrespect for men's dichotomies. When they swore as Jehovah was their witness that there were only two poles—good and evil, friend and foe, yin and yang, monogamy and non-monogamy—I started looking for the third—and fourth, and fifth. The dichotomousness of the monogamy/non-monogamy choice was in itself enough to convince me that there was at least one and probably hundreds of other ways to connect with people that had no relation to either of these concepts or this either/or worldview. It also told me that these other ways were so productive of joy and power that they would wipe patriarchy's leer right off the face of the earth; otherwise the dichotomy wouldn't have become one of its prized tools of mind control and couldn't have been used to focus us so intently on the wrong question for so long.

The knowledge that our magnificent creative powers, our inherently beneficent sexuality, had been turned against us and made the malevolent agents of our captivity sickened me. So I rejected forever both sex as patriarchy's minion—i.e., as a means of control—and the red herring of numbers that focuses us on how many lovers we are taking naked to bed instead of what condition our souls are in and what is in our hearts as we lie with them.

I realized pretty quickly that monogamy vs. non-monogamy had never been the real issue, that it had always been a ruse, distracting us from the truly revolutionary questions: How can we associate intimately with one another and be totally free—never compromising, never negotiating, always choosing independently exactly what we want every moment? What is intimacy and how can we have it? What is the connection between freedom and power? What is power and how can we have it? How can we keep our power and still have intimacy? How can we get our legitimate needs for touching, companionship, and comfort met without merging or being responsible for meeting anyone else's needs? What are the links between and among freedom, power, creativity, intimacy, and integrity that bind them so closely that we can't have one without the others? Do we mate only in captivity? What would love look like in freedom? Over the following months, I dwelt upon freedom and its connection with all I most cherished. As I turned my attention upon the amazing creativity and power and integrity and intimacy possible among free people, the words monogamy and non-monogamy lost all meaning. They finally became as empty and meaningless as the word "rug" or "supper" repeated aloud for the fiftieth time.

At this point I made an important connection: These words have meaning *only in the context of phallocratic relation Ships*, just as an image in a poem holds a particular meaning only in that specific poem as it exists upon that page. The image taken off the page, out of the poem, ceases to be. The words monogamy and non-monogamy, taken out of the relationShip poem, do not exist.

The farther I moved from my programmed relationShip thinking and behavior, the less relevant monogamy and non-monogamy actually became. Finally, I so thoroughly rejected the form that these attendant concepts no longer found a niche in my mind anywhere. Outside my conditioning they were not even ideas. They had become not only totally irrelevant; they had ceased altogether to be.

Jealousy, another idea that exists only in the context of the marriage/ownership poem, also became a non-concept. Bizarrely enough, we have been taught to perceive jealousy as evidence of love: The more jealous a person, the greater her love.

But from my own personal experience then and since, I learned that jealousy has nothing whatever to do with loving another person and everything to do with *not* loving my Self. I observed to my astonishment that my feelings of jealousy were really feelings of competition for first place—for the one/up position—in another's woman's heart, and I knew that competitive feelings constituted blatant evidence of low self-esteem. Knowing that when I did not esteem and love myself, I could not possibly love anyone else, I had to accept that jealousy existed only in the presence of no-love. More than that, that in any given situation, the fervor of my jealousy was directly proportional to my lack of self-love.

With this discovery came the understanding that, instead of love, jealousy signaled in me dozens of self-defeating and destructive attitudes and reflexes: The feeling, for example, that my loss of first place was a loss of "face," that my being passed over for another personally and publicly humiliated me, proved me inadequate, and justified my anger; the fear that my partner's breach of the unspoken contract giving me total rights to her time and attention would leave me without the emotional support on which I had become dependent; the fear of forfeiting present possibilities—and who knew if or when there would be others?—of what I perceived as intimacy; fear of loneliness; fear that I couldn't rely solely on my Self, that I wasn't reliable; fear that if I lost possession of my lover/sexer my Ship would sail off over the horizon leaving me marooned and wretched; fear of loss of Self: Who would I be if I weren't someone's most special friend, if I weren't her "chosen" one?

But I had learned not to be too hard on myself about the deep powerlessness that reared its ghastly head inside me whenever I or someone close to me violated the sacrosanct relationShip form. I reminded myself that it was through profoundest oppression that I had learned the feelings and responses of jealousy; that they neither represented my basic nature nor my own thoughtful choices. So even as I writhed in jealousy's toils, I comforted and forgave myself for it, concentrating upon loving myself fully just as I was and believing in my power to free myself utterly in time. Jealousy is unimaginable to me without the concept of ownership, and ownership only makes sense in a world of dire scarcity, of severely limited and dichotomous choices. It must have taken centuries for the fathers to destroy the goddess cultural mind in which abundance was assumed—the pagan psyche that understood abundance as a natural law of this planet, like gravity. Without the imposition of the construct of scarcity upon the human mind, the fathers could never have persuaded anyone to own anything. If ownership were not a concept, jealousy could be neither posited nor experienced. I feel certain that in the goddess planetary mind scarcity, ownership, monogamy, and jealousy were not even possibilities.

Bringing about the death of these concepts in my own mind—part of the task of freedom upon which I am so passionately bent—is difficult, of course, but not as difficult as I thought it was going to be. Daily practicing my belief that freedom with its attendant wholeness and power can come only from being true to my Self, I have for the most part left the ownership mind—with its progeny, jeal-ousy—behind. (I say "for the most part" because I still have occasional atavistic pangs, and expect that I shall for some time.) I am finally to the place where even to consider being "true" to someone else undermines and subverts in me everything that I have come to value.

Still, it took me many more months to imagine generally what a world would look like in which concepts of exclusivity and ownership did not exist and what their absence would mean for my own life. I had to make serious distinctions between a possible new non-coercive, non-exploitive mode that would evolve out of my changed focus—from numbers of sex partners to personal freedom and power—and "sleeping around," which objectifies women and uses them as means to ends. I had no tolerance left for anything that hurt women. That was the old, male style. For me, peace and joy had to be inherent to any new world view, and as givens, not as aberrations as they are now. I was sure that women's authentic way of loving—when we rediscovered it—would suit and benefit everyone.

I also thought a lot about what happened when women tried to "open" their relation Ships, how seldom, by my criteria—no pain to anyone and satisfaction for all—they did this successfully. I concluded that part of the reason for this high failure/anguish rate was a lack of understanding of the inseparability of form and content in relation Ships.

Sexual exclusivity is inherent to the marriage model.[1] It is what that model most profoundly *means*. Therefore, to be ethical, two people following the marriage form *must* be sexually exclusive. If this were not what love meant to them on a non-conscious level they would not be coupled up at all. Whatever they may think, they have committed themselves, have in a very real, very clear way, promised fidelity—*regardless of what they may think or of any pronouncement they may have made to the contrary*—simply by acceding to the

---

[1] Even though phallocracy allows men more leeway in extramarital sex, the form ostensibly demands fidelity from both sexes.

form. To follow the form is to agree to and to make the promise. It says yes to all the assumptions and expectations of "love" as dictated by the officer on the Ship's bridge. When this fact is ignored, terrible suffering ensues. A large part of what woke me up to the dreadful state of our relationShipping was the enormous anguish it was causing. I knew that to hurt women for whatever reason is never "natural," never justified. It is always unacceptable and always avoidable.

It therefore seemed to me then, and seems to me still, that those who are following, or mostly following the form—i.e, in conventional or semi-conventional relation Ships—are ethically bound to adhere to the content and be monogamous. Since it is not possible to divorce monogamy from relation-Ships/marriage (the inherent meaning from its form), to be sexual with someone while harboring a Ship in another living room is to break a promise, however tacit, and to betray a trust. Though these behaviors are both immoral and unethical, they are rendered almost inevitable by the very nature of relation Ships.

Looked at in this light, the fact that serial monogamy has now become society's norm is puzzling at first. It seems contradictory in a culture that professes to believe in "Til death do us part," but since it is the monogamy that is essential, apparently as long as there is *some* guard on duty, it really doesn't matter whether it is the *same* guard. The only reason, it seems to me, that "Til death do us part" maintains its preeminent position in phallarchy's brainwashing scheme is that in the space of time between guards, it prevents the prisoner from escaping. Thoroughly schooled in the necessity of non-freedom, she oppresses herself in the interim by focusing on and hungering for—rather than for escape—the next guard.

Thousands of us are completely fed up with the self-betrayal of marriage of any sort, including the serial betrayal of "serial monogamy." (Perhaps "serial agony" is a more apt description.) The thought of going through even one more relationShip cycle, to say nothing of one after another until we die—ecstasy, contentment, boredom, numbness, pain, misery, breakup, recuperation—makes us feel suicidal when it doesn't bore us senseless.

For those of us no longer willing to suffer or to inflict suffering in the name of bogus "love," it seems to me there is only one honorable choice and that is to refuse to climb aboard the relation Ship, with its shallow emphasis upon numbers, ever again. For us this means no longer playing the current game of love at all, rejecting everything we thought we knew about it. It means erasing the old brainwashing tapes and their pain-producing potential forever.

As we do this, however, it also means inviting misunderstanding from just about every imaginable quarter, as others perceive us mistakenly as lusting like men for free access to more women's bodies, or as irresponsible, or as lacking compassion or emotional stability or depth, or as selfish and hard.

Mostly, however, it means that we have the chance to dare to dream of a love that encompasses everything and possesses nothing. Perhaps we have even the obligation to do this, to bring this entirely different—this women's way—of loving into the world.

11

Memo
To: A Lover
Re: Commitment

I 'm excited about our talk on the phone last night. I'd been thinking about commitment for a day or two before you called, thinking about the part it plays in OurBS, thinking how we're conditioned to long for it and how so many women do, how so many of them are in "committed" relation Ships, how this is deemed a great and positive good among couples, Lesbian and otherwise.

But it's only to be expected. Since relation Ships, necessary to the survival of mensgame, are impossible without commitments, obviously we're trained to desire commitments, and commitments of many kinds. We're taught to believe that they are what ensure our safety. This is one of the ways we're encouraged to externalize responsibility for our well-being, to put it upon someone else.

But, you might protest, I don't want to love someone who won't be true to me.

Okay, let's take a look at "being true" in the context of OurBS. Here's another blatant reversal. Since compliance with being owned is called "being true" in relation Ships, being true means being faithful to one's owner and validating one's slave condition. "True," then, is sadomasochistic code for falseness to Self, for self-betrayal.

How could you believe I'd be true to you, for instance, if by being what you perceived as "true" I was false to myself? As Shakespeare has Polonius urge Laertes, "This above all, to thine own self be true, and it must follow as the night the day thou canst not then be false to any man [sic]." Even though it is silly Polonius saying it, he's right: Only by being absolutely true to myself can I ever be true to anyone else. True is simply true, the same internal state whether I am alone or connecting with others. True is having integrity—wholeness, authenticity.

Despite fierce indoctrination to the contrary, sacrifice is faithlessness to self. If I sacrifice something I want or need for myself in order to please you, I have been false to us both. I have betrayed my desires, and I have deceived you. This is why compromise is so erosive of integrity and hence of well-being, and I can't for the life of me see how to have a relation Ship without compromise. But more about this later.

It's beyond me why anyone still has faith in relationShip promises. Would you feel satisfied and safe if I promised you I'd stay with you forever, if I'd "commit" myself, when from your own experience you know that no one can possibly predict such an outcome? No one can tell today how they will feel tomorrow. They can only pretend to, or want to, or extrapolate from past experience.

But life is about growth and flux and change, and when we promise something we cannot possibly produce at will, we hamper its free unfolding. We also deceive ourselves and others, and since deceit shatters our inner unity—which is the stuff of life—we plunge into a coma. Since the truth is that this moment is all we ever have of life, we can honestly say to one another only such things as, "This is how I feel right now. I can't promise you how I'll feel or what I'll want in the next moment because I have no way of knowing. But you *can* count on me to be as true to myself every moment as I can be, and in this way also true to you. You can know for sure that when I am being and doing exactly what I want every minute, not sacrificing, being in my power as much as I can, I cannot deceive you or endanger you. Because there will be no subterranean motives, no manipulation, no murk, you will also always know who you are dealing with.

"That person is someone who is not expecting or needing any specific behavior from you, not depending on you to make her feel safe, or loved, or alive; not waiting for you to rescue her, or to take care of her, or to meet any of her needs.

"In turn, you can't rely on me to make you feel safe, or loved, or alive either, or to rescue you, or take care of you, or to meet any of your needs."

I wonder what evidence couples who long for commitment have that others who have made commitments to love each other forever experience genuine happiness and intimacy together. What evidence is there that such commitments have kept such couples together? Even if they stayed together, mightn't they have just dozed numbly through those years? Have I somehow missed the actual proof that the committed are more able to grow and change, widen and deepen freely in their bonds than the uncommitted? More questions for you. Why are so many people so impressed by relation Ships of great duration, as in, Wow! That Lesbian couple has been together for thirteen years! I know that numbers are excessively important in mensgame, so much so that we often forget that it's only quality that ultimately counts, but still . . . .

When I think about the hooplah over longevity of unions, all I have to do is look at my parents, at parents of friends, at high-school friends now thirty-five years married, to discover couples who, though they have stayed together because of legal, socially-demanded commitment, have been wretched with one another or numbed out for entire lifetimes. It's pretty discouraging to watch Lesbian and straight friends struggling to emulate that ghastly example.

I don't think they do it because they have seen so many wonderful marriages that they can't wait to follow suit. Denial and irrationality are classic evidence of brainwashing. Few, if any, discerning people have seen at close range many wonderful marriages—or at least marriages that *stayed* wonderful. You and I agree that what all of us have seen most often is loss of identity, dependency, eventual boredom, misery, dysfunction on all levels, disillusionment, betrayal, heartbreak, violence, and/or a deep, deadening despair that passes for contentment.

But the propaganda of every song, every movie, every book insists that coupling up is happiness ever after, so in the face of the overwhelming grim reality, we believe it. What the propaganda assures us is that it will be different for us, that it is a matter of individual, not systemic, failure. So even though nearly everyone else failed in the end, we won't. You know that I believe that when all evidence points to one conclusion but still we persist in believing the exact opposite, we can know we have been brainwashed. You and I talked a little last night about the misnomer "free love," how love has no place at all in the exchange system or in the language of commerce. Love is outside the economic mind—literally priceless. It does not demand that we pay anything—not our identity, our time, our attention, our freedom, or our joy.

We noted that relation Ships, on the other hand—deeply embedded in the adversarial exchange model—are very, very costly. This includes those Ships that seem to us to be "good," but particularly those that have lasted longest: These have demanded exorbitant payment. Such exorbitant payment, in fact, that those who have made it for ten or twenty or sixty years have difficulty facing the truth that their life's blood has not been able even to buy them security or comfort, let alone intimacy.

You insisted that any of us could make a list of what each party in any enduring relation Ship had to do to stay in it; that there's not a one of us that doesn't know on some level what each had to forego, ignore, sacrifice, squish down, falsify, give up. I was impressed by your belief that whether we can articulate it or not, we know—because we have experienced it ourselves—the fear of personal power, the fear of living fully, the fear of the deity inside—of the wild magnificence—that leads to such self-betrayal.

It seems to me that one of the major purposes of commitment is to lull us into emotional and psychic slumber, to put us on automatic pilot. I was delighted that in our conversation we progressed from thinking that we would make only one commitment to each other—to communicate—to deciding that instead we would only commit to being honest, and from there to thinking that we would commit ourselves to being conscious instead, to realizing finally that we could make no commitments to each other at all. I felt enormous relief when we finally got to this point. Along the painful path Susan and I had to walk that grim, though memorable year, various well-meaning friends had us making commitments to each other that turned out to be serious roadblocks to our understanding.

For instance, we agreed to make a commitment that for a certain length of time we would not "abandon" each other. I wonder now why I didn't object powerfully to that, particularly to the word "abandon." "Abandon" is a concept that applies only to helpless things: Domesticated animals, babies, children, invalids—people or animals or objects (an abandoned automobile) that cannot be expected to take care of themselves. There was no way Susan and I, both capable adults and completely able to take care of ourselves, *could* have abandoned each other. The word simply did not apply.

I've thought today that though commitments between people are not only useless but generally deceptive and probably immoral, commitments to oneself, especially if reviewed, revised, and discarded when necessary, *may* help keep us conscious. I must admit I hated to give commitments so much as an inch, but I realized that I've been making them to myself, and that so far they've been useful. (I'll let you know if this continues to work.)

For example, I've promised to know and to be honest with myself about how I feel and what I want; to consider what's best for me first; to center my life in myself; to realize that my safety comes from within.

As I thought about these, I recognized that they include the understanding that knowing and being with someone like you is a marvelous gift and addition, not the daily stuff of my life, that the daily stuff comes from inside me, from my unconditional love for myself.

So I make no promises, no commitments to you, dear lover, except that you can count on me never to do anything I don't want to do. Though I truly am as you see and know me now, a large part of who I am is my determination not to remain emotionally or intellectually anywhere long enough to fall asleep again and doze my life away. I am committed to deepening and expanding and flourishing as my Self dictates for the duration of my life.

And I may choose to do this in ways that cause our paths to diverge. Maybe you are a lover whose path will cross mine many times before we're finished here. Maybe this is the only meeting of our destinies. Whatever the case, it's really irrelevant, isn't it, since now is all we have and this moment in my life couldn't be lovelier, more life-enhancing.

I'm glad we're lovers today.

12

No Negotiation, No Compromise

During the difficult years of my mutiny, I often heard the menstream's tiresome lie that compromise and negotiation are necessary for successful relation Ships, that each partner must sacrifice something in the present on the promise that this loss will be made up to her in the future. The lie insists that there is no other way to connect closely with each other.

Everyone seems to accept it. No one points out to us that both compromise and negotiation are forms of exchange, and that exchange (including barter) is an adversarial, conflict mode, the war model in miniature, intrinsically win/lose. We are unaware of how it pits us against each other, making each of us struggle to gain more control than the other, to win: I know you don't want to go to the dance tonight, but if you'll go with me just for a little while, I'll go with you to the movie you've been trying to drag me to, or I'll type that paper for you after all.

In addition to being an instrument of control, compromise/negotiation (sacrifice) is the mainstay of the scarcity-mind so necessary to tyranny: If you'll give up this for me, I'll give up that for you. This dynamic between partners, in focusing on relinquishing something valuable, creates the illusion of deprivation; each partner feels as if she is giving—and giving *up*—more than the other.

This occurs because when we sacrifice any part of what we want, nothing can repay us for the consequent loss of our birthright: All the resources, the power and opportunity and energy that we want. Therefore, whatever we are promised in order to get us to give up something we really want can never satisfy us, and we will always view ourselves as cheated. As indeed we are. It is through compromise and negotiation under the rubric of "love" that we take from others their freedom and are ourselves pressured and deprived.

In fact, when we ignore the evidence of our perceptions, or deny how we feel, or give up even a bit of what we want for some "good" in a nonexistent future, we are cutting our Selves off from the moment, off from life, out of creativity and power.

This is so because, despite all the "new-" and bygone-age nonsense to the contrary, our lives are not means to some end. Since time is not linear and past and future do not therefore actually exist, it doesn't make sense to believe that we live to learn lessons, to become better, to grow, or to get off this planet's existence wheel—beliefs that demand a linear time mind.

In our atomic universe, *now* is what time *is*. The only reason to live that makes logical sense in such a universe, the only possibility—and in nonlinear time it is a limitless possibility—is to *be*. To be whatever is possible for us at this moment, to create and experience our Selves joyously, richly, fully, and magnificently, right *now*.

To the degree that we are in good emotional and spiritual health and free from our conditioning, to that degree we are able to be and to be present now—fully alive. In this state, we do not merely have access to creativity, we *are* creativity; we do not merely have power, we *are* power. That underlings should *become* such power, such creativity, is anathema to tyrants. One of their most compelling reasons to brainwash us into believing in the construct of linear time is to persuade us to distrust and defer, indefinitely and habitually, the gratification of desire that is *being* now—our power.

To the degree that we are in good emotional and spiritual health and as free from our conditioning as possible, to that degree we are in our power. In that state, our desires, pure and authentic, are our surest definitions of our Selves.

By habitually denying or betraying through compromise the desires that *are* us, we deny and betray our Selves, driving them underground into numbness, preventing them from being wholly and exquisitely present every moment—the meaning and purpose of our lives.

It seems to me that one of the reasons sex therapy doesn't usually succeed for any length of time is that PRBS prevents this issue of freedom—doing exactly what we want to do *at this moment* without negotiation, without compromise—from being perceived as even important, let alone central. Instead, the officer on the bridge in most therapists' as well as most clients' minds most often recommends false/linear-time, goal-oriented behavior to cure relationShip malaise.

But if I were asked for advice by couples who were having problems around sex (assuming that they had otherwise assiduously and effectively deprogrammed themselves of manunkind's dangerous dogma), I would suggest that they look for any of the thousand tiny coercions/compromises of their lives together, the constant onslaught against each other's freedom that takes place in even the most loving connections, and stop *all* such behavior at once. I would strongly advocate that they never do or say anything that they don't genuinely mean or feel like doing—that they follow their desires no matter what they perceive what the possible consequences might be. I would suggest to them that emotional/physical numbness is the result of frequent self-betrayal, of giving in to the tender tyranny of lovers who certainly never intended to be oppressive. I would warn them that such unwitting enslavement erodes all hopes for intimacy because, contrary to our socialized beliefs, nothing free or joyful can come from self-denial.

But I know, and am glad, that regardless of my opinions— though some women will consider and agree with some of them—each woman is ultimately going to live her life as she pleases. Each of us following our desires, and being happy and willing for others to do the same, is the way women's free world will become reality.

Though I can't see into this new reality clearly enough to discern it in any detail, it seems to me that allowing ourselves always to have and do what we want and extending this right to others, is evidence of the freedom from conditioning and of the self-love and trust that are the bases of power. I believe that if we honestly and courageously, with neither negotiation nor compromise, followed our desires, miracles would take place between and among us.

In weak moments during my mutinous months, such thoughts gave me courage, and made me hungrier than ever for the possibilities that I knew lay within women's scope. So though I still couldn't imagine how I could always do only what I wanted in a relation Ship and still have intimacy; though I couldn't imagine how, if I cared about someone, I wouldn't have to do at least a *little* something I didn't want to do now and then, how I wouldn't have to take them into consideration at least some times when I didn't want to; though I still didn't understand where recognizing and getting for myself what I wanted ended and selfishness began; though I couldn't imagine how I could have desirable connections with others that involved *no* compromise, *no* negotiations, *no* ifs, ands, or buts, my Wise Old Woman persuaded me to believe that all this was possible. Not just this but—as I suspected—miracles, too.

Trusting her, my goddess Self, against every precept of patriarchy embedded within me, I believed. And though it was still far off, with every small step I took in my own behalf I was drawing closer to the place of understanding.

13

House Arrest

After taking my memo to a lover out to the postbox, I returned to my notes to see where I was in my examination of OurBS. When I did I realized at once that I needed another close look at my hypothetical couple—they were being heavily pressured by OurBS to make a home together, and I wanted to know why. I wanted to know how such behavior benefitted the minions of Mammon and Mayhem, and therefore in what ways they had subverted and lethalized it.

From sources as divergent as feminists and accident experts, I had heard repeatedly that the most dangerous place for everyone is "home." It's where we trip on broken basement steps, where our smoke detectors fail, and where our kids eat the drain cleanser under the sink. It's the place where women are beaten and children are abused and neighbors and police are most loathe to interfere. Homes are the berths of our Ships, and as our Ships are understood to be at all times in international waters—out of the jurisdiction of local authorities—our domestic decks are rendered effectively off-limits to all but inept social service organizations.

What I saw when I observed my happy couple's establishing a home together for their Ship was that they were totally convinced that they were doing it—living together or planning to live together, sleeping together most nights, and spending most of their time together—simply because they loved each other and enjoyed each other's company. I had no reason to doubt that they loved each other or that they found each other enjoyable companions. But I distrusted their unshakable belief that their delicious feelings were facilitated by such behavior. What evidence had they for their assumption that the amount of time their partner spent with them was directly proportional to the depth of her love? What made them think that such cleaving to each other would make them happy? Why should the gradual narrowing down and down and yet again down of external stimuli increase one's joy? How did their wonderful feelings for each other get transmogrified into such constant surveillance?

Knowing phallocracy's cunning, deceitful ploys to take away our freedom, I could rapidly surmise some of the answers to these questions. For instance, it is important to the maintenance of mensmachine that we live, sleep, eat, and play together because in this way we can constantly monitor each other's behavior. This is the way we can each be sure that the other is not making independent, autonomous choices to do with her body, her time, and her attention what she damned well wants to. That she is not being subversive to the system of oppression: That she is not being free.

Not letting our lover long out of our sight or out of our psychic ken is clearly the easiest way to maintain ownership control, the surest route to guaranteeing that some bond servant will always be there to meet our needs. Such, alas, is our profoundest brainwashing about what constitutes a romantic relation Ship. It is as if only by staying as much as possible at our captive's side and speaking in her ear that we can drown out the distant echoes of her wild archaic jubilation and prevent her escape back to it.

Whatever inspires it, typical possessive behavior—knowing where the other is at all times, what she is most likely doing and for how long, and assuming that evidence of these facts is available upon request; knowing pretty much when she will return (at least what day if not what hour or half-hour) and expecting notification of any of her changes in plans—indicates worry that she might remember and return to her Self if her OurBS conditioning is not constantly monitored and reinforced.

It seemed odd to me that two women can be intensely connected for many months, savoring each other's conversation and company, and yet no one begins anticipating a change in their living arrangements until they learn that the two have had sex. It is a powerful given that once two people are sexual with each other they will live together if they possibly can. Few ask them, "*Are* you going to live together?" Rather, the questions are, "*When* are you going to move in together, and *where*—your place or hers?"

Suddenly this appeared as curious to me as some custom of an exotic tribe in a part of the world I'd never heard of. Like something out of *National Geographic*.

I remembered a story a friend had told me. When she and another woman with whom she was occasionally sexual moved in together, largely for economic reasons, everyone assumed that they were now a "couple." Considering themselves nothing of the sort, however, they each had their own separate bedrooms and generally slept there.

One day a couple of Lesbian friends dropped by, and as this friend showed them through the house she announced, "This is my room. I just barely got my bed made before you came!" At this evidence of nonconformity, she could almost hear them thinking, "But are they having a relation Ship or aren't they?" She admitted to me that she got a perverse sort of pleasure from the agitation her lack of orthodoxy caused them. "The jolt probably did them good," she chuckled.

Feminism had taught me many of the reasons for the invention of marriage. Now I began to observe men's need for it from another point of view.

In pre-patriarchal times, before jehovah toppled the goddess (i.e., the knowledge of female divinity) from her throne in the hearts of the human species worldwide, every living woman knew she was the goddess—that her essence was pure creativity and power. She didn't look for guidance to some smarter, more powerful woman in the sky. The goddesses in her mythical pantheon were representations of aspects of her Self, as were all icons and sacred paintings.

So when men began their take-over of heaven and earth, what they were faced with were female deities on every hand, a planet full of goddesses. Among the many strategies they found for stripping us of our power was one that has come in handy for them in subsequent, though smaller, wars.

My formative years were spent during men's so-called Second World War.[1] From that war and from reading since,

---

[1] There has been only one war fought literally worldwide, affecting every living thing, and that has been men's all-out, non-stop, millennia-long war against women, a war that not only continues to this moment without the slightest abatement but intensifies hourly.

I learned some of the tactics that had had to be invented to prevent the escape of prisoners.

Generally, when a group of men was captured, as soon as possible the captors got them into some sort of holding corral—some cordoned-off space—and set guards to watch them. Among the prisoners, leaders would soon arise, those men who might, for instance, urge others around them not to cooperate with the enemy until they were all given water. In some way, those who were less afraid, surer of themselves, and therefore most likely to organize rebellions or escapes, soon identified themselves.

Their captors discovered through trial and error that to prevent trouble they had either to execute these leaders immediately or to put them in solitary confinement—one man to one cell with his own private guard.

The analogy is obvious. When men dreamed of controlling women and hence the world, every woman was just such a leader—one of those who would disrupt and defeat the hell-plans. So during the war men have fought against us for thousands of years, they have had either to kill us or to put us in solitary confinement—one woman to one guard in one cell.

But at first women were so incredibly strong and the bonds between and among us so indissoluble, that these tactics alone could never have succeeded. Our eventual subjugation was accomplished, as all seasoning is accomplished, by a lethal combination of brainwashing and terrorism. It was the slow work of many, many centuries to tame us, to persuade us that this captivity, violence, and isolation was in our best interests, that it meant that we were loved and respected, that it was pleasant, that we liked it, that we wanted it, that we couldn't live without it, and—the ultimate doublespeak—that it was freedom. They called it "marriage" and it was literal house arrest. I have often been asked, "If we were so strong, how did we become such patsies? How do you brainwash a goddess to act in self-destructive ways?" But those who understand conditioning—the slow, steady dropping of the water on the rock—are surprised, not that we gradually capitulated, but that we held out for as long as we did.

Looking at my own life and the lives of my friends in the context of my thoughts about "home," I was saddened that we were still believing the lies, that we continued daily to collaborate in our own and each other's domestication. By living together, sleeping together, monitoring where each other is most of the time, spending most of our free time together, narrowing down our outside contacts, and behaving in dozens of ways as dictated by the relation Ship, we were keeping each other under nearly constant surveillance and control. Ignorantly but deliberately following the masters' "imprison and disempower" stratagem, we were doing the work of oppression for them.

But as I observed us, I also saw evidence that our untamed, our feral Selves that had lain buried for so long, were only silenced, not killed. In my own breast and among women everywhere I travelled, they were calling to us again. And we were listening.

14

TweedleDee and CoupleDumb

Script: Liz: "What's going on with Marilyn lately?"
Debra: "You may find this hard to believe, but she
and Rebecca are now a couple."
Woman in audience: "A couple of *what*?"

That Marilyn and Rebecca—two individuals—can be
melded into one entity, ironically called "a couple," is
one clue that relation Ships are designed to un-Self and un-
power women.

Calling themselves a couple, Marilyn and Rebecca
announce that for much of their time they willingly relinquish
their distinct, separate Selves, and choose instead to be
subsumed into a unit that, because of its superior political and
social uses, has far higher status in the menstream.

In their circle of friends as well as in their wider women's
community and perhaps in every arena of their lives—except,
usually, their workplaces—whenever others think of Marilyn,
their thoughts also automatically include Rebecca. Every time
anyone speaks to or about Rebecca, they envision Marilyn at
her side: "Where's Marilyn?" they ask, peering around. Or
"Say hello to Marilyn for me." It becomes nearly impossible

for anyone to see and respond to Marilyn or Rebecca as individuals. And it becomes nearly impossible for them to *be* individuals.

In this way the concept and experience of "couple" constantly reprograms into them the acceptability, the inevitability in love, of loss of Self.

We joke about how one half of a couple can't be invited to dinner without the other half. We giggle about being joined at the hip—"Co and Proud!" as a couple I know laughingly describe themselves.

The discomfort that causes us to snigger is that we are getting too near the truth—two halves make one, not two. One what? Why, one relation Ship, of course. But where then did the *women* go? They went where they had to go to avoid the demands and responsibilities of freedom, where they had to go to maintain a Ship. Submerging themselves into a "couple," their Selves went underground.

A look at "couple" as a verb—as in "to couple with"—reveals an equally negative picture. Meaning "to plug into," this is obviously an apt description of men's connections with women; powerless on their own, they need our creative juices like machines need electricity. But women all too often also "couple" with—plug into—each other, one or both of them seeking to find in the other the definition and sustenance they have not learned to provide for themselves.

A friend once said to me, "If you can't find a vise to get into, a couple will do just as well." The restrictiveness inherent in coupling is exacerbated by artifacts such as the "biography"[1] each partner perpetuates about the other, and

---

[1] Suggested by Becky Phipps at the Michigan Womyn's Music Festival, 1989.

the "couple history," a sort of Ship's Log that they both contribute to keeping.

Members of couples often come to believe that they "know" their mate through and through—almost better than she knows herself. She can hardly make a move without its being prejudged on the basis of who her partner thinks she is: "Sandy go to a country western concert? You've got to be kidding! She's strictly into opera." How is Sandy going to find out if she could enjoy other kinds of music? How will her partner feel if Sandy ceases to be a high-brow opera buff?

"Jill just loves children. Wherever we've lived before, she's been 'Auntie' to all our friends' kids. It's one of the things I've always loved most about her." If Jill is actually tired of being "Auntie" to everyone's kids, how long will such shoring up of her former feelings postpone her discovery of her new ones? How much harder will her change be made by her partner's cherished picture of her? How many of such strains can the relation Ship sustain without sinking?

"I'll drive you home," Barbara says. "Eileen finds freeway traffic too overwhelming." With this kind of reinforcement, will Eileen be able any time soon to revise her view of herself as a fragile, incompetent driver? How will such a change affect Barbara, who enjoys feeling superior to Eileen in this way?

Because each partner in a couple thinks she knows exactly who the other is and projects this upon her all the time, and because each needs the other to continue playing a certain role in the coupledrama, often neither of them is quick to recognize or welcome change in the other.

Also, it is often the case that each of them believes that in order to keep her lover she has to conform to the picture her lover has concocted of her, thinking and acting as she has in the past, as she is expected to, as she knows will keep her lover comfortable. Leaving so little room for difference, the couple biography adds its serious limitations to each partner's scope and growth.

In addition to the "biography," couples compose a "couple history"—or Ship's Log—that works much the same way to stunt growth and fend off change. Couples bond by agreeing upon what they will record in the Log as the characteristics of their union.

For instance, let's take Joan and Sue who have been a couple for fifteen years. We are interviewing them for an article about Lesbian marriages. To get them talking unselfconsciously so that they will reveal their couple history, we begin by asking them a general question such as, "Tell us something about yourselves—what you like to do together, how you interact with each other, what's important to you in your relationship, stuff like that."

"Well," Sue begins, "we like to do the same things—backpack in the summers, fix up the house, travel, cook." She turns nervously to Joan.

"We're both vegetarians," Joan smiles. "About ten years ago we decided that we would never again eat anything that had a face."

When we finish laughing, she continues. "Fortunately we've never cared much about material objects. We live simply and get pleasure from small things: A tasty supper, a long hot soak in the tub, a chapter or two of a murder mystery, and each other's soft, loving body snuggling us to sleep."

"Tell us more about your relationship," we urge them, "how it is that you've managed to stay together so long."

"Well," Sue smiles, "we're very open with each other. I think that having no secrets has helped a lot."

"And we don't let a day go by," Joan adds, "without spending some quality time together—we even call each other every night when we're apart. We also think it's very important to sleep together every night if we can. And we're lucky that we've always been able to talk things out sensibly, without getting angry or having fights."

Sue, more relaxed and forthcoming now, says, "We see eye-to-eye on the kind of people we want to associate with, too. We've found that we can't have meaningful friendships with women who wear pantyhose, or high heels, or make-up, or who shave their legs, or have been Saved by Jesus, or who waste water, or are into S and M."

Joan wraps it up. "I think it all comes down to having the same values and being considerate of each other." Pause. "And of course," she deadpans, "never eating sugar."

We know that these snippets come to us directly from the invisible pages of their co-authored couple history.

As we leave the house after the interview, we speculate among ourselves about what would happen if Joan or Sue were suddenly to discover that one or more of these facts was no longer true for her.

We imagine Sue giving in to an overmastering craving one evening for a Wendy's hamburger on her way home from work. We see her later slinking guiltily into the house to bed. Then we watch her wake up in a sweat in the wee hours of the night, remembering that she left the Wendy's container in plain sight on the front seat of her car. She slips out of bed, careful not to wake Joan, and sneaks out to the car. Opening the door, she snatches up the evidence of her perfidy and clutches it to her bosom. But what to do with it? If she puts it in the house garbage, there's the danger that even if she buries it deep in the sack it might be discovered. She ponders a moment, then, glancing furtively over each shoulder, stuffs the greasy box and napkins under the passenger seat and quickly shuts the car door. Tiptoeing up the stairs, the crisis past, she lays plans for disposing of the evidence at work tomorrow.

But is the crisis past? She has doubly violated the sacrosanct couple history: Once by eating meat and again by keeping it a secret from Joan. This is such unkosher behavior in her Ship that she is likely to suffer a degree of distress from it that will catapult her right back into conformity with the expectations and assumptions of the Ship's Log.

But perhaps even more dangerous is that it will also create resentment, resentment that she will not direct sensibly toward the Ship, but irrationally against Joan. On some level, she will be at least annoyed—and probably upset—that her knowledge of Joan's disapproval is making her feel and behave like a guilty child.

We also make up a hypothetical scenario for Joan. Suppose one day she discovers that one of the bald-legged, pantyhosed, made-up women in her office is actually very intelligent, witty, and interesting, and that she would like to have her for a friend.

If she wants this fervently enough to rebel against the inertia of the couple history—"we don't associate with women with such low consciousnesses"—what will she do? Phone High Heels from the corner drugstore? This is too much like clandestine courting for comfort, and in other ways doesn't jibe with Sue's characterization of her in the couple history as "very open," and "having no secrets." Trying to keep in character, will she explain to Sue—to whom this particular "political correctness" matters most—in the hope of reframing the couple history to include "unenlightened" friends? Will the situation become so fraught with peril that she will just forget the whole thing? How many times has she had to forget whole things and how much resentment has consequently built up inside her toward Sue?

Whatever she chooses to do, Joan has a difficult emotional task ahead. The couple history has a momentum of its own and unless she is adamant, it will prevail. Then sooner or later her growing store of resentment will eat away her fondest feelings for Sue. But the Ship has her clamped into its classic dilemma: If she *is* adamant, she also risks losing Sue. Damned if she does, damned if she doesn't.

I know how it feels to chafe against the constraints of the couple history. In my experience, it made doing or thinking anything even slightly outside its purview a major performance, requiring the expenditure of so much time and energy that I decided the price of subversion of the Log simply wasn't worth it.

As I painfully uncoupled from Susan, I promised myself with great fierceness that I would never be a "couple" again, never again compose a couple history with anyone, never keep another Ship's Log.

I also finally decided that as long as there was going to be one entity, that entity was going to be me, and me alone, not a couple. Never Soniaandanyoneelse ever again. Just Sonia. Period. No more sharing of hip bones or, even worse, of vital organs. I was never again going to be part of a package deal.

Finding the word "single" as strong a relationShip programmer as "couple," I was equally firm in my refusal ever again to think of myself or any other uncoupled woman as "single." It seemed to me that women were nearly apologizing when they described themselves this way, as if being one-whole instead of one-half were not legitimate or healthy, but instead something one hoped soon to recover from. It was as if they were not really living but simply on hold until they plugged into someone else, became one-half of a couple, and turned on their lives again. I knew they would never think to call themselves "single" if they didn't accept coupledom as the natural and therefore more desirable state—a state I now dubbed "coupledumb."

We are taught to accept the menstream assumption that one-half is better than one-whole because two is necessary for oppression. A woman's not joking when, after divorce, she shouts ecstatically, "I'm free!" She is being true to her deepest knowledge and desire. She *is* free, at least in the sense that she has escaped her one particular assigned guard and is now out in the larger prison yard. If she is frightened by the responsibility this new spaciousness demands, however, she will soon begin looking for another guard to rescue her from her fear of her immense power, put her back into her familiar cozy cell, and control her life.

But it may be argued that I am making this too absolute. Women are loving beings. We want affection and tenderness and companionship. Why am I then turning this perfectly natural desire around and making it appear threatening and evil?

I admit that, indeed, it is all turned around. But it was reversed by masculine force. I think men took our worthy and natural desires and, in a truly diabolical way, turned them against us—making us, under threat of death, do to one another in the name of love what most of us would be too merciful to do to someone we hated.

146

It is phallocracy that insures our obedience by lying, "When you have a wonderful moment with someone, you must quickly capture and own her so that you can be assured of having more of such moments. If you don't get possession of her, someone else will, and you will be left with no one to touch and hold and love you." It is the fathers who continue to misname these feelings of powerlessness, scarcity, and desperation "love."

Realizing this, coupling began to look not merely dumb but deadly: CoupleDoom.[2] But I didn't recognize until much later the basic and profound flaw at the heart of it. Before I could acknowledge this, however, I had to continue step by step through OurBS with my mythical couple as my guides.

---

[2] Courtesy of Vivian Goldstein of New York City, New York.

147

15

Just Friends

F riends—as expected—slip almost off the bottom of our
affection scale as soon as we "fall in love."[1] When I
looked at the comparative merits of the words "lover" and
"friend" in our culture I confirmed the obvious: "Friend" is so
much lower in prestige that it almost never travels in the
same social circles as "lover."

I was aware that it occupies this lowly position in the
relationShip program largely because it is not an efficient
vehicle for the control of others that mensmachine values
above everything. I also knew this didn't mean that friends
are perfect peers, but that friendship does not lend itself easily
to domination and that therefore friending *can* be a mutinous
act, one that actively subverts the bullies on the bridge.

But because society doesn't value friendship, most of us
can give up friends without too much heartache—move far
away from various sets of them often during our

---

[1] A telling phrase in itself, as many of us have long noted. It makes love
sound like a pit, or a trap, in which we are helpless, unable to get out. For once,
the language has some integrity. This is precisely what love is in patriarchy—the
pits.

lifetimes—because in general they don't count for much. Certainly not for nearly as much as lovers, from whom we do *not* usually pack up and move away forever—at least not as long as we perceive that we are still having a "good" relation Ship. And when we are forced to leave lovers behind, both we and they usually scurry about in all directions trying to figure out how to arrange to live with each other again—and we almost always manage it.

Since most feminists would agree that nothing can really be more important than friending, this attitude toward friends would be baffling if we didn't also recognize sex as menstream's crucial link to control. The closed romantic system, the padded cell called "lovers," *matters* because it is the perfect vehicle for tyranny.

The Ship not only bosses couples around, it bosses their friends around as well. I could be reasonably certain, therefore, that when the two women standing in each other's arms in my study became lovers their friendships underwent a change. The frequency with which they saw their friends probably dropped off drastically and at once. They may have nearly stopped seeing anyone but each other, at least for the first six months or so. In addition, most friends they opted to keep up with had now to fit into a few rigid categories: If they were "single" friends of one of the lovers, they had to pass her partner's rigorous inspection, subject to her constant evaluation of their sexual interest in her partner. If a friend appeared too intimate, she would be dropped—gradually, perhaps, but quite definitely, at least until she found herself a partner, becoming safely owned and monitored.

In my workshop at the Michigan Womyn's Music Festival in 1989, an insightful woman named Helen pointed out that being in a couple is very like being in the convent: In neither can you have "particular" friends.

The couple's friends who were safely coupled up themselves would therefore become the couple's primary outside contacts, but even as couples they wouldn't see as much of each other as each one when "single" used to see of her "single" friends. In short, friends—who are all too often viewed as mere stopgaps until a lover comes along—now find themselves abruptly dropped or at least playing a far less important role.

The conventional relationShip drama is about domination, and domination becomes harder to maintain successfully in direct relation to the number of players. Players other than the couple open the action, increasing the chances that influences and viewpoints dangerous to the status quo will enter the dynamic.[2] With a cast greater than two, it might become obvious to everyone that no one person can mean everything to another person.

Being everything to someone else—because it is impossible—is a high-frustration, low-reward job. As I discovered later in my search, it spawns the kind of stress that inevitably destroys whatever was once pleasurable between lovers.

---

[2] This is why battering men almost always close off and narrow down the external reality of the women they abuse. The smaller the number of distractions, the easier dominion is achieved and maintained.

16

Meet My Needs, Make Me Happy

S o far every detail, every feature of OurBS that I'd
ferreted out, was more disheartening than the last. This
pattern persisted now as I looked at the next bit of encap-
sulated programming: Being lovers means that we should
meet each other's needs and make each other happy.

I knew full well by this time—nobody better—that
obeying "shoulds" was lethal to integrity. I also knew that
obeying these particular "shoulds" was the point in the
relationShip poem where we most give up our power.
"Shoulds" do us as much damage as any of the conditioned
responses in the coupling program.

Like most women, I was bombarded from birth with
messages about what a "good woman" is, many of which in
my culture are about what a "good woman" wants.

Since a good woman's happiness comes from making
others happy, she puts their needs first. A good woman
believes that her wants and needs are incompatible with what
is good for other people, and therefore that she would be
immature and anti-social if she did and had what she wanted.
In addition, everyone would be very angry, call her a bad
woman, and not love her. A good woman thinks that it is

legitimate to have what she wants only after everyone else has everything they want. But since everyone else never has everything they want and it is therefore never legitimate to have what she wants, she never really has to risk in her own behalf.

A good woman has focused so hard and so long on never giving in to "selfishness" that early on she ceases to ask herself what she wants. This becomes such a habit that she loses the ability to tell how she feels and what she wants, and mistakes conditioned relationShip beliefs for her own genuine idiosyncratic desires.

A good woman is convinced that pleasure weakens individual and societal character. She believes that the nature of life is such that, for the smooth functioning of relation Ships, families, countries, and all other institutions, everyone has to do many things they would prefer not to do. She believes that she is morally strengthened by doing these less-than-pleasant things, and is certain that any woman who does only what she wants to do is outrageously selfish, hedonistic, and unloving—a bad woman.

I realized now as I looked at relationShip commandments that my "good woman" habits of thought had caused me to view my feelings as really very much out of my direct control. I saw that I had come to believe that they were externally determined, that other people's behavior and opinions, situations, even objects, were what "made" me feel certain ways. If someone said something unkind to me or I failed an exam, my assumption was that of course I would feel bad. It was simply cause and effect. Having been taught that certain feelings were appropriate—by implication, "natural"—to certain situations and that others were not, this had not appeared to be a matter in which I had conscious choice.

So I felt powerless to change my feelings, out of my own control and at the mercy of every thing, every person, every situation on the planet. Since a large part of who I am is how I *feel*, where then was my Self if everyone and everything but I could determine how I felt at any given moment? There's no better definition of Self-lostness and powerlessness.

Most of what I now know about my power I figured out as a mother. It seems to me that a significant piece of patriarchy's Motherhood Belief System (MomBS?) is that a good mother's feelings are determined by how her kids are feeling and what they are doing. If her kids are suffering, a good mother suffers. If her kids are worried or behaving foolishly, a good mother worries. Only if her kids are happy and well can a good mother be happy without guilt.

Several years ago,[1] [when my third child was seventeen, he and I had a clash in the kitchen one night, one of a great many throughout his adolescence, this time about drugs. He stormed downstairs to his room and slammed the door, leaving me standing in the middle of the room feeling wretched and powerless.

Even having already reared two adolescents, I had no more idea how to get the present one to do what he should than I had had with the first two. The task seemed impossible. I had lived in terror for years—terror that they would be unhappy, that they would do drugs, that they would self-destruct—and doing everything I could think of to prevent these disasters had neither lessened the fear nor changed their

---

[1] The following story—enclosed in brackets—is excerpted from my book *Wildfire: Igniting the She/Volution*, Wildfire Books: Albuquerque, 1989, pp. 89-93.

behavior. Although the first two had made it through somehow, I wasn't at all sure if or how my actions had helped or hindered those outcomes, and the trial-and-error of it had nearly undone me. I couldn't imagine, standing there that night, how I was going to live through two more adolescences.

Suddenly, I began to feel very angry—in my experience always a first sign of returning health. I realized that I was furious at the anguish I had suffered so long as a mother and the misery that seemed still to stretch so endlessly before me. I felt as if I couldn't wait to be happy until all my kids were over thirty and safe. (Besides, mothers of over-thirty's had told me that their kids were still never safe.) I'd been the best mother I'd known how to be for over twenty years and I deserved to be happy. What's more, I deserved it *now*! I was nearly fifty years old. When had I thought I was going to begin?

Then, thinking of my tyrant son sulking down in his room, and feeling an unaccustomed invulnerability, a new firmness at the center, I thought, "That kid can go to hell in a handbasket! I would be sorry, because I love him, and I'll do what I can to prevent it—but not like before. I can't live his life for him; I can't make him do what I want him to do. He's just going to have to decide for himself whether he's going to self-destruct or not, and I'm going to have to be happy no matter what he decides."

I felt as if I had been holding his heel as he hung upside down over the abyss. One cannot live one's own life while holding someone else's heel. I decided I needed to love and be true to myself first, do what was best for me, assuming that whatever is best for me is best for everyone around me.

Though I didn't understand for a long time the scope of my change that night, and though I still had much work to do to make that change permanent, looking back it is clear that I was finally beginning to understand the dynamics of how I gave away my power. I was getting hold of a basic principle of power, that when we make our feelings of well-being or security or safety dependent upon someone else's behavior, we hand them the opportunity, even the invitation, to destroy us.

I realized that night that I would never have control of my life if I continued to make my internal climate contingent upon whether or not my children or anyone else outside me did what I wanted them to do. It had become unmistakably clear in that flash that because I couldn't control anyone or change anyone but myself, it was emotional suicide to put the responsibility for my happiness in someone else's hands.

In some inchoate way that night, I knew that I had to hold *all* responsibility for my feelings in my own hands or I would never be safe or free. Since no one can care about me as much as I care about myself, I would always get hurt, sometimes very badly. I felt as if I could not bear the pain of being a "good mother" another second.

Without knowing exactly what I was doing, but for the sake of survival, I detached myself from my children then as sources of well-being for me, took the responsibility away from them, where I couldn't control it, back into myself where it belonged. At the same time I realized, momentarily at least, that I was not responsible for any other person's well-being or security or safety either; that there comes a time when we must each learn to put our own lives first, realize that no one else can or will or should consistently bear the burden of making us feel safe and loved, and find our source of satisfaction and safety *within ourselves*. In any other thinking, disaster looms.

That night in my kitchen these ideas were largely still feelings—strong, internalized feelings of love for myself and a dedication to my own happiness, the basis of power. With these feelings full upon me, without thinking of a plan, without asking, "What shall I *do?*" I went down and confronted my son. I have no idea what I said; there is a limited repertoire in such situations. Certainly I didn't say or do anything I hadn't said or done a dozen times before. I couldn't have put into words the change I'd just gone through enough to articulate it to myself let alone to him.

The difference was in how I *was*. The instant he reluctantly opened his door to me, he knew the old game was over. He knew he was standing in the presence of New Mom, Mom who could not be manipulated or bullied, Mom in her power. Regardless of what his ears were picking up, all his antennae were quivering with the message that had become a part of my being, of my aura: I had let go of his heel. He knew without conscious thought that whether or not he plunged to his death in the abyss below or decided to change his course was now entirely up to him. I was handing him back the responsibility for his life.

Overnight—and I mean that literally—the chronic disquiet in our home disappeared. My son's life changed dramatically in the direction I had been trying to get it to change for years, and it has stayed changed. Of course, he could have chosen to self-destruct, though most people, given the responsibility and the choice, do not. But even if he had made that choice, I would have been all right. I would have grieved terribly, but my heart's fire would not have been extinguished with guilt as it would once have been.]

That night I had realized that since at any given moment at least one of my kids might very well be wretched about something, if I were a "good mother" I could look forward to continual misery until the day I died.

So I decided to be a bad mother. Being a bad mother meant that I could be sorry when my kids had sad times, but *I* wouldn't be sad. Their being sad was already enough sadness. They could be in trouble and suffer, and I would commiserate and help in whatever appropriate way I could, but *I* would not suffer.

That day I chose power. I chose to feel how I wanted to feel no matter what was happening to others, no matter how others behaved toward me, no matter the situation. I chose not to be, victim-like, at the mercy of external circumstances, but instead to be potent in magnifying the joyful, free spaces in my soul. I made a deliberate choice to jettison from my beliefs the nonsense that it is nobler to suffer—particularly as long as any other living thing is suffering anywhere on the planet—than to be at peace in spite of everything. I accepted accountability for being who I wanted to be.

When I had believed that my feelings were contingent upon others—not only Susan and my children and friends, but bishops, pornographers, legislators, rapists, judges, and presidents—I had to try to get them to do the things that would "make" me feel the way I wanted to feel—safe, worthy, lovable, intelligent, important. I had to manipulate situations in the same way, since I had also granted them the power to determine my well-being. It was a big job and took lots of time and energy. So it was with great relief that I gave up my struggle to make external circumstances yield up what I needed and concentrated upon accepting and using my own considerable power in behalf of my own beloved Self.

So being in my power came to mean taking total responsibility for feeling the way I felt every minute—whether I liked how I felt or not—and for feeling the way I wanted to feel all the time, despite everything. I noticed that the more I lived in this internal security that I knew was power, the more I could allow other women to be themselves, without my having to try to change their beliefs or behavior. Knowing that I wasn't responsible for their feelings or beliefs or behavior any more than they were for mine, I could also be more myself around them without fear of what they might say, what they might do.

I realized that when I wasn't covertly relying on or expecting anyone else to act in certain ways or to do certain things to make me happy—when I chose friends freely, no strings attached—I saw that our loving one another didn't depend on what we did for each other.

I discovered that I liked others most when I was being most myself. This encouraged me to continue to dare to be that way. I wanted to experience the freedom to be myself that only disinterested affection offered, caring that didn't need to control because it wasn't a means to something else, had no agenda but itself. I was learning the truth that I was totally lovable just as I was, that other women were lovable just as they were, without having to *do* anything.

As this change was taking place in me, I tried to articulate it to Susan. "I would love you even if you never got me another speaking engagement, never took care of Noel[2] another second. I appreciate what you do for me, but it does not *make* me love you. I love you because you are smart and

---

[2] Noel, my last child, was eight years old when Susan and I obeyed the mandate to live together.

160

brave. I love you because you sit like that in the chair with your foot up and your hair shining in the lamplight. No, none of that's right. It doesn't matter how you look or act. What I love is your *Susanness*, the essence of you that remains the same no matter how much you change." I would add now, "The more I love myself and am willing to provide myself with all I need, the more I am able to let you simply *be* that wonderful Susan."

I vowed never again to see any woman as an object, as a means to certain ends—such as filling up my emptiness, giving me feelings of security, keeping me from loneliness, or "making" me happy in dozens of other ways. In addition to exploiting women, it was a tragic lie that any other woman could do this for me. I promised myself instead to see truly *who she was* and to be most pleased when she was most herself, to love *her* so that she didn't have to *do* anything to be lovable to me except to be herself.[3]

When I stopped depending on other women to meet my needs, I affirmed my supposition that if I were no longer obscuring their real faces with my projected needs, I could "see" them more clearly, begin genuinely to know them. Because I understood that getting my needs met and feeling the way I wanted to feel all the time had nothing to do with them, when they were around me they didn't have to do anything special or be anything but exactly what they wanted to do and be. And I didn't have to do anything but really see and hear them. When I was in my power, other women's

---

[3] Back in the days when Joyce Marieb and Linda Barufaldi owned The Amazon Sweet Shop in San Diego, Joyce once wrote out for me on the back of her business card: No amount of hard work, struggle, suffering, or success will make you any more worthy of love than you are right now.

simply *being* in my presence gave me the purest of all my life's many pleasures.

What a gigantic relief, too, to give up the obligation of critiquing other womens' political correctness, not to have to decide whether they were being patriarchal in any way—racist or elitist or agist or able-bodiest—and oppressing them about it, trying to force them to stop. I knew that pressure or coercion of any kind for any purpose—even purposes I might perceive as crucial—was always part of mensgame, always oppressive, always sadomasochistic, and could change nothing except for the worse. I knew that I couldn't change anybody but myself for the better. And I also trusted that other women were doing the best they could at the moment, as I was, and that, like me, all they needed from others in order to get on with their personal work was to be unconditionally accepted as the experts on their own lives.

I could only give them this when I felt it for myself, when I loved and accepted myself completely, so I assumed that they could only give this kind of freedom to me when they were also in their power. From observing myself become less and less critical, I knew finally that all critical feelings toward others are motivated by a lack of self-love, by self-denigration.

At the same time that I stopped looking to other people to meet my needs, I stopped feeling responsible for meeting theirs. I realized that there comes a time when learning how to meet our own needs becomes more important than having them temporarily met by others. I didn't want to disable other women by stepping in—assuming the one/up position and forcing them into the one/down. I had to believe that they could be depended upon to get what they wanted.

Part of what this came to mean to me was that none of us is on this planet to meet any other person's needs, including children's. This is not the reason for being. Like rainbows, we are here simply to be. Everyone understands that a rainbow just is, that it has no extrinsic purpose. No one demands that a rainbow meet their needs; they simply enjoy its presence.

That we have *had* to fill others' needs, even children's, that we have been coerced into putting their needs first *whether we felt like it or not, wanted to or not* at the moment, is evidence of the gross, and I think deliberate, mis-organization of society into nuclear family units based on ownership. There isn't a woman living who couldn't design a model more freeing and humane, and it's a good thing. Because in order to have a new world, we must figure out how everyone's needs can be completely filled without any of us doing a single thing we don't really want to do, *without even the smallest sacrifice.*

The denial of Self and life, the lack of integrity and power inherent in sacrifice, is deeply disfiguring to all of us, children and adults alike. Children are damaged—just as we are—by having their needs met by slaves, by people who are not making free choices out of love but are instead acting much of the time out of the despotic coercions of apparent necessity and guilt and needs for approval and desire to control. From this, kids internalize all life-hating, joy-destroying messages of manunkind and start on their own progression into numbness and robotitude.

What if every piece of clothing we put on, every tool we handled, every bit of food we ate were made, grown, or prepared by someone who chose freely to do it because they so enjoyed the actual doing of it? Imagine eating food prepared by someone who loved preparing it, who chose to do it right then for her own enjoyment. Imagine how infused with her integrity and power, how much more tasty, more nourishing and wholesome such food would be than that cooked by someone primarily because she knew it had to be done.

It is true that the woman who chooses to cook because she feels like it right now also gets great pleasure from watching others enjoy it. But this is not the reason she does it. That there is no linear time signifies that the means are the ends, making the journey truly the destination. Therefore, since she chooses to be alive—to act out of the integrity of her real feelings at the moment—the cook's food preparation is both means and end. She does not project her pleasure along a fictitious line into a non-existent future and fix food for the purpose of enjoying others' enjoyment of it in an hour or so. Being true to her Self every moment is her source of life-stuff. It is freedom.

She can and of course does still care very much about others' well-being, even more deeply perhaps because she cares so very much about her own. She often feels like surprising and delighting others, and helping them when it is appropriate. But her overriding motive for doing anything for others remains that the actual doing of whatever it is gives her pleasure at the time. She knows that when any behavior becomes a means to another end, it carries the genes of oppression in it.

Doing something for another person might incidentally accomplish some goal other than delight—such as making life easier for them for awhile, or proving to them (and to her) that she is a good, caring person with the right politics, or causing them (or her) to think more highly of her, or making them like her better—and that would be fine. But none of these secondary benefits could persuade her to do something she did not, at that moment, actually want to do. No outcome, no matter how worthy in the old social sense, could compensate her for the devastation wreaked in her own and other lives by such betrayal of Self.

Though I was greatly relieved when I realized that I wasn't on the planet to meet anyone else's needs and that no one was here to meet mine, like the woman who loved cooking this didn't mean that I stopped caring about others—their difficulties and pain, triumphs and joys—or that I didn't help or rejoice in whatever non-sacrificial, non-guilt-motivated, non-hierarchal ways I could see. It meant that I recognized other women as able to take their own power as I took mine.

I recognized sacrifice as a virulent form of control. By this time I knew absolutely that power cannot exist in the presence of coercion, under even the merest, seemingly most innocuous, pressure. Just as I facilitated personal power in my children by trusting them to feel their own feelings and live their own lives and by being the best example I could in my own life of how to do this, I knew I had to let go of control in a global sense. I had to stop believing that focusing on other women's problems was desirable behavior, that through my own personal sacrifice I could somehow "save" them.

I had to keep on believing despite massive propaganda that how I helped create a world in which everyone got their needs met was by creating within myself the ability to meet my own; that how I helped create a universe of freedom for everyone was by creating a free inner universe for myself. I had to believe that this was not only the most I could do but that it was abundantly, miraculously enough.

17

Shipwreck

E ven though by this point in my research I could feel drastic shifts taking place in my soul, and knew absolutely that I was changing in so many and such profound ways that nothing would ever be the same again, I was reluctant to let go of the Ship. No matter that my intuition kept urging me to; my heart was broken, not just about Susan but also at the prospect of relinquishing forever the sweet dream of love.

Though I hungered for freedom, I also wanted affection and intimacy. Every so often I would feel a frisson of panic as the thought crossed my mind that these might turn out to be antithetical. But I would deliberately reject the dichotomous, binary mind behind that panic, the mind that posed the inevitable question: If I find that they *are* contradictory, which will I choose—freedom or love? Instead, I held firmly to my belief that I could have them both, and more. I could have it all—whatever "it" turned out to be.

But I couldn't help grieving at the passing of a defunct ideal. And in that grief I grew to hate the term "breaking up." It not only hurt me, it confused me as well, suggesting as it did that something that had once been whole was now coming to pieces—like ice breaking up on the lake. This bore no resemblance to my experience. Instead, through it all I had had the profoundest sense that I was personally coming together at last and that therefore my connection with Susan now also had the chance to be whole. I knew by then that the problem wasn't that something was wrong with either Susan or me or that I simply hadn't found the "right" person yet. I knew absolutely, deep in my innards, that relationShipness itself was the villain, but I hadn't yet realized that "breakup" was an integral part of it.

Though *I* might have perceived that Susan and I weren't "breaking up" but were instead regaining our individuality, I knew that this distinction would be lost on most of our *friends*—as it would have been on me a few months earlier—and that the moment Susan moved out they would pronounce us "broken up."

I had known dimly from the onset of my clash with OurBS that there was always a possibility that, in its terms, we *might* break up. But the idea seemed absurd and the inescapable misery of it unnecessary. I therefore stubbornly refused to consider it. Why should I have to wrench Susan out of my heart? Why couldn't we remodel our relation Ship without trauma? Why couldn't I always have her and all the women I loved and ever would love in my life? It seemed to me both possible and desirable.

My decision to regard as spurious the necessity for breaking up, plus the continual commands from the officer on the bridge (who lived inside me, one foot in my conscious mind, the other deep in the cordoned-off sector), plus my genuine affection and respect for this amazing Susan woman, caused me to prolong agonizingly what I now know was the inescapable breaking of our marriage/ownership contract.

Long after the event, my poem analogy returned to help me figure out why we hadn't been able to change our mode without finally having to go through "breakup." It was then that I realized that "breakup" was an integral part of OurBS poem, a basic metaphor, an amalgam of form and content as unique as it was essential to marriage. Though in no other context has it any meaning at all, in the context of relation Ships "breakup" plays a very powerful and compulsory part. Every couple that ever truly wanted to change how they connected with each other had to cut the Ship loose from its moorings in their souls and let it sail out from between them. They had to do this because acquiescing to the dictatorship of the officer on the deck prevents the reintegration of the psyche. Reconstruction of Self is possible only in freedom.

I had long since discovered that at the point where fear prevents me from recapturing my Self, I sink into a coma, a deadness at the center, because it is only in this stuporous state that I can endure captivity. From this, I had deduced, as so many of us have, that having a free and independent Self is a necessary condition for full, conscious life.

Though the only way to get out of the relationShip form is to break up, some of us manage to do it more kindly and gently, more quickly than others. A great deal depends upon the tenaciousness of OurBS's grip on our imaginations. It had a steely grip on mine. The situation would have been infinitely more humane for us both if I had been able to let the flawed dream go and simply broken up with Susan early on in the process. Despite the incredible heartache of it all, however, and for selfish reasons, I'm glad now that I wasn't able at the time to do it in any other fashion. I learned more about myself than any other experience had ever taught me.

I'm grateful, too, to the starry-eyed couple I called forth to show me the way. With their help I forced most of OurBS piece by piece out into the open, though I overlooked the most obvious and single most freedom-killing relationShip element for at least another year. Nevertheless, I thought I was finished with the major part of the task and sat back to view as a whole the form and content of this relationShip poem that patriarchy had transcribed directly onto the pages of our psyches.

It was then, mulling over the connection between form and content in poetry and in life, that I finally understood why I hadn't been able to tell how I felt about sleeping with Susan until she moved into her own place—i.e., until we broke up. As long as I was immersed in the form—living together, sleeping together, and so on—I was a captive of the content, at the mercy of the expectations and assumptions that are integral parts of the structure and upon and around which it is organized. Choosing the form, I was automatically restricted to the feelings and behavior that it dictates, the only ones it allows.

Therefore, until I rejected the form, it was a given that I wanted to sleep with Susan. Believing that we always want to sleep together is a perfect example of the union of form and content that constitutes relation Ships.

But the minute I tried to take the form out of the content—I would still love her (how could I help it?) but I wouldn't live with her, sleep with her every night, do everything with her, be sexually exclusive—the poem fell apart. No longer governed by the assumptions of OurBS, I was not only free to feel how I genuinely felt, to do what I really wanted to do, but also outside the form suddenly I couldn't *help* feeling in new ways.

I won't quickly forget the day when, with pain and relief battling furiously for ascendancy inside me, I held my mind and heart wide open and let the Ship that had alienated me from myself and from Susan sail out of my life forever—or so I naively thought. As soon as I closed the door behind it, I noticed without surprise that it disintegrated on the front doorstep.

So I set about immediately to retrieve from its wreckage the resources it had commandeered from me for so long. I knew I'd need my full attention and powers for pioneering the wilderness left inside me as the stereotypes and categories of men's society decamped from my psyche. I figured that my liberated capabilities would come in handy as I walked step by step into shining possibilities, unlimited scope, precious freedom.

Though there's still much talk about co-dependency as a disease, my experiences lead me to believe that it is instead patriarchy's Relationship Belief System that is the disease and that co-dependency is only one of its many symptoms.

I am finding, as are others, that as I continue to deprogram myself of OurBS's false and deadly picture of intimacy, in wondrous ways I change both the form and content of my connections with others. I love to remember that in doing so I am helping to write another, truer, more lasting, happier love poem for women and perhaps for everyone.

18

Whence and Whereto Bliss?

On the day, long after we had "broken up," that I finally understood "breakup" as an unavoidable stanza in the relationShip poem, I glimpsed another aspect of patriarchy's Relationship Belief System (PRBS).[1] I was thinking about Susan and me, how we'd met, how I'd felt, how our story had unfolded. I saw the stars in our eyes that first year, the same stars that had sparkled in the eyes of my blissful, mythical guide couple.

It was the bliss that I fastened upon in those memories. What had it been all about? Where had it come from? Where had it disappeared to, and why?

I figured out for starters that while the stuff of relation Ships that I had uncovered might be thought of as the warp, fabric also had woof. Perhaps the woof of PRBS was our conditioned assumption that relation Ships have a certain natural rhythm or progression. Wallowing in delirious

---

[1] At this point I stopped calling it OurBS. It certainly wasn't mine or my friends' any longer. I also thought the call letters PRBS were very apt because of course men do the preponderance of their indoctrination through their various media—Patriarchy' ' Relationship Broadcasting System.

lustiness is considered normal behavior for a couple transported to the first stage. Equally normal behavior is their eventual return to "the real world," i.e., their graduation to a contentment that society insists is more desirable despite how it seems.

Though the last phase is also considered normal, society definitely neither advocates nor condones it—in fact, scarcely acknowledges its existence. In this stage the couple becomes disillusioned, bored, miserable, and ripe either for "breakup" or coma.

"Who said this progression is 'normal,' that this is the shape of love?" I asked myself. "And who decided what constitutes 'the real world?' The same guys who brought you Vietnam, *Hustler*, chicken factories, and an ozone layer that rivals swiss cheese," I replied. "Since I obviously can't believe a word of this, what *shall* I believe?"

I thought about new relation Ships, about their headiness, their glory. I remembered how, when I "fell in love" with Susan, my senses woke up wonderingly as if out of anesthesia, then grew quickly keen and avid. How greedy I became not just for her but for the whole world—tasting, smelling, hearing, seeing, touching—experiencing those miracles as if for the first time, sensuously vivified and aware every moment.

Could this be the same drab, sorry world I had lived in last week, I marvelled? Could this wildly energetic, optimistic, joyous person really be me? I felt more vital than I had in years, brimming with love for everyone. Every face on the street was beautiful. Every dream was possible.

Unfortunately, phallocracy sees to it that such power doesn't get out of hand. Quickly announcing that experience will prove this a passing phase, it ensures the fulfillment of its prophecy by channeling our vast ecstatic energy into the narrow, prescribed gangways of a Ship. It seemed to me as I thought about it that in the relationShip poem bliss is *calculated* to be only the first stanza, designed not to last. Propaganda subliminally assures us of this, and tells us that we should be glad that it doesn't last. Otherwise, we'd never get anything important done—meaning we would soon stop doing the miserable work of non-life eight or more hours a day.

I wondered what would happen if we believed that we could live forever in that vibrant aliveness? What might happen is that we might ask the obvious question, "Is there anything more important to do than to be aware of and enjoy being alive every moment?" Our asking that question would mean that, already knowing the answer, we were forsaking the old dead world and venturing into life as we intuited it could be—vital and heady. Everything on earth would have to change to match us. We would be dangerous.

Because of this, because the condition of being fully, sensuously, and joyously alive is so generative of power, I asked myself what could be more natural than that those who rule the world make sure it doesn't become a permanent condition. Certainly, society seems set up to ensure that it doesn't. It channels this great energy into the maintenance of relation Ships that, by paring all this lifestuff down to control, causes it soon to waste away and die.

In the past I had looked at being "in love" quite differently from this. In *Going Out of Our Minds: The Metaphysics of Liberation*, I call it a "patriarchally induced coma," in which "women lose their identity, their autonomy, their survival instincts, their will, and their good sense.'[2] Clearly I was referring to the first stage—"falling in"—and more conditioned than I realized, I smugly perceived myself as safely and sanely beyond that.

Ironically, at the time that I described "falling in love" in that derogatory way I was almost at the total mercy of the Ship in my living room. Though I was unwilling, and I think unable, to look critically at my condition then, the words that my Wise Old Woman wrote through my hand ostensibly about "falling in love" may actually have applied directly and purposefully to the second phase—"contentment"—the phase I was buried alive in at the time.

Since we channel ourselves when we write, we can search our own words for directions to the getaway routes. If I had dared pay attention then, for instance, I might have waked up right away and speeded up my escape from the tyranny of the Ship by as much as a year.

But that experience of ignoring my Wise Old Woman as she tried to alert me to my plight at least taught me compassion for myself and other women. I once also denied, as many women do, that I lacked freedom in my relation Ships, I once also insisted that because my Ship was not like others, relationShip problems were individual matters, not results of deep systemic decrees. It keeps me humble to remember that for a long time I also chose safe oblivion over scary ambiguity.

So though I once viewed "falling in love" as a patriarchal plot, I began to see that the real plot was the transmogrification of something basically lovely, free, and life-enhancing into doomed relationShipness. When we "fall

---

[2] The Crossing Press: Freedom, CA, 1987, p. 105.

in love," we fall into prefabricated mindtracks that prevent us from seeing and knowing our loved one as she is and therefore from having an authentic experience. We are highly likely to objectify her, viewing her as something that exists for our delight or safety or other use. We have strong tendencies to project our ideal woman upon her. And carry false assumptions and unexamined expectations into our every encounter with her.

I knew, too, that "in love" is "in reaction"—that is, a set, conditioned response to a stimulus—and that reaction is neither a creative nor a free choice.[3] I knew I was loving and not "in love" when I was not losing my Self[4] but was instead more and more reclaiming my Self, was not becoming dependent but was instead finding my own way, was not becoming part of someone else or submerging my Self in "us," but was living and thinking autonomously, not *falling* for someone else but *rising* for myself.

I understood all this cultural overlay, and was aware of having lots of ambivalence and unsurety about this subject. Language continued to warn me about this state, too. After all, if one does not fall *in* love, one cannot fall *out*, and I still intended to find a way to maintain intimacy with all the women I loved, never to have to "break up." I was incensed at the all-too-prevalent custom of throwing women and their affection away like paper cups. To me, respect and affection were not disposable. Having to part, as Susan and I had to

---

[3] Conversation with Sally Tatnall and Phyllis Balcerzak, Cleveland, Ohio, December 2, 1988.

[4] Adele Gorelick, from Rockville, Maryland, tells me that one of the ways she keeps from losing herself, from emptying out and waiting for her lover to fill her up, is—when she finds herself dwelling on thoughts of her lover—to repeat her *own* name until she is again centered in her Self.

part, was a signal to me that as women we had not yet found our own true way of loving.

Despite everything, I had—and have today—a persistent hunch that there may be something about the "in love" feeling that is pure and true, some clue we can glean from it about how it is possible for us to *be*.[5] And not just how to be for a short while every now and then but all the time. Feeling zingingly alive if only for five seconds gives us the supremely important information that such feeling is possible. It seems only reasonable to assume from this that—since as atomic physics tells us there is actually no linear time, no time "passing," but all time present at once—any feeling we are capable of experiencing for five seconds we are just as capable of experiencing for five hours, five years, or five decades.

In the last part of *Wildfire: Igniting the She/Volution*, I relate my experience of seeing the world for a few moments as it really is—the "real world"—without the scrims of linear time and powerlessness with which the men's millennia-long rule by force has so successfully veiled my eyes.

Entering this world, I suddenly felt very large, very healthy and strong, and hugely capable of pleasure. I also knew at once and without question that I was beautiful, brilliant, and witty, that I was irresistibly lovable. I felt full to bursting with goodness, creativity, and psychic power, and was awed by the vastness and nobility of my soul. For my short sojourn in that world, I was completely alive, truly and magnificently myself, free.

The heart-stopping revelation during those few moments was that such feelings were *possible*. Although I experienced

---

[5] I learned later to think of this state as "arousal." See Chapter 22.

their incredible intensity for only a few seconds, I knew that because I could feel them at all I could feel them for any length of time.

As that world began to fade from my vision, I tried vainly to maintain the internal climate it had created. Men's small drab "reality" quickly dulled the brightness in me, though, and stopped the singing. For long periods of time I forgot that I had ever seen the glory of my real home, women's world.

But during the years that I struggled to understand how we might love one another in freedom, I returned again and again to the memory of it, until finally, longing for it with all the power of my life, I determined to figure out how to recapture it. Though I didn't know how to break through my brainwashing and conjure it at will, I remembered clearly the feeling of extraordinary aliveness and well-being. The closest I had ever come in my patriarchal fog and numbness to that shining awareness of beauty and power and delight that truly pervades everything was when I had "fallen in love." Though my "falling in love" feelings were dimmest echoes of that other wanton embrace with the goddess, in my exile from her they were the best analogy I had. So I re-opened my mind to the "falling in love" syndrome, studying it for clues to living in a state of sensuous and perceptual arousal.

To my mind one of the falsest and most destructive aspects of "falling in love" had been that we are conditioned to attribute that marvelous feeling to the presence of the loved one in our lives. And not only the marvelous feeling but any positive feelings at all. How many times in the past had I thought I'd die because I couldn't be in someone's arms? I looked back at my life and saw blank periods—a year, two years—when all I had done was long for and obsess about someone else, feeling totally unable to stop.

During those times, regardless of the activities of my days, I hadn't really lived at all. Oblivious to my own beauty, to that of other friends and of the natural world, dead to the rich variety of emotional and intellectual experience within easy reach, I might as well have been interred in the nearest cemetery. I had lost years of life in "in love's" dead space.

I longed now for freedom from that bondage. I was determined never again to be so in the phallocentric mind, so under its illusions or so operating out of its assumptions that I lost life if I lost a lover's arms. I wanted to find out how to generate and live in that creative ecstasy without focusing upon any other person.

I began to theorize about the nature and origins of the bliss of new love and postulate reasons for its meteoric life cycle. I returned to my first questions: Where did it come from so suddenly? Where did it go so quickly and why? What *was* it?

These questions, coupled with the fact that my own sexual desire was waning at an alarming rate, began to lead me into ethical thickets so scary and dangerous that in the past my conscious mind had refused to go near them. But I so longed to feel again that I was willing to risk all my comfortable illusions, ready to take on the rest of the monsters in my soul.

So with trepidation I turned my spotlights on that part of my experience I most feared to examine. I began to look searchingly at my sex life.

PART III

SEX ABOARD THE SHIP

19

In Bed with Men's Misery Machine

That I felt sexually numb—despite my genuine love for Susan, despite how desirable I found her in other ways—distressed me more than I liked to admit. We had begun so passionately, my senses had been so extraordinarily awakened. It hurt to admit to myself that almost none of that lovely stuff was left in me, and I had a vague feeling of guilt—as if I done something wrong, hadn't tried hard enough, were somehow lacking.

Even after I first allowed the recognition of its absence to flit across my conscious mind, it took a year or two for me to become really alarmed. I believe this was because I continued to take the greatest physical pleasure in Susan—looking at her, caressing and kissing her, holding her, sleeping in her embrace. We touched dozens of times a day. I felt as if we were in these ways sexual all day long, so I tried not to worry about my anesthetized body and our non-pursuit of orgasm.

But in spite of myself, I did worry. Sharing the deep programmed belief with other members of the fathers' planetary tribe that sexual excitation and even more particularly orgasm is central to a relation Ship—and that the hotter and more frequent the healthier—I found my growing numbness more and more disturbing.

Finally I found the courage to examine what was going on between Susan and me in bed that might be precipitating it. As I did, the pattern that emerged shook me to the core. I saw that we had, in all innocence, invited into our bed our most dreaded enemy. There in all its destructive inequity was manunkind's current model of interaction: Dominance/subordination, master/slave, patriarchy.

What I saw was that despite our feminist consciousness, despite our awareness of the snares and our determination to bypass them, we had nonetheless fallen into them. We were playing roles. Since roles are behaviors that are societally essential, in our sadomasochistic society role-playing is sadism—no matter how gentle, no matter how subtle, no matter how often participants switch roles. I felt stricken when I realized with what increasing frequency Oppression had made a third in our bed over the years. That this had been entirely unintentional made the problem no less shocking or formidable. I was determined to understand and to reverse it.

Examining my genital relation Ship with Susan with as much honesty and fearlessness as I could muster, I recognized that in our sex-in-bed adventures, I was nearly always the initiator and that I controlled whether we went ahead or stopped somewhere along the way. I winced at the realization that I had freer access to her body than she had to mine. I saw with grim clarity that though we acted our roles very subtly, I had nevertheless become the husband and Susan the wife.

This so alarmed and sickened me that I could no more have continued this model of "making love" than I could have aligned myself deliberately with the builders of nuclear power plants or the bulldozers of the Amazon forests. I knew that the dominance/submission paradigm is the war paradigm, and I refused to perpetuate it by "making war"—by "making self-hatred"—with Susan ever again if I could help it. Though I had surprised Grossest Inequality in my bed and routed it out for the moment by becoming celibate, I had little idea where or how to begin to banish it permanently. I realized that as an active third partner in my life with Susan, it had not limited its arena to the bedroom; I had recognized it there first only because my socialization made that the likeliest place to spot it. I felt wretched knowing that we were not only "playing house" in bed but that we were playing it everywhere.

In our unfree embrace, Susan and I had neither been fully living our own lives nor connecting with each other much of the time. While we had often hovered dimly, on hold, in the background somewhere, our roles had lived our lives, relating to each other with almost perfect compatibility. Moving our bodies around and wagging our tongues, they had been having a grand time.

Susan and I had fallen easily into the trap patriarchy lays for us all. To keep us under house arrest, it entices us to lock ourselves into what appears to be a loving embrace but is actually the same dreary struggle for control that both defines and constitutes male rule. If it were a truly loving—and therefore free—embrace, instead of a subversion and mis-direction of power, our combined individual stores of personal power would synergize, becoming greater than the sum of our individual potentials. Because such pools of power would be devastating to the status quo, patriarchy pits us against each other—from couples, the smallest unit in society, to nations.[1]

But I couldn't even *think* of a genuinely different model. Any alternative I came up with turned out upon close inspection to be merely a reversal of roles. If I were truly honest with myself, I could see that though the control differential might be narrowed, it could not be made to disappear altogether no matter what alternative I examined.

I hungered for peerness, and my growing awareness that not a single aspect of my relation Ship with Susan was as peer as I had believed it to be was profoundly humiliating and troubling to me. It kept me awake to the implications of my feelings and behavior as nothing else could have done, and prodded me to keep searching.

But I began to fear that my not being able even to *imagine* a non-hierarchical, non-sadistic way was not simply a function of Susan's and my relation Ship, but that it was far more sinister than that. I feared that if I looked more closely I would find that peerness is so non-paradigmatic on this wretched planet that almost no one, and certainly no one without terrific intuitive powers, is able to relate to anyone else without some degree of hierarchy and therefore of sadism and oppression. For obvious reasons, I shied away from this conclusion for many months.

Then, when I couldn't avoid it any longer and before I realized that it couldn't be done that way, I tried to think my way out of the sadism that was at the root of my sadness and pain, at the root of the sadness and pain of relation Ships, at the root of the sadness and pain of the world. I resorted to theory.

---

[1] Conversation with Susan Horwitz, November 1988.

20

No Way Out?

I turned first to the information that women who consciously choose sadomasochism have given us. They say that this practice overcomes the emotional numbness inherent in our oppressive world and in doing so heightens feelings of aliveness.

Since my earliest feminist days I had understood that hierarchy is the present paradigm of this unlucky planet, and that hierarchy is always established and maintained by physical, economic, and psychic violence and terror. Since hierarchy always necessitates that some people control others, it is simply another word for sadomasochism.

I had since come to a deeper understanding of the thoroughness of a global paradigm such as this, how it is the basic determining pattern of thought and action in everyone's lives. I could not even intuit how any of us were going to learn to think and act outside our present model of sadomasochism, though I believed absolutely that it could be done and that women were going to find the way to do it.

I therefore assumed that when the self-proclaimed sadomasochistic women called us hypocrites—insisting that we were doing "it" too—they were right. After all, they were the experts. They knew it when they saw it. And how could we even imagine how we'd act in a nonlinear, nonhierarchical world when all we've known as a race for thousands of years is the violence of hierarchy?

So, perhaps, I conjectured sadly, sadomasochism is at the root of the exhilaration of "falling in love."

But there were problems with this theory other than my resistance and discomfort. Since domination through threatened or real violence is the way we find excitement in our sadomasochistic world, it didn't make sense that violence-induced excitement would be the *first* phase of loverdom. Rather, it seemed logical to me that if this excitement were sadistically achieved, it should increase as the relation Ship developed since lovers become more, not less, controlling of each other over time.

In addition, I couldn't understand how the same kind of violence and terror that are responsible for our emotional numbness in patriarchy could also be the instruments for alleviating it. Could the principle here be like that underlying homeopathic medicine, that a little of the same disease cures it? Or does conscious sadomasochism heighten awareness simply by increasing the apparent violence and danger quotient present at any given moment? Even if it does, it doesn't explain why more control over time doesn't equal more bliss over time.

Concentrating on the connection between time and control, however, soon took my thoughts in quite another direction. What if the reason for the excitement at first is not domination but freedom? After all, though none of us is yet free in an ultimate sense, when we first come together as individual uncoupled women we are at least temporarily free

188

from menstream's principal and most ruthless tyrant: The officer on the bridge of a relation Ship. What if the deliciously heady feelings of power and creativity and joy result from the coming together of women in freedom? This seemed to me to be at least one possible theory, and one I found hopeful and exciting. It would not only clarify the essential part freedom plays in the possibility of all other desirable emotional states, but it would also explain why, in our sadomasochistic style of love, these states are so transitory. Almost the instant we become "lovers," we begin to take away one another's freedom in all the ways our current love poem prescribes. As soon as we invite a relation Ship into our lives, the uniformed minion of patriarchy high on his bridge in our souls begins his serious work of domination.

In men's world of contrived scarcity—of love, of touching, of everything we need and want—when we perceive someone as "making" us feel this wonderful way (instead of merely providing us with one of the few socially condoned occasions to experience a tiny bit of the magnificence that is always in us), or as "giving" us these rare feelings of wholeness and aliveness, our programming works on several levels to make us try to capture and cage them. It has taught us to fear that we may lose them or have to share them (and goodness knows there isn't *enough* to share!) We feel as if we must have access to this magical person at all times as a guarantee that the good feelings they "give" us will be available whenever we want and need them.

The terrible irony is that the feelings we crave are totally dependent upon freedom—ours and theirs. And owning is as non-free as being owned. When we take away others' freedom, we kill all possibility of freedom feelings in ourselves. These feelings are manifestations of our wild, creative, powerful Selves, and they cannot live in captivity. We hear the apparent paradox expressed often these days that in order truly to have something, we must let it go. But freedom *is* paradoxical. Everything we want and need, and an abundance of it, depends on our learning to let everyone and everything do only what they want to do, to go their own ways and be free. Doing this frees us as well. The question this raises is, "How then can we come together each time, always, as women free of our relationShip brainwashing?" In women's world—the paradigm I glimpsed briefly that one day long ago—least coercion equals most integrity, power, and delight. What I therefore needed to believe right then was that despite still being trapped in the madness of the dominance/submission pattern I could somehow learn how not to coerce anyone else in any way to any degree. Even though it meant leaping out of the planetary mind-set, and therefore perhaps right out of existence, I resolved to act as if it could be done and that I could do it.

With this resolve, I found myself bustling about and getting nowhere in the pro- and anti-sadomasochism thought-loop. Though I perceived that sadomasochism was a daily constant, and in my estimation the most grievous fact of all our lives, at the same time I was inordinately hopeful about banishing it. I believed naively that if I would only give it my attention and learn to identify it in specific instances, I could erase it from my repertoire. To my credit, I knew that both recognizing and disentangling myself of it would be exquisitely difficult, but I so hungered for freedom that I glossed over any doubt that I would finally prevail.

Until Sally Tatnall came to visit from Cleveland, that is. It just so happened that she and her friend, Phyllis Balcerzak, were writing a book on this very subject. I listened eagerly to their ideas—and my optimism about escaping from the clutches of dominance and submission flew out the window. They confirmed my suspicion that at least at that point in human history sadism was nearly inescapable on this planet.

With liberation now appearing less likely than ever, I became seriously depressed for the first time since my teenage years. All the wretchedness of my prolonged breakup with Susan, added to the seeming impossibility of changing my life in as profound a way as I craved, plus the impending adolescence of my fourth child and third son, combined with the daily grinding boredom of menstream society—all this suddenly made life seem very bleak. My gloom was nearly impenetrable.

I say "nearly" because even in the face of what appeared to be incontestable proof that there is no way out of phallacracy's paradigm of oppression, there was a part of me that stubbornly refused to give in. *Still* stubbornly refuses to give in.

After several weeks of trying to pick my spirits up off the floor, I finally felt enough like my old self to continue with my experiment. I planned to face up to my sadism, to reject it at once whenever and wherever I found it in myself, and to figure out how to replace it with peerness.

Why not!

21

Hey, Big Woman!

I began with the easy stuff.
I had noticed for instance, that through my use of language I subtly belittled Susan, keeping her trapped in the one/down slot and myself securely one/up. I intensified the already marked nonpeerness between us by using the word "little" in addressing her and in referring to her.

I called her, as if it were her given name, "Small" or "Smallest," "Little" or "Littlest," "Tiny" or "Tiniest," as in "Smallest, where's the Marlene Mountain file?" or "Hey, Little, do you want some watermelon before I slurp it all down?"

I also often sang to her, songs like, "Oh, li'l Susie, li'l Susie Lu, Oh li'l Susie, I'm in love with you," and "Sukyahlah, you're my darling that's why I'm in love with you, little Sukie, little Sukie." It was my habit to say in passing, "You have such a sweet little _____"—fill in the blank: Body, tushi, face, footie, paw, leggie, head. "Little Susie"—a matronizing, disparaging, reductionist epithet.

She called me "Big," "Large," or "Biggest," "Largest."

As soon as I noticed this habit of ours, I realized that it alone should have made glaringly obvious what was going on

193

between us. But if I'd been called on this before I discovered it myself, I would have said that we were simply teasing about our huge difference in size: I was three-quarters of an inch taller, ten to fifteen pounds heavier. Perhaps I also felt that it was all right to address her as if she were an infant because it was just "love talk." But of course it wasn't right and it wasn't love talk. It was hate talk—Susan is an adult, not a baby—and hatred of any woman has its origins in self-hatred.

As I became aware of this habit, I determined to break it. I deprogrammed myself of perceiving her as weak and helpless by emphasizing at all times her largeness, her grown-upness. Though it often felt ludicrous, I persisted. Not for Susan's sake but for my own.

So I began to say, for instance, as I passed her 100-pound-body at her desk, "Hey, big woman!" Or now and again throughout the day, "You have the most beautiful huge hands," (or "massive curly head," or "immense and admirable ways"). I rechristened her such names as "Largest in all the world," and "Bigger than Anything," and "Biggest Possible Fully Grown-Up Woman of my Heart"—"Biggest" for short. We were amused that each of us was now calling the other "Biggest."

Though we laughed a lot at the strangeness of "big" words to describe Susan, switching to them changed my feelings dramatically. Immediately she *felt* more grown-up to me, she *seemed* bigger, more important and capable. I was delighted that at least in this one simple way I was loosening sadism's fierce hold on my psyche.

In the next couple of years, when a certain lover talked about her "little hand" or "little foot" or announced that she was retiring to her "little bed," I had to be very careful not to mimic her. I determined never again to call any part of any woman "little," even if it was, never to use diminutives to express affection—at least not until hierarchy became extinct. I knew that such habits with me were not benign.

22

The "Woofer-Tweeter" Blues[1]

Having tasted even this limited success gave me great optimism and encouraged me to declare "peerness" my word of the month for several months running.

That is, until I realized the utter futility of it. Through my daily-expanding conduit to her, my Wise Old Woman persistently brought me back to what I knew about society's structure under the rule of the phallus: That so long as patriarchy (i.e., hierarchy/sadism) prevails, peerness is not possible between or among anybody. So long as we are trapped in patriarchy's dichotomous mind, there are only two possible positions to choose from in relation to others: Above or below. With any other person at any given moment we occupy either one or the other of these. There is no place else to be in the phallocratic paradigm. And unfortunately no other route then to most of what we perceive as the keenest possible excitement.

---

[1] The Woofer-Tweeter concept and name are courtesy of Sally Tatnall and Phyllis Balcerzak of Cleveland, Ohio.

For many obvious reasons, both of these facts are most strongly borne out in romantic/sexual relation Ships. As Sally Tatnall and Phyllis Balcerzak write:

> *If two people are in a primary coupled relationship or looking forward to being in a primary coupled relationship, then . . . they are in a sexual place that supports hierarchy. Even if orgasm has left a relationship, they are probably still 'doing it' because stimulus/response is still present. By [our] theory, stimulus/response is hierarchy, is primary relationships, is sex.*
>
> *This is the only construct available to us. This is the conditioning of patriarchal society. . . . Without stimulus/response—i.e., dominance/submission or power imbalance—sexual excitation is not possible.*
>
> *Power imbalance, hierarchy, sexual response, dominance/submission, patriarchy, bondage and discipline, and sadomasochism are all the same.*[2]

In a later paper, they clarify what they mean by "stimulus/response" and why it is so dangerous for women:

> *The identifiable characteristic of the sexual dynamic is the presence of stimulating behaviors that expect a response and responsive behaviors that expect a stimulus. We carry this model of sexual expectation everywhere and have learned to measure success and so-called power by how effective we are at stimulating others or responding to them. These behaviors form the s-r dynamic which directs [and*

---

[2] The Woofer-Tweeter Theory of Sexual Response: A Challenge to Power in the Patriarchy, unpublished paper presented at the National Radical Thought for Women Conference in Cleveland, Ohio, May 1987, pp. 6, 9, and 10.

changes] the energy of arousal and creativity—or power—into the energy of excitation and sex—or control.

[Our] theory states that at the moment of arousal, energy is raised, and as soon as it is raised, it is misdirected from arousal into excitation.[3]

Because they both care deeply about women and cherish the dream of a women's loving, peaceful, plentiful world, Tatnall and Balcerzak are distressed at women's menstream conditioning to direct all available energy into this closed-circuit of stimulus-response. They lament that we allow this conditioning to transmute our passion for our visions—a passion they term "arousal"—into mere excitation and consequent sex behavior.

Sex behavior, they attest, grounds and dissipates the energy that we could otherwise use to make our dreams come true, to create the world we so hunger for.[4] "A Wild Woman," they write, "recognizes the energy of arousal as a clear connection to passion and creativity and power."[5]

When I began consciously to look at sadism or status behavior in general—mine and others'—I soon verified the ever-present, though in many cases extremely subtle, hierarchy among us. With experience I grew fairly expert at spotting it.

---

[3] "The Woofer-Tweeter Theory of Sexual Response," unpublished paper delivered at the National Women's Studies Association Conference in Akron, Ohio, June 1990, pp. 1-5.

[4] Ibid., p. 1.

[5] Ibid., p. 2. For a Wild Woman scenario by Tatnall and Balcerzak, see Appendix IB. For their theory of how Wildness was lost, see Appendix 1C.

What appeared undeniable was that though our jockeying for the one/up position might be so delicate as to be nearly indiscernible and though the outcome might place us on only microscopically different levels, nevertheless such levels are invariably present. We might come close, but we are never peer with any other person in any stimulus/response situation—i.e., in any "interaction." Instead we are always somewhere along the continuum from very much to barely more or less "important."

As long as we are "interacting"—a word that describes stimulus/response behavior—we may shift positions with the same person several times in any one encounter, or at least narrow or widen the space between us without actually changing places. I'm not talking about what happens only in quarrels or debates, but in pleasant, friendly conversations as well. For example, first she may have the upper hand, feel more confident, more relaxed and comfortable, then for a few minutes we might usurp the catbird seat, then she may rally and regain control of the tone and direction for a while, only to have us take it back from her—a dozen shifts in position and perhaps even a few actual switches without so much as the slightest effort on either of our parts and usually without the faintest awareness.

It is also probably true that we could not associate at all if we could not find our comparative rung on the status ladder. Our conscious men friends tell us that two men meeting one another must decide instantaneously which is one/up and which one/down before they can make the first overture, say the first word to each other. If this psychic state prevails in patriarchy, it means that until we move out of the sadomasochistic paradigm we cannot even acknowledge or speak to a person if we accidentally find ourselves on the same status rung as they and neither of us moves to correct the situation.

It means that at this moment in history if we are peers we cannot *be.*

"So what?" I usually interrupted myself rudely about here. *"Any second it could change. And one of these seconds, it will change."*

My confidence arose out of my knowledge that the reason women are rising all over the world is to dethrone patriarchy by eradicating sadomasochism. I still believe what I believed then: That when enough of us are aware of it enough of the time, when enough of us desire passionately enough to be released from it and to take the next step, an entirely new possibility of human interconnection will be born. Perhaps it will happen before this book is published and invalidate everything I've written here. I profoundly hope so!

One of the things that occurred to me to do to help make sadism passé was to learn how to tell which position I was occupying in every interactive situation. I immediately stumbled over several large blocks to doing this.

To begin with, I had trouble really believing that sadism was inevitable, despite full awareness of the conclusive evidence. Propaganda had rendered the hierarchy inherent in every interaction invisible to me. In fact, conditioning had softened the sharp edges of my awareness so much that I thought that, though there were definitely strata among us, at least some of us were on the same level some of the time and were at that time "peers." Or, I thought, if we were not yet peers, we could become so by trying.

Sadism was also difficult for me to discern in my thought and behavior because it contradicted my fondest beliefs about myself. I couldn't bear the evidence that I was not only capable of sadomasochism but that I was at that moment incapable of anything else. I enjoyed viewing myself as above it, as the active enemy of all oppression—and sadism is oppression's archetype.

But the fact was that while I may have been the enemy of oppression, I was still captive in its camp. I had difficulty acknowledging that my major excitement has stemmed, and may still largely stem, from inequality—momentary or longer-lived.

Knowing that I wasn't alone in this only made me feel worse. I was not cheered to read in Tatnall and Balcerzak's first paper:

> *It is important to recognize sexual response as an institution. An institution is any establishment devoted to the promotion of a particular law or custom. In this case, the institution of sexual response is promoting the law and custom of stimulus/response, dominance/submission, power imbalance, and hierarchy.*
>
> *We believe that patriarchal investment in hierarchy is so strong that even homosexuality, lesbianism, or any sexual response choice is not a threat to patriarchy as long as it supports hierarchy. Primary relationships do support hierarchy. It is well within the scope of current patriarchal boundaries for two lesbians to live as a suburban couple, have children, own a home, have two cars and be accepted at a progressive block party. Heterosexuality may be a prevalent example of male dominance, but it is not the prime mover of patriarchy—hierarchy is. If women choose to challenge patriarchy at its root, it will be in*

what we create with equality and not with whom we have sex.[6]

I had noticed all along that my sexually-based sadistic behavior infused every social interaction, and I didn't believe I was alone in this, either. Though in sexual activity it is far more virulent, apparent, and nurturing to patriarchy's roots, I saw from my own life how we carry this stimulus/response, dominance/submission dynamic into every aspect of our lives.

Most of us feminists, for example, individually or as part of a group, have spoken negatively of or attacked a woman from some supposed morally superior position—calling her racist, or classist, or able-bodiest, or homophobic—and have enjoyed the unmistakable and heady sensation of rising above her, of looking down upon her.

Judging again from my sample of one, I am fairly certain that most of us still occasionally get such a rush at another woman's expense. Even when I am fully conscious of what I am doing, I have lapses into saying or thinking something slighting about another woman in a self-defeating attempt to feel better about myself by feeling superior to her.

Recently I noticed a distinct sense of disappointment when a woman with whom I was talking praised a friend we had in common. I was disappointed because she had seemed to be heading toward making a derogatory remark, not an accolade, and I was anticipating the quick jolt of pseudo-superiority and well-being that I knew I could get from it. When her comment about our friend was unexpectedly positive, the faint but unmistakable prick of disappointment I felt shocked me into full awareness of myself. Once again, in the illumination

---

[6] Woofer-Tweeter Theory of Sexual Response: A Challenge to the Patriarchy, unpublished paper, May 1987, p. 6.

SEX ABOARD THE SHIP

of that moment I recognized sadism, my old companion. Though I find that I rely less and less on him for reassurance nowadays, I am always saddened to find him still lurking about inside at all. This brings me back to the most basic reason I had trouble admitting my deep sadomasochistic patterning: I despaired of finding a way to extricate myself from it, to operate outside it. Try as I might, I could not seem to break entirely free. I would have loved to be able to continue to ignore and deny it; I had brief but strong waves of homesickness for my former ignorance. But I was no longer ignorant, and I could neither ignore nor deny it.

As I travelled in my thinking from sadism in general to sadism in sex, I arrived at additional unpalatable conclusions. The grim fact now about sex on this planet seemed to be that since we are all more or less conditioned to need sadism for excitement, we might find truly egalitarian relationships sexually boring.[7]

Or perhaps, I thought in my more upbeat moments, we might find them sexually disappointing only at first. Maybe we would soon dispel all dissatisfaction by beginning—in psychic, intuitive ways—to remember how to awaken our senses other than by stimulus-response/sadomasochism. Subtler, more interior, independent, non-relational ways generated from places and understandings within us to which our species has not been attuned for many thousands of years. Ways I couldn't even imagine.

---

[7] Assuming, of course, that we had the least idea how to have egalitarian relationships. As things stand now, "equality" and "relation Ships" are contradictory, even antithetical, concepts.

Tatnall and Balcerzak also taught me that my way of defining and looking at hierarchy had been too narrow, that I was seeing only one aspect of the problem. Contributing the idea to my consciousness that there is an enormous and crucial difference between sexual excitation—i.e., stimulus/response—and arousal, they helped me understand that arousal was not the culprit; *it* was pure passionate, creative energy. Excitation was the danger—the conditioned, hierarchical response that reduced our potential for creativity and power, siphoning them off into mere orgasm. As they say, "Sex/stimulus-response is not creative, it is not power, it is not Wild Woman."[8]

Sexual excitation—their model of sadomasochism—turned out to be evident in many, many ways. The authors contend, for instance, that when a dynamic, creative woman in the community suddenly disappears after getting involved with a lover, or when creative projects bog down in dissention among the women working on them, it is because women's original arousal—passion, creativity, and power—is derailed into the closed system of conditioned excitation, with power-lessness as the result.[9]

They give other examples of how our power is diverted, subverted, and inverted by this dynamic:

Whenever the loudest complaint gets our attention, time and energy, we are in stimulus-response and we are doing sex. Whenever we produce the loudest complaint, we are intending to bring another into stimulus-response and we are doing sex. When we

---

[8] "The Woofer-Tweeter Theory of Sexual Stimulus-Response, "June 1990, p. 9.

[9] Ibid., p. 6.

are doing sex we are calling another into excitation or responding with our own excitation.

Whenever we withhold approval until another displays a desired behavior, we are in stimulus-response and we are doing sex. And when we are doing sex, we require approval for our behaviors and withhold approval until the other displays a desired behavior.[10]

Tatnall and Balcerzak are of the opinion that the entire external approval, reward-and-punishment, system of patriarchy has its foundation in this sexual stimulus-response, sadomasochistic dynamic.[11]

They list "Compulsive production or rescuing, persistent complaining or appeasement, bickering or fighting" as other examples of the kinds of substitute stimulus-response behavior we indulge in to squander our precious creative energy when genital sex is not possible. "Whether the result is orgasm or argument, the process is stimulus-response to excitation," another way of saying sadomasochism.[12]

Though I nearly lost heart when Sally and Phyllis's findings so corroborated what I was reluctantly discovering, they approached the monster with such good humor that I was able to follow their example and face the unfaceable.

They succeeded at this primarily by talking about "woofers" and "tweeters." Having wisely determined that the terms "sadist" and "masochist" were so politically and emotionally loaded that women might not want or even be able to listen to their theory, they substituted for them these

---

[10] Ibid., p. 7.

[11] Ibid.

[12] "Woofer-Tweeter Theory of Sexual Stimulus-Response," June 1990, p. 7.

funny, non-threatening, labels. Women, they reasoned, would be much more likely to examine themselves for "woofer" behavior than for "sadism" and "tweeter" behavior than for "masochism."

It worked with me. Thinking "woofer" and "tweeter," I was able to consider the conclusions rising out of my own experience with less dismay, and to face the same difficult implications in their theory. They conclude, for instance:

Females, males, homosexuals, heterosexuals, and lesbians all display woofer and tweeter behaviors. Woofer and tweeter behaviors can be displayed by the same person, but for sexual excitation to occur, only the dominant behaviors are displayed in the presence of submissive responses and only submissive behaviors are displayed in the presence of dominant stimuli.[13]

This terminology made me able to laugh about what I had been feeling so desperate and dire about for so long. As I had tried harder and harder to behave outside sadomasochism and found more and more conclusively that it was simply not possible for me, that no matter what I did the strata were there, instead of killing myself as I sometimes almost felt like doing in my despair—if patriarchy couldn't be eliminated in us as individuals, there was no hope for the world—I learned from Sally and Phyllis to joke about it. Being able to laugh about sadomasochism's seemingly irredeemable presence was a huge relief, the healthiest behavior I could have stumbled into.

---

[13] "Woofer-Tweeter Theory of Sexual Stimulus-Response," June 1990, p. 5. (For a partial list of Tatnall and Balcerzak's matching woofer/tweeter behaviors, see Appendix 1B).

To these two approaches to the seemingly unapproachable—keeping sadism's manifestations in my life as conscious as possible, and laughing when I saw them—I added a third: Making the hierarchy of the moment—who was one/up and who one/down, who was woofer and who was tweeter and what behavior signified it—as overt and visible as possible.

So I might say, for instance, as I was sexually engaging with a lover, "You've been a terrific tweeter for the last hour or so, and I've had a great time woofing, but my elbow is killing me. How about taking over the woofery and letting me relax and tweet?" Or she might say to me, "How does it feel to be the world's best tweeter?" Or "I haven't woofed up such a storm in years!"

Though at this point in their understanding, many women choose celibacy, I didn't. I reasoned that I was immersed in sadomasochism in my every interaction, not just in my sex life, but that it was so much easier to see in my sex life that I didn't see how either as a hermit or celibate I could come to grips with it. So though I sympathized with and admired women who chose celibacy, my plan to wrest sadism from my soul did not include trying to avoid it, since I didn't believe I could.

What my plan *did* include was to enjoy each moment I was close to someone, to delight in it freely without any misgivings, without searching its sweetness for the bitterness at the core. To enjoy sex, if I could, knowing that the incredible heat of it came direct to me from patriarchy's kitchen, the ovens of sadism. And that other than relying on my inner wisdom to move me out of their way, there was little I could do to escape them.

When I noticed that I was too often in the "on top" position—literally or figuratively—I could roll over. And though I knew it wouldn't change anything, though I knew that hierarchy would still be present, I was an activist and it relieved me to *do* something.

So I went on batting my head against this obdurate fact over and over again. Trying to fix it by increments, trying to reform it by eliminating or reversing small behaviors.

All this effort, though it had no effect on the sadism, had at least the merit of keeping me awake in the midst of the general stupor that is menstream society.

Being kept awake was—and is—worth a very great deal to me, so I still try to remain aware of as many shifts in control between me and others as I can discern, stay as conscious as I can of which of us is "on top" at the moment and what transpired to put her there. In this way, I never become inured to the presence of my enemy, never forget long enough to sink into complacency and forget that it is sadism that is keeping me from the ecstasies of freedom.

Also, I discovered back there somewhere that I could either choose to be awake and wretched in the knowledge that I couldn't think or act my way out of sadism, or I could be awake and full of faith that my inner Wise Sonia, who has never yet failed me, was every moment preparing me for new ideas and modes of being and creating in me a new mind.

Of course I chose my Wise Woman. She assured me all along that if I would continue to be conscious, to shine the light of day onto my oppressive behavior and thinking, and to enjoy myself as much as I could while I was doing it, in some way I couldn't foresee I would find my way out of the sadomasochistic paradigm. I would discover that somewhere along the way I had abandoned the patriarchal mind forever.

Then one day I remembered something important. Driving along in the mountains of New Mexico talking about my growing impatience with this regime, complaining that despite my sincerest efforts to follow it, it didn't seem to be making an iota of difference, I stopped in the middle of a sentence. My Wise Woman had just reminded me that the surest route to transformation is not what we *do* but how we *are*, that it's not doing but being that rearranges the stars of destiny. The surest method of erasing hierarchy, she said, is to be the kind of person to whom it is inimical, in whom it cannot find a niche. And she promised that out of who I *am*, out of who we *are*—not out of acts of desperation or resistance—is coming the new world.

Trusting my Wise Old Woman's promise, every day I feel inexplicably nearer the possibility of genuine peerness in my own life and hence on the planet. The vertical distances between me and others are decreasing in both directions—at least I am having more difficulty more often figuring out whether I'm on top or on bottom—a wonderful sign! Though I'm not yet able to see how the shift to peer behavior will occur, I don't need to. If my Wise Woman says it is happening, then it's happening.

When we each do finally manage to function to any degree outside our profound patriarchal mandate, it will be because it has been a group effort—every woman who has searched out a fissure in the seemingly solid wall of hierarchy and with her passion for liberty has pried it open has made it easier for the rest of us to find our own ways out.

I know that since I am engrossed by this task, countless others are also even now so engrossed. I know that their success ensures mine, just as any success I have in escaping sadism ensures their escape. This is a community prison break.

I am hungry for other women's accounts of how they are breaking free.[14] When any woman successfully escapes any border of men's world into no-man's land, I am avid to know her escape route. I want to know how she kept the baby quiet.

---

[14] Sally and Phyllis assure me that they are making headway. Hurray!

23

Stale Sex and Fresh Resentment

All the while I was pondering my own sexual/emotional numbness, I knew that I was facing more than a purely personal problem, that this was a generic condition, not limited to me or to just a few others. From my wide acquaintance with Lesbians, I was aware that many were experiencing similar perplexing sexual disinterest—disinterest, that is, in the women with whom they were harboring relation Ships. But few seemed to be making much headway in dealing with it.

Many of their attempts to understand and remedy it—except for the truly revolutionary emphasis on recovery from incest[1]—seemed to me to be based in the myths and methods of mensgame prevalent in society at large: "Romancing" their partner, changing partners, having casual sex, consciously choosing and intensifying sadism, attending sexuality workshops, reading technique manuals, poring over erotic literature, masturbating, experimenting with sex toys,

---

[1] But since those of us who have never experienced incest also experience this deadening, I have reason to believe that when their incest trauma is mostly healed, women may still be numb. Clearly, incest is not the only culprit.

introducing third parties into their sex lives, consulting therapists, objectifying (and in doing so disconnecting emotionally from) themselves and other women, disembarking from their relation Ships to begin the sad, cyclical dance of misery all over again with a new partner.

All these seemed to me to be pitifully superficial and futile attempts to deal with the real issue, the deep intractable fact of our times, that every human contact is tainted with hierarchy. In hierarchy's lethal presence women's most positive values, such as genuine affection and intimacy, can hardly be born, let alone survive.

Earlier, in my investigation of the Kiss in Bed, I had caught a glimmer of understanding. I had learned that using sex or any physical closeness as a means to an end and not for its own sake detached me from the genuineness of the moment and thence from my capacity to feel. I had learned that integrity in touching was necessary for fullest feeling, that a touch must be precious to me in and of itself in order for my senses to rejoice. But I had no idea how to untaint touch from the conditioning surrounding it in menstream thought.

I came to believe then that to the degree that any of us used kissing and hugging and genital sex as a means to some end other than pure delight—to feel safe, for instance, to reassure ourselves of our coupledumb, our love—to that same degree we robbed physicality of pleasure. Now I wonder what I meant by "physicality." But that's another story.

About this time, I discovered an article by Diana Rabenold and was elated to read her theory of the decline of sexual desire among Lesbians. (I was not elated that it declined, but that there was theory about it.) In her opinion, desire drops off in couples who have fused identities—who *are* each other—because it comes to feel incestuous.[2] No matter how lovely touching oneself may be, most of us prefer some physical connection with other people at least part of the time. And when I read that, I thought, "Yes, they probably feel as if they are alone, as if there isn't anyone else present."

Rabenold describes these "fused" couples as typically being together much of the time, "mutually supportive and generally content in their domestic 'nest,'" but suppressing resentment and individual needs out of a fear of being "selfish,"[3] and, I might add, of upsetting the Ship.

There is at least one other dimension to the incestuous feeling of sex. In their childhoods, many Lesbians (as well as many heterosexual women) experienced actual incest, the most egregious coercion of all coercions. It makes sense that because of this, incest survivors often have more difficulty with sexual behavior than other women. The subtle coercion present at times in even the best and most healthy of their relation Ships is identical in kind to the gross coercion these women experienced at the hands of their sexual abusers. Differing only in degree, it restimulates the old feelings of powerlessness, outrage, and self-hatred, and makes being sexual with anyone very problematic.

Because I wanted, finally, to feel as much as I could feel, and because I thought then that this was a matter of intensity of sexual excitation—not, as I came to believe later, of power and creativity combined to generate real intimacy—I couldn't deceive myself any longer. Whenever I rejoiced because I

---

[2] "Love, Politics, and 'Rescue' in Lesbian Relationships," Herbooks: Santa Cruz, CA, HerBooks Lesbian-Feminist Essay Series, 1987, No. 2, p. 10.

[3] Ibid., p. 10.

thought that my kisses, my embraces, my small acts of gentleness and affection were not burdened with other chores but still had integrity, were still fully and only kisses and embraces and caresses, I felt as if I had to be sure that I was rejoicing legitimately.

But how could I be sure? Because I hadn't yet discovered Sadism in my bed or made Sally and Phyllis' distinction between excitation and arousal, I really had no way but the old entrapping way to think about sexual feeling at all. Certainly at this point I couldn't have suspected the ubiquitousness and ignobility of its relation to all "touch" in patriarchy, not just physical, but emotional, social, and psychic touch as well. So as much as I wanted surety, I remained distressingly uncertain about what was behind or under any given touch, any given desire, at any given moment.

But I had learned a thing or two from the Kiss in Bed, the most important being the part coercion plays in the death of desire. Since the day I discovered that dynamic, I had in my travels stumbled upon lots of examples of it. A situation I heard described many times typically went like this: To prove any number of things to herself—among them that her lover still loves and wants to be with her—a woman expects her partner to make love at some acceptable-to-her intervals, perhaps as often as every night: It's 9:30, time for sex.

Since no one can become aroused on demand for long, her mate soon begins to dread bedtime. In her search for escape, she notices that if she has a good excuse for refusing and makes clear that it is only a postponement, her partner accepts it in good grace and all is well.

If she says, for instance, "Honey, we'd better go to sleep now. We have to get up early to catch that plane," or, "I'm awfully tired. Let's wait until morning," she forestalls her lover's demands without panicking her.

But though she may succeed in postponing the inevitable until morning, in the morning or the next evening she's trapped. She *must* perform, or spend endless and fruitless time "processing" with her partner. The thought of the wrangle that may ensue defeats her, and also since chances are good that she's not totally clear about what's going on in the situation, she probably doesn't want to try to talk about it anyway. So she tamps down her resentment and goes ahead with what has become the sex routine. All she has accomplished by her subterfuge is the delay of stale sex and the production of fresh resentment.

The resentment builds, becoming ever hotter under increased pressure. Finally, it burns out her sexual interest and takes its place. So even if, without such coercion, she might occasionally have felt like being sexual, she is so filled with resentment and with the necessity of keeping it from exploding into her consciousness and destroying the Ship, that she dares feel nothing. When we close down on one front, all other areas of our lives are dimmed. We become generally blurred and muffled to ourselves.

Though this is an extreme case, the understanding that it was different only in intensity, not in plot—and the immense implications of that fact—took many months to unfold upon my understanding. At the time, I hadn't grasped the one essential point about coercion that I needed to know in order to change.

But even then it was slouching along its wicked way into my life, getting ready to hit me full in the face down the road a piece.

PART IV

A SHIPBOARD ROMANCE

24

"How About Me?": A Cautionary Tale

B y the time this story opens, I was able to remain aware more and more of the time that something was deeply, fundamentally wrong with accepted ideas about sex and sexual behavior. But because I was still straddling two worlds—with the preponderance of my weight resting in the old one—my immense capacity for self-deception had hardly shrunk at all. I was full of contradictions.

On one hand, I firmly believed that sexual excitation inevitably led one along a Ship's sadomasochistic route, and was determined not to sail another second on that unfree course. On the other hand, however—and, amazingly enough, at the very same time—I still believed deep down somewhere that sexual excitation was "natural," that if I were emotionally and physically healthy, I would feel like being sexual with others in the conventional kinds of ways. I still felt that a large part of being free meant being free—of hang-ups, of guilt—to engage in the sexual acts beloved of phallocracy, not yet aware of the irony that these are the least free acts of all.

In this confused condition, I examined my loss of sexual interest with the singular lack of clarity that epitomizes the

work of my old programmed mind. This antiquated thinking turned up in many of my letters to lovers. For example:
"Helen of the honeycomb, beloved of the bees,
    "I'm sure you've noticed how the motif of sexuality has wound itself through my letters to you. Perhaps that's true because, as I explained early on, when one part of me gets free, it seems to radiate that message and desire to all other parts—in this case sex, that most problematic part.
    "If I were a mansion with dozens of rooms, each room representing some aspect of my personality or character, I would say that by the time you knew me, nearly every room had had much attention—been remodeled, refurbished, cleaned, and aired—and was in reasonably good shape. Every room, that is, except that terrifying and chaotic one that housed my sexual assumptions, conditioning, experience, and feelings.
    "Though I suffered none of the obvious sexual traumas—rape, incest, overt brutality—Mormonism early left its ugly sadistic mark on me. Women's conditioning to feel as if our prime purpose in life is a sexual purpose—to give sexual pleasure and to have babies—was massively intensified in my experience as a fundamentalist christian. So was my indoctrination to model my sexual conduct—even if in kindliest terms—along sadism's party line.
    "By the time I became conscious that all was not well with the way I functioned in relation Ships—six months or a year before your advent—I was seriously and painfully confused about sex. Desiring not to blunder on without some enlightenment, I knew that someday soon I would have to be brave enough to

222

break open the boarded-up room where I had hidden my sexual artifacts, and face what was in there.

"Though I couldn't even imagine how to deal with the sadism intrinsic to sexuality on this planet, I was confident that, though I was afraid, I *could* change many of my perceptions and feelings about sex and about myself as sexual, and that I could heal a major part of the sexual hurt done to me in my childhood.

"I was so overwhelmed by the events of my life at the time, however, that I paraphrased the famous prayer, 'make me brave—but not yet.' Still, I knew the need was there and felt it beginning to press itself upon me with some urgency as the pivotal year of 1988 progressed. Not because I was physically attracted to anyone; I felt as dead as a stone—*that* was the issue. I knew I was a passionate woman. I responded lustily to life in all its other manifestations. I could only conclude that patriarchy was holding my body in thrall as it had for so long held my mind.

"That conclusion made me angry. I'd be damned, I thought, if those thieves of joy were going to take away from me permanently the deep pleasures and possibilities of my wonderful woman's body!"

When I was thinking in this conventional mode, I forgot to identify as my greatest sexual hurt my profound training to dishonor my power by ransoming it to excitement. Wanting to be "normal" and "healthy," I forgot that what manunkind says is "normal" and "healthy"—in this case, sexual attraction/excitement and behavior—is always alien and deadly. I neglected the work of distinguishing my conditioning from my Wild Self.

But as soon as I apprehended these backslidings, I forgave myself for them freely. I chose then and continue still, no matter how many times I regress, to tell myself honestly that I am doing just fine, that there is no way to do this work wrong, that I am doing it perfectly. But still in retrograde, I decided that I could rectify my abnormal and unhealthy state of sexual deadness by experimenting sexually with some "safe" woman—i.e, a woman who would not be tempted to let a Ship sail into her living room. Feminism to me had always meant experimentation. I had believed for some time that if I always did what I'd always done, I'd always get what I'd always got. So because I wanted a new world, I had no choice but to at least try to do something else—*anything* else. I knew from experience that taking such risks could jettison my mind out of its ruts and expose it to a vast range of new possibilities. Never mind that what I was thinking of at that time was the same old thing, I absolutely perceived myself as embarking on something new.

With my children gone and the tyrannical Ship finally out of my house, I was freer than I had ever been in my life to try what I imagined to be new ways of being. I had dozens of experiments I was eager to begin, many of them having to do with sexuality. Though all along my old unexamined belief that I needed someone else to do the work with—it takes a couple, doesn't it?—was really the problem, the difficulty *seemed* to be in finding the "safe" co-conspirator.

I assumed that, as had always been the case before, I was not the first or even close to the first to think as I was thinking. So there had to be thousands, maybe hundreds of thousands, of other women out there who had reached the point where they refused ever to have another Ship in their lives, and at least a few thousand of them who had also figured out why the very thought of having one repelled and sickened them. I reasoned that among these thousands, there might be hundreds who were eager to experiment with other possibilities and had their eyes out for other experimenters. But I had no idea how to find one of these, to say nothing of how I would know which was most "suitable"—i.e, most free of relationshit and most in her own power.

In ways other than my selective memory of my conditioning and the general befuddlement this caused, I myself was hardly a promising candidate for sexual experimentation. Up to that time, I had had only two fully sexual relation Ships in my life (which eliminates all the groping about in dark cars, all the furtive teen-aged stuff the '50s were notorious for)—my marriages to Rick and Susan—and hadn't felt sexually attracted to any woman except Susan in my life.

But there were some points in my favor. Though I had grown up during one of the most sexually repressive periods in American history and in one of the most sexually repressive subcultures, and though I had suffered agonies of guilt over sexual misdemeanors in my youth, and before marriage arduously damped down the fires of passion that threatened to destroy my life if left unchecked, somehow I had retained sparks of the physical freedom and wildness with which I had come into the world. I liked my body and had no false modesty. Also by this time I was almost totally free of guilt about sex.

I admit that I didn't have my experiments sorted out with great clarity. I knew I wanted to practice being sexual outside the purview of a Ship and to examine my feelings and insights as I did this. I knew I wanted to discover the scope and depth of feeling that my body was capable of. I knew I wanted to listen for the voice of my conditioning in such circumstances so I could continue to eradicate it. I knew I wanted to learn what intimacy really was. I knew I wanted to practice taking responsibility only for myself, doing only what I wanted to do all the time—behaviors that were impossible under the despotic eye of the officer on the bridge of a relation Ship.

Though these experiments were possible without genital or other sex behavior, I didn't think so then. I thought that because I wanted to learn how to connect freely to others in every way, sex had to have some overt place in it—this was what mensmachine had drilled into me all my life.

Still, it was hard for me to think about being sexual, a difficulty that I could have interpreted much differently, as I later did. But at the time, I thought the problem was that for at least a year and probably longer I had felt little if any sexual desire. Sometimes I thought that these experiments might reveal why I felt this way, what had happened to that enormous store of physical passion with which I believed I had begun life. I wondered if it had disappeared when my menstrual blood stopped flowing. Assuming again that they were "normal" and "healthy," I wondered if those fierce fires of the flesh could ever be rekindled.

Though I had little actual hope of it, I thought wistfully that this experimentation *might* give me some insight into what was sexually "natural." But figuring—correctly, as it turned out—that I was so deeply programmed to be unnatural about sex that my small experiments would be hopelessly contaminated, I dropped that as a hoped-for result. Actually, I had no projected goals in mind for any of this. I merely wanted to see what would happen—to my feelings and my thinking—when I tried something different. The "something different" was for me to be sexual without climbing aboard a Ship.

While I was in this adventuresome, though occluded, state of mind, a friend from California came to visit me. I had known this woman for nearly a year and liked all I knew. One of hundreds of lovers, her spiritual gift was an unusual understanding—not always wordable—of friendship between women, and I had had the good fortune of learning from her.

One afternoon, sitting with her at the kitchen table, I briefly outlined my plan of experimenting with sex as solely myself, not part of a couple, ending with the supposition that I might meet some woman in New Mexico—where I was planning to move—who would be appropriate to do it with. Very quietly she asked, "Why not me?"

I realized immediately of course that she had been in the back of my mind as a possibility all along. It wasn't that I had been being devious; I really had not been conscious of having already chosen her until that moment. But before we made a decision, I had to be honest with her about one thing. "You know I love you to bits," I said, "but perhaps you don't know that I have never for a second felt any sexual interest in you."

"Don't worry," she said, "It's just an experiment, not a marriage. We can call it off any time we choose."

"Right!" I laughed with relief. "The instant we see the Ship on the horizon, we'll run for our lives!"

Big talk, but largely bravado. Though I thought I did, I really had no idea how to be sexual without inviting a Ship into my life. And despite her protestations to the contrary, neither did she. But we had little suspicion that we were still deeply mesmerized by the same tired old sex tapes that we'd always had playing in our heads. In addition, new Ships are very deceptive, assuring us all the time that they are an entirely different species than the old ones. We are so desperate to believe this that of course we do. And she and I both did.

So, thinking that we were off on some exalted spiritual quest instead of going to sleep in another Ship's cabin, we began our experiment as sex friends.

Oh, the headiness of fresh sex, its sweet, exquisite chains of brightest steel! Oh, the delight in learning that my body was not dead after all! I was soon as caught up in romance as I had ever been, deeply "in love," but disguising it from myself in expertly cagey ways.

During this bliss stage, I constantly confused arousal—power and creativity—with excitation, as evidenced by a paragraph I wrote in another love letter:

"I am stunned by the richness and possibility of sexual experience, not just for being wonderfully exhilarating and joyous, but for being a meditation, a vision quest, for connecting the great forces of life within us to those in our universe. Though patriarchy has stripped it of its real meaning, I have learned for myself that our sexuality is power and holiness. As the body's creators, women all through history must surely have known its sacredness, the splendor of the flesh, how permeated with spirit and mind it is as we wear it among our days."

Not just headiness, not just delight, but also, oh, the ironies! Both of us totally disillusioned about relation Ships and absolutely determined never to be snared into bondage by them again. Both of us aware that our deepest programming would always be trying to get us to do it again, and that we would have to be on the alert, almost preternaturally wary, every moment. But both allowing ourselves to be reassured by the fact that we lived many hundreds of miles apart, both reasoning that this should keep us from fembotically following the prescriptions of the PRBS. Both, that is, unsuspectingly lashed to the Ship's mast.

Since we didn't even live in the same part of the country, let alone the same town or same house, we thought naively that we would avoid the PRBS problems of living together, sleeping together in the same bed every night, spending most of our time together. Since we weren't going to get caught following the form, we thought smugly, we should have little trouble keeping free of its attendant content.

We also agreed that each of us would be passionately committed only to her own comfort and enjoyment, that I would take no responsibility for hers nor her for mine. That insofar as we could tell, we would do only what we wanted to do all the time.

Intent upon our experiment, we visited back and forth often in the next six months. I had moved to Albuquerque during this time, which closed the gap between us by more than a thousand miles but still kept us safely un-relation-Shipped. Or so we imagined.

But I wasn't comatose, just sleepy. All along in a drugged sort of way I really did understand the danger. In another co-conspirator letter I wrote:

"Knowing how hard sadism is to spot in the connections of kindly, largely contented women—by them*selves* even more than by others—I know that one day I might wake up and discover that you and I have been kidding ourselves all along. It is highly possible that, like thousands of well-intentioned folks before us, unbeknownst to ourselves somewhere along the way we will secretly marry. This sour knowledge keeps me awake, resolutely conscious through the drifts and dreams of sweetness that surround you."

About this time, however, I began to be seriously troubled by familiar and unpleasant feelings. Though they were subtle—merest flickers in my consciousness—there came rapidly to be so many of them flickering so constantly that I couldn't avoid them any longer. In a very blizzard of déjà vu, I recognized them as classic relationShip reactions: Calling long distance five or six times a day to consult her about small things, feeling as if I had to take all her calls despite my resentment at having to interrupt my work, finding her family annoyingly insensitive to her, worrying about her lawsuit. Seeing dependence, fusion, choicelessness, coercion, and resentment all still arrayed within me, I fell off Cloud Nine with a thud. Somehow, despite all my brave efforts not to, despite everything, willy nilly, I was—*damn it all!*—once again having a relation Ship.

Though I was crushed, I can't say I was terribly surprised. After the first shock wore off, mostly I was intrigued. Clearly there was a hole in my theory, something I hadn't looked at, a missing part, or some idea that was more critical than I'd thought. I began to scrutinize my behavior, searching for the invisible assumptions and expectations at its roots. What programmed behavior was I still engaged in and why?

Part of what was happening was relatively easy to see, and though I was chagrined at the discovery, I also had to laugh. I have such a terrific talent for self-deception that if, in addition to having been frustrated and embarrassed by it over the years I hadn't also found it a little endearing, I couldn't have gone far with my research. This time I was amused at my innocent but totally illogical and erroneous belief that distance would act to increase choice. It was very clear that it does just the opposite.

Take this sample scenario. When, after we have been absent from each other for a few weeks, the other conspirator arrives at the airport in my city, I assume that I have to drop my work on the article for *Woman of Power* that is moving along so well and go pick her up. That I can choose not to do this doesn't even occur to me. So whether I want to or not—and I don't ask myself whether I want to do something when there appears to be no choice—I go to the airport to meet her.

When she walks into the terminal from the plane, neither of us has much choice but to greet the other with a hug—that is, if we want to keep the relation Ship in our respective living rooms without expending a lot of time and effort. (She brings her half of our Ship with her when she comes, the part that has been monitoring her behavior while she was away. It immediately reconnects with the half that stayed to monitor me.)

The briefness of her stay in my city calls forth dozens of assumptions that usually would not apply quite so automatically since my bearding of the Relationship Belief System. The major assumption that slips by me at the time is that we will spend most if not all of her short time here together. So we eat all our meals together, several of them at restaurants though there is actually little or nothing on the menus that I can eat or over which I would not prefer my own simple food; she accompanies me on my walks—and slows me down, but it would be bad-tempered of me to suggest that she not come; though I try to do some of my most pressing work and feel anxious about the rest, I put off

everything put-offable until she goes; we try to think of something special to do in the evenings though there is not an evening in the world that I wouldn't really rather read.
And we sleep together.
Even though we understand the important place in PRBS of sleeping together every night, nevertheless we sleep together every night of her visit. We do this not because we have examined whether this is actually what we prefer to do on any of the possible nights but (1) because according to PRBS, it is what lovers do, and willy nilly we are all unsuspectingly back on a Ship; (2) because we don't get the chance very often; (3) because she has come such a long way; and (4) because to suggest otherwise when the time is so limited would be churlish, and women's deepest programming is not to be unpleasant, to be *nice*.
Either of us would probably accept the other's desire to sleep alone with good grace—this is, after all, our experiment. But we have only two or three nights to spend together, and the panic caused by scarcity overcomes us. Even if we can tell that we would rather sleep alone—and this is a tricky discrimination to make in the best of circumstances—under the added pressure of time we are even less likely to be able to tell.
Because of all this, we feel awkward about making such a suggestion. Why start even small ripples in the smooth surface of this beautiful connection and risk having to use some of our precious time "processing" away any misunderstanding or discomfort that might come from it?
We run through this litany of reflections and judgments almost instantaneously and usually with almost no awareness that we are doing so. In reality, in our fear we have reverted to the PRBS's ready-made decisions. So we sleep together.

And chances are very good that, because of this very delicate, very subtle coercion—so subtle that it does not prevent our being delighted by each other's company, our having a wonderful time together—we are sexual this weekend despite the fact that possibly at least one of us would rather not be. We feel an inner coercion to have sex also because, according to the officer on the bridge, we need reassurance—no, *proof*—that we still feel about each other as we did last time we were together, that nothing has changed unless it's for the better, that all is well. In short, we are back where we started, needing verification that we can keep someone loving us, control our lives so that we will not be lonely, make predictions about our lives—all the major duties of sex in a relation Ship.

Thus, the description of our behavior during our weekend together is a description of nearly constant, unwitting coercion. Neither of us yet has the freedom *in our souls* either to figure out what we really want to do or to choose to do it.

But it's not for lack of interest or effort. We stick our feelings and observations up on the wall on memo paper and talk about them—what they signal about the PRBS in us; we scrutinize ourselves for merging patterns, pounce upon them, and try subsequently to subvert them; we try to maintain our awareness through the day of who's woofing and who's tweeting, why, and how it makes us feel, analyzing how our feelings change when we switch roles; we consciously choose in specific situations not to rescue each other, allowing the other full responsibility for her own feelings and behavior, and try to figure out why we can sometimes do this and sometimes can't; we acknowledge the ways in which we allow ourselves to be coerced and why we coerce in our turn;

we feel satisfied that we are doing very good, very important work, and that we are doing it well. And we are.

But our most fervent attempts to remain conscious of and to eradicate our conditioning have obviously not kept us from salivating when the bell rings, have not freed us from the Ship's comfortable, dear, sweet vise.

The irony is that the almost constant but low-level coercion that promises us intimacy if we act out the detailed, prescribed drama of relation Ships in our lives is precisely what makes intimacy impossible. This is particularly obvious with sex. The unconscious pressures that too often get us into sex are the very feelings that eventually kill our desire.

Travelling around this country and several others during the last decade or so talking with women, I had gradually identified an intriguing phenomenon among us: In Lesbian couples, one of the partners almost always wants to be sexual more often than the other, usually to a marked degree. And when I began asking about this in the last couple of years, every couple knew instantly which one of them it was. This was true even in cases where neither partner was very interested and the couples were seldom sexual.

At first I thought, "What a coincidence that so many Lesbians are pairing up in this way. How strange that those who want lots of sex seem always to be choosing those who don't." But as time went by and I saw so few exceptions, I decided that it was not a random, coincidental occurrence.

Still, for some time I couldn't figure it out. It seemed ridiculous to assume that women with high sex drives were so attracted to women with low sex drives that they were always searching them out and wedding them. On the contrary, such a disparity in sexual rhythms would almost certainly be a source of tension from the first, serious enough to give pause

234

even before the relation Ship formally began. Surely no one would *ask* for this problem.

The most sensible conclusion was that both women began with reasonably similar requirements for sex—and all that sex means in their culture—and that something happened along the way to make one back off. And in the many cases where both partners lost interest, something happened to make them both back off, though always one more than the other.

I developed a hypothesis about it. Let's say, I proposed to myself, that two typical couples—i.e., couples in which one woman wants more sex than her partner—meet and that each partner discovers that the sexual appetite of one of the other partners matches her own almost exactly, whether she is the one who wants more sex or the one who wants less.

Let's say, I continued, that the two who want more than their partners fall in love with each other and that the two who want less follow suit. Oh, what bliss, they would all exclaim, finally to be in a relation Ship where the subject of sexual frequency is not surrounded by anxiety!

My hypothesis, however, was that within a few months—about six or eight—the old configuration would again reign: In each couple there would again be one who wanted to be sexual more often than the other, and to about the same degree as before.

The PRBS exerts its coercive influence in this syndrome in yet another way. The axiom that "the retrograde rules" applies here: The partner who wants less sex is at the helm of the relation Ship. She decides if and when and maybe how and where sexual activity takes place. This puts her firmly, though probably not deliberately, in the one/up position—a pleasant spot. So though she may worry over the repercussions of not having as much sexual interest as her partner, the pleasures of control make up to her for any anxiety she may suffer.

But what was all this about?

The phenomenon was so widespread and so similar everywhere that I began to look for a common denominator. I figured it had to be in the Relationship Belief System somewhere, and it made sense to me that because the central motif of mensgame is enslavement, coercion was the most likely common denominator.

Of course, such corroboration of my theory increased my determination to search out and eliminate in my life all the subtle, sweet, loving pressure that makes a Ship a Ship. But coercion had already been my prime suspect for a couple of years. What I needed was more and other sorts of information before I could make good use of this knowledge. Understanding some important aspects of Ships and having no clue about others, I was off-balance, careening tangentially toward freedom like a car that needs a front-end alignment. But as wild as it was, I never once thought of calling off the journey.

So I continued, understanding better as I went along the connection between honoring my desires and being in my power. This prepared me for the day when, talking with some wonderful women in a cafe in Honolulu, I suddenly grasped what had been eluding me for so long—the central, controlling metaphor of the PRBS poem.

Then, with a much clearer map at my disposal, I drove straight into my dreams.

25

Wallowing in Mindless Lasciviousness

Knowing that all sex was sadomasochistic but not understanding what to do about it except to stay conscious, and before the distinction between arousal and excitation struck mortal blows to my relationShip life, I conducted dozens of informal sexual experiments with my co-conspirator. I thought that if I persisted, I might find ways out of the ethical swamp of sex. I wanted ferociously to believe that other affectional and sexual modes were possible between people, and was particularly avid to discover my innate, untamed inclinations. I knew that menstream sex—which was all I or anyone knew—had thrown up mighty barricades between them and my perceptions, and I longed to tear them down and discover my authentic sexuality, what I was like stripped of my sex-slave mind.

Still determined somehow to salvage sex—though I didn't deceive myself that I could sort out this skein of life most tangled by patriarchy—I hoped for at least enough enlightenment to integrate it differently, more wisely, into the rest of my life. I wanted it not to be something separate, with boundaries and demarcations: "Oh, now we're doing it!" I wanted it to blend invisibly with every other aspect of me, as I believed was "natural."

I also wanted to understand better the connection between sex and intimacy—or lack of it. I was aware of the reversal: Though we are brainwashed to view sex as the path to intimacy, the way mensmachine teaches us to be sexual actually prevents intimacy.

Clearly, because patriarchy does everything in its power to prevent it, intimacy was somehow in cahoots with freedom. My mind was full of questions. What *is* intimacy anyway? If sex isn't synonymous with intimacy—and obviously it isn't—how can we experience intimacy? What is its connection with freedom and with power?

Searching for answers[1] I examined my feelings and attitudes toward sex. It didn't take me long to uncover the vein of puritanism running through my socialization. Puritanism—quintessential patriarchy—had seeped into me as much through my being reared in the United States as through being reared christian. They are nearly identical experiences, the values of one being the values of the other.

Much of this puritanism was centered around pleasure—pleasure versus the work ethic. I wasn't surprised to realize that I still viewed pleasure with distrust, even as dangerous. I didn't have to think very hard to realize why I had been taught that pleasure would deceive me about the nature of life. Life, men have insisted, is brutish and short,

---

[1] One night after a speech in which I said that if I could think of the right questions, the answers came easily, a woman pointed out to me that my belief in questions and answers revealed a dichotomous mind still at work. "You're right, "I admitted, "there are probably no answers." She said, "There are probably no questions." The time will come when none of us any longer thinks in the Q/A mode.

demanding almost unremitting, largely unpleasant, toil for any reward.

Because we are taught that hardship and difficulty strengthen us, we draw the obvious conclusion about pleasure: It weakens us.

Since sex is about pleasure—or at least reputed to be—I could be pretty certain that deep down I believed that too much sexual pleasure would soften not only my bones but my brains as well, and would certainly rot my ethical fiber. Imagining myself experiencing hours and hours of continuous sexual pleasure, I couldn't see how my jelly bones would allow me to rise from my couch of bliss. Would I even *want* to? Might I not lose all moral muscle, develop a terminally flabby will?

Also, the fathers have taught us that since there is so little time and so much work to do, it is incumbent upon us all to spend that precious time doing the really important work of earning a living and making the economic world go around. How much work we do and where on the scale of menstream values it falls determines our worth. Work is good; idleness is bad. Pleasure is idleness, so pleasure is bad.

I found that, despite more than a decade of raging feminism, I was still oppressed by men's work ethic. Even though I was self-employed, I had to "earn" the right—by working extra hard beforehand—to take time off without guilt. True, this syndrome was rapidly loosening its grip on me, but I still had to struggle against feeling worthless if I didn't put in so many hours of work every day.

I had a hunch that this was going to be a barrier in any sexual experimentation. As I thought back on previous experiences with sex, I saw clearly how my beliefs about time and pleasure and work had prevented me from exploring its limits. To observe the dynamics created by these beliefs became one of my experiments.

My first sexual experiment with my new cohort, however, had centered around the desirability of orgasm. Patriarchy swears that it is the "natural" and most desirable conclusion to sexual excitation, elevating it to a position of be-all and end-all. Millions of people—particularly women—seek therapy in an attempt to overcome their supposed blocks to orgasm.

Long before Sally and Phyllis wrote their second "Woofer-Tweeter" paper about arousal versus excitation, this incredible emphasis on orgasm had caused me to suspect that orgasm was a patriarchal ploy to con us into squandering our wonderful sexual/creative energy, to pour it into others, including the Ship. At the same time, I wanted to believe that I was wrong, that instead of sapping it, orgasm augmented our supply of this powerful stuff. I wanted to know what would happen if I reached the pre-orgasm level of excitation and didn't dissipate my expanded supply of creativity by having an orgasm. Would I go about the rest of the day full of inventive vigor and enthusiasm that I could use in my work? Or would I feel dulled out, tired, or "unfulfilled"?

So I tried it, and discovered to my disappointment that I couldn't tell the difference in my energy level one way or the other.[2] I conjectured that this probably told me less about orgasm than it told me about my sensitivity to my body and to the interplay of body and psyche.

---

[2] I think now that I couldn't tell the difference because I was almost always—until the experience I am about to relate—experiencing only excitation, not true arousal.

Nonetheless, I liked knowing I could choose whether to have orgasm or not, and assumed that with practice I would become more perceptive about the effect of both orgasm and non-orgasm upon my level of creativity, my mood, and my physical well-being. At least I had learned from my experiment that just because I was able to have orgasms didn't mean I had to, and since then I often, purposefully, hadn't.

Still, I continued to be perplexed about orgasm. Though I hadn't found it true yet in my experience, it seemed to me that by not driving toward orgasm but bypassing it deliberately I could build up tremendous inner power that I might pool with similar power in others. I figured that many of us together could generate enough power to fuel a spaceship to the Pleiades.

With the orgasm experiment behind me—inconclusive as it had seemed at the time—in a half-conscious way I planned several others. One autumn afternoon as we two confederates embarked upon an amorous adventure, the moment seemed right for another experiment. I didn't reveal beforehand that I was going to be conducting an experiment throughout because it wasn't an actual defined plan. Instead, the knowledge that that afternoon I could observe my puritan patterns lay on the periphery of my cognition, somewhere in the right brain, not spelled out.

It wasn't until the middle of things that I realized that I was looking and listening for clues, and not only to one aspect of the experience but trying out several ideas at once—doing a multi-experiment.

Part of what I was observing about myself was what would happen when I dared do only what I wanted to do the entire time—not worry about her pleasure unless I felt like it, for instance, just touch her in ways that pleased *me*.

What *did* happen was that soon my initial excitation had so intensified that I found myself on that sexual plateau from which at any instant I could, if I chose, spin into orgasm. Before my first experiment, I had almost always had an orgasm when I reached this point, maybe not immediately, but pretty soon—wasn't that what it was all about?

Now, however, knowing that I could control my body and choose what I wanted it to experience, on this particular autumn day I decided to see how long I could stay in the exquisite pre-orgasm state of excitement and what would happen as the time lengthened.

So in the heat of wanton lustfulness I began my research, slipping out of my wordless, thought-less, sensuously sophisticated right brain enough to be aware of everything I was doing, all that was going on—inside and outside me.

Immediately and with astonishing lucidity I could hear the voices of my conditioning, including the voice of the officer on the bridge of the Ship. Trying to prevent my pleasure from expanding into subversion, they were hitting me with every guilt trip in their repertoire. In my head, their incessant admonition and intimidation sounded something like this:

"Shouldn't you find out how she's feeling? Maybe she's getting cramped, maybe she'd like to change positions. She may not know whether you are enjoying this. You need to tell her how you feel so she won't be uncertain about her part in it, so she'll feel successful. Shouldn't you check to make sure she's enjoying what you're doing, too? Surely you wouldn't want to go on if she *weren't* and maybe she's too shy to tell you that she'd really rather you'd do something else. Shouldn't you be paying more attention to her needs? She probably needs you to tell her you love her and what a delightful lover she is, how lucky you are to have her in your arms and in your life. This will help her enjoy herself more. What if she has to pee? Shouldn't you say *you* have to so she will feel free to do the same?" And so on.

Interspersed with the imperatives to focus on her or else feel guilty and worthless were the orders to stop wasting time or else feel guilty and worthless. Though several hours had passed, I was, with minor fluctuations, maintaining that lovely near-orgasm level of excitation. Afternoon had lengthened into evening, as I could tell by the dimness of the room. The taped voices of the fathers were all but shrieking in frustration at me now, but still I persevered.

Although warnings about wasting time had been interspersed all along with the imperatives to take care of her, as evening deepened into night, these predominated and became almost abusive:

"Look, hasn't this gone on long enough? It's pitch-dark outside, for heaven's sake. You must have been at this for *hours*! It's irresponsible and disgusting. How can you allow yourself to wallow in this mindless lasciviousness? You have *important*, things to do, remember? like a book to finish. You're wasting precious time with this nonsense. Get up and get busy doing something useful and admirable, something that really matters."

Even in my less-than-fully-alert condition, I thought I recognized patriarchal reversal. Since the voices of the fathers were admonishing me to limit the time I spent in such activities as that I was engaged in, insisting that other things were more important, what I suspected was that what I was doing *was* the important thing to be doing right then and that what they were trying to get me to do was inconsequential. The implication seemed to be that there was potential in sexuality that frightened the socks off them, a potential they didn't want me to discover.[3]

Since then it has occurred to me that the propaganda of the fathers may be much more subtle than I suspected. I think now that, as I had sometimes done with my children, perhaps they were using reverse psychology on me. I remember wily Brer Rabbit begging Brer Fox not to throw him in the briar patch, and wonder if, knowing my rebellious nature, what they *hoped* I'd do was, in rebelling against them, take sex very seriously indeed. I think now that sex may be their most effective red herring of all.

But this didn't occur to me until much later. So that day I hung doggedly in there withstanding the voices, thinking that maybe if I refused to listen and went ahead being "irresponsible and disgusting" they might eventually give up. I remember wondering idly what the experience would be like without the relentless effort of my conditioning to counter it, and considered the possibility that I hadn't heard silence since I was born.

The experiment continued for several hours and the voices of my socialization didn't stop even once for breath. Finally, exhausted from resisting their demands and manipulations and realizing that they weren't going to give up, I began to think about how to bring it all to a close.

Actually, I didn't *think* about it so much as I turned some inner attention to it. Would I choose orgasm this time or not?

---

[3] Now I suspect that that possibility of arousal—which they fear—may be present in sex, but only in rare instances. Because of the experience I am about to relate, I continue to think this despite my contradictory belief that sex behavior, being sadomasochistic by definition in patriarchy, makes true arousal—i.e., creativity and power—impossible. With more time and thought and experience, I am certain that I will come to some clearer understanding.

It wasn't as if I made a conscious decision, but more that I observed myself moving in a linear way along the continuum from no-orgasm to orgasm. Though I had been trying for years to rid myself of dichotomous, either/or, linear thought, I didn't realize until that moment that I hadn't succeeded in doing this with sex. Clearly, my belief right then was still that there were only two possibilities: Orgasm or no-orgasm. This, despite the years I had been saying to myself and everyone else who would listen that there are never only two choices, that dichotomous thought does not represent the possibilities of life in our universe, that it has been imposed upon us to take away our freedom, that any time anyone says, "There is only one way," what we know is that there are dozens, hundreds, maybe even thousands of other possibilities, all equally or more useful and good.

So there I was, watching myself head along the road toward orgasm, when suddenly, just before my anticipated destination and entirely without intent, I stepped off the dichotomous road onto a path that I had had no idea was there until I found myself on it. During the split second that my foot was in the air before it came down in that unexpected place, I knew absolutely that the path I had inadvertently stumbled upon was only one of thousands, millions, actually innumerable paths off the plateau of sexual excitement that I had been on all afternoon and evening.

But I didn't have time to think about this then because as soon as my foot touched the path, I found myself—to my great astonishment—up in the night sky.

26

In The Night Sky

I have since wondered if what I was having was an out-of-body experience, but I have no way of knowing. What I do know is that it was not like a vision. I was behind my eyes there in the indigo sky, not seeing myself but seeing the sliver of moon to my right and the millions of stars all around me. Not merely seeing them, but *feeling* them.

The state I was in can, in our clumsy language, perhaps best be termed ecstasy, though ecstasy seems a small word for it. I was full of love, I *was* love.

As I looked at it, I could feel how it felt to be the moon. I knew it from the moon's point of view, from inside it. It let me into itself, and I saw and experienced everything through its "eyes," and "heart." As I did, love for it rose and broke over me in waves again and again, flooding me and sweeping me away.

But the exquisite part was that I knew that the moon was experiencing me in the same way, that it knew for that moment how it felt to be me in a way that no one and nothing else ever had, that it knew, as I did, from *inside* me, from for a moment *being* me.

The stars and I also danced together like this in spirit, in an instant learning one another completely and adoring what we learned, on our hearts' knees before one another in awe and gratitude. I was so overwhelmed by bliss I was afraid I might die there in their midst.

Patriarchy has taught me to bear unbearable pain and to bear it stoically. After more than a half century in its wretchedness, I have developed such a high pain threshold, have become so inured to misery, that I can bear almost any sorrow for almost any length of time. The years of my life between twelve and twenty-three, for instance, were so terrible that each day I marveled that I had lived through yet another one without dying of grief. I don't know how I survived that empty, loveless time—empty of self and of love of self. Though somehow I did, all I learned from it was how to endure pain.

What endurance I didn't learn on that rack I learned from motherhood, and what I didn't learn from motherhood I learned from loverhood. All in all, I became a perfect patriarchal product—pathetically low expectations of joy and hardly any experience in surviving it.

Standing there in the sky that night, known and knowing, I felt so engulfed by happiness that I thought it might suffocate me. Because I had had too little experience with joy to learn how to bear it, it was literally unbearable. My spirit felt like a balloon that someone had put in the freezer overnight and tried to blow up with a hot-air machine as soon as they took it out. It was too stiff and cold, too rigid for this, too likely to shatter.

So, in fear for my life, I brought myself hastily down from that dangerously expansive love and back to the safe bed. I could bear lifetimes of agony but I couldn't bear sixty seconds of joy.

Only then, safely down, could I begin to think about what I had just done, to ponder the messages in it, and to turn its portents over in my mind.

I thought about how male philosophers have told us for centuries that we are ultimately alone, finally unknowable to anyone else. They have assured us that the nature of our beings is that we can never know others as they know themselves—from the inside out—nor can we ourselves ever be fully known. We are all then inevitably strangers to one another forever.

Our experience corroborates this. We see that, in fact, we have never known others as we know ourselves and we have never been so known; we see that we are alien to one another. But we haven't asked ourselves often enough whether this apparent "fact" obtains truly because of our natures or because of millennia of profoundest brainwashing.

After less than a minute in the night sky, I knew that the fathers had lied to us once again, this time about human possibilities for connection. I knew at last what a miserable substitute for intimacy they had fobbed off on me in relation Ships. I had experienced genuine intimacy in the sky that night, and it bore no resemblance to what I had previously called intimacy, neither in degree nor in kind.

I called to my mind those occasions in the past on which I believed I had felt intimacy and, sending my memory back into them, sought to uncover what the feelings and perceptions really had been that I had been persuaded to term "intimacy." My findings nearly broke my heart.

What I realized I had mistaken for intimacy were those moments when my lover and I had felt most securely owned and most securely owning—her most mine, me most hers. Patriarchy had deliberately and diabolically trained me to adore my chains, to long for and seek non-freedom in its guise as intimacy. And then, when I had resisted, had told me through its therapeutic minions that I was afraid of intimacy.

I should *think* I was afraid of it! So should everyone be if I am right that intimacy as defined by mensgame is the feeling of being most possessed. If so, no wonder they hold it before us as the goal, as the ultimate achievement of relation Ships. No wonder they teach us to love our condition and to perpetuate it ourselves as the most desirable of all things.

I may have been horrified and angry at this discovery but frankly I was not surprised. This brand of perfidy, this evil turning of our best instincts against us—making us believe slavery is freedom, making us believe it feels wonderful—this is characteristic of the twisted mind of manunkind now controlling the planet.

I began to understand the fathers' fear of genuine intimacy and why they have had to lie so hard for so long. Though there are many avenues to intimacy—meditation, music, dance, conversation—my journey toward intimacy that autumn afternoon had begun, as inexplicably to me then as now, on a plateau of sexual feeling.

Women have suspected for a long time that what mensgame isolates as sexuality is actually only a minute part of the fountain of creativity and that that creativity embraces the whole of us, not just our bodies, not just our genitals. I thought that on that plateau I had been in my power—in a state of nearly complete creativity. I decided that I had got there by obdurately refusing patriarchy's taped messages and being true to my Self, doing exactly and only what I genuinely felt like doing. I interpreted this as being free, having integrity, and credited it with my ability to feel powerful and fully creative. I concluded that this combination of freedom, integrity, and power was essential for intimacy.

Later, I pondered again the impossibility of couple Ships, struggling to imagine what might really come naturally, without programming. I remembered that many women were thinking, researching, and writing now about how the world might have been during those hundreds of thousands of years before men introduced control into it, those millennia when every living person on the planet worshipped the goddess. Not as some now worship god—as an all-powerful person in the sky—but as the personification of freedom, integrity, power, and generativity, as the connecting principle, the principle of intimacy.

To experience true intimacy had now begun to be for me a puissant reason for living. After my brief love affair with the planets, the possibility that humans could know and love ourselves and others in that same total way seemed well worth sticking around for. If reincarnation were a fact, I was sure then that what lured me back again and again to Earth was the longing for this experience.

I saw clearly that the patriarchs' lie that we are all inescapably alone had been needed to make a new kind of deity attractive to us. Jehovah, or whatever name is used for the male god who has temporarily supplanted the goddess, was touted as an actual male *being*, a big, controlling guy, easily offended. His living in the sky facilitated the myth of his being everywhere at once, as the sky is. Longing for closeness, for being known, humans must have found highly appealing that this god could *know* them, not only as they knew themselves, but even better. Though they couldn't know *him* in this way, they could be assured of a semblance of intimacy. A one-sided affair, of course, but better than they could have with one another, and at least they were rescued from irrevocable loneliness.

But since this god of men's is a sorry substitute for genuine deity—the creative power which resides in our own breasts and in all living things—he hasn't been much of a comfort. There cannot be another planet in our universe or any other where there is so much comfort needed and so little available.

Since the day I had finally shucked christianity off my back a decade before, I hadn't paid much attention to the bible except as a record of the jehovah-directed slaughter of the goddess peoples. But I knew that everything that the men who wrote and transcribed that book thought about women and women's world was upside down and backwards. Because of this, I felt safe in assuming that when they denounced the pagans as debauched and reviled them for their "orgies," something quite different was actually going on, something so outside the emerging masculinist paradigm of sadomasochism that there was no place for it in their imaginations.

As soon as I asked myself what it might have been, across the screen of my inner vision scene after scene began to flash as if I were watching a movie:

Women are living as we might have lived ten thousand years ago, part of a large community of women of all ages, a community like a town in which we know and love every woman in a way that transcends expression. We come together often, formally and informally, with various purposes, for many reasons, and for no reason at all. But whatever else we may do, we always rejoice together, taking delight in ourselves, in one another, and in the unspeakable glory of being alive.

This particular evening we are gathering in the glade of the forest to re-create our bonds of intimacy. It is tender twilight in late summer, the air soft and sweet. Walking singly, in pairs, in small groups, we come from all directions to this familiar and beloved place. We know many ways of renewing our deep heart connections, each with its own distinctive ambience and benefit, and tonight we choose the way I stumbled upon unintentionally that autumn afternoon.[1]

After the singing, after the dancing, after the poetry and drama, after the story telling, after whatever ritual grows out of us at the moment, we are ready. Laying our clothes aside—if we still have them on, and I can't think why we would—and in whatever configuration we wish, in twos and threes and fours and more, we begin caressing one another.

Though we live in present time and enjoy every moment of this thoroughly for itself alone, we also know that in some other present moment, we will all be on the creative plateau from which an infinite number of paths lead to an infinity of possibilities. We know this because we have traveled this and hundreds more of these paths together, having loved one another completely since we were infants.

Because we also have the advantage of living in spiral—not linear—time, we have no concern about the time it takes. There is an abundance of time.

Now, communicating without words as we do much of our lives, we are aware of the exact moment when we have

---

[1] Because I hadn't experienced any other, this was the only way I could imagine.

all delighted in our own and others' mounting creative energies as fully as we desire. Together we step off the plateau onto the path nearest orgasm, eager for the night sky and our sisters the moon, stars, and planets. Eager for one another.

Suddenly we are there, bathed in starlight, our arms around one another, our spirits expanding with joy. After we exchange greetings and affection with our bright celestial sisters, we turn to one another. Each one of us may then renew intimacy with every other woman there—since there is enough time—or with only one or two. There is no one right way or one best number; we simply do what we want to do.

I choose to remember again why I so love the woman directly across the circle from me. So I focus on her, and as I do, she opens herself to me.

Because desire is cherished, if she so desired she could shield parts of herself from me without the slightest risk of displeasing me. But since she is concerned neither with pleasing nor displeasing me, she feels no compulsion to reveal anything she doesn't genuinely want to reveal. In our society, we do not have even an unspoken understanding that the woman who reveals everything is somehow braver or better in any way than the woman who shields various aspects of herself—or vice versa. There is no judgment of one another's *behavior*, only acceptance in love and delight of who each of us *is*.

Standing among the stars, I look at her and know her. I know her as she knows herself: The taste, the smell, the aura of her deepest self, how she feels and perceives herself from the inside out, as if I were behind her eyes, within her body and spirit. As if I *were* her. In an instant I experience every incident of her life, laugh her happiness and mourn her grief, watch her come into her wisdom and power.

Understanding her creation of Self, I am in profoundest awe. I want to kneel before her and weep on her feet, to adore her. I feel worshipful of that in her that is deity, her glorious power to *be*. I love her unutterably, as I love myself, forgive her anything, as I forgive myself, and want for her every blessing I myself desire.

The next day as I go about my life I meet her on the path and am overwhelmed with gladness at the sight of her. She is so incredibly dear to me that it would be impossible for me, even for an instant, to wish her ill. Not only am I incapable of saying anything negative about her, I cannot even *insinuate* to anyone else that she is anything but totally acceptable just as she is. I am eager to hear others praise her, and am delighted when she is successful and well and powerful. I see only good in her because, though she may have flaws, I could never come to the end of counting her virtues. Besides, dwelling on her faults causes me not to love myself and reduces my power. On the other hand, I get endless and profound pleasure from noticing all that is beautiful in her. Rendering me sensitive to the beauty in myself, this increases my self-love and power.

I experience this intimacy with every woman I see and meet and talk with every day. Every bite of food I eat has been grown and prepared by the hands of women whose hearts beat in my breast; every article of clothing I wear, every tool I use—everything is created out of this love. My life is deep and rich and satisfying beyond telling.

I thought as I observed this union of freedom, integrity, power, and creativity in my mind's eye, "*This* is intimacy!" This was the way I wanted the world to be. I didn't realize that in some ways this vision was a product of my old linear, dichotomous, stimulus/response conditioning. It felt wonderful and free to me, and my longing for freedom surpassed every other longing of my life, since I knew it was the basis of everything else I desired. I was prepared to do anything, challenge any assumption, leap off any cliff into any apparent chasm, die as my old self and be reborn, to bring a new possibility of loving into the world.

So I continued to deprogram myself by undertaking to know and to be faithful to how I felt, and to do all the time only what I wanted to do. I practiced being completely accountable for my own feelings and perceptions—not only answerable for taking care of them but for having created them—*all of them*—in the first place. I also accepted the entire obligation of getting my needs met. Insofar as I knew how, I believed no old givens about myself or others, and lived as much as I was able in the incredible power of the moment.

I was buoyed up in this endeavor by my knowledge that in this same way, hundreds of thousands of other women were also making a world where the deepest connections among all living things was again possible, where we could once more be what we were capable of being, where we could experience the intimacy that was the reason we lived.

27

But We Did That Already!

"Hey, you're not talking about anything new," women in my speeches and workshops sometimes objected. "We tried this in the '60s." They went on to warn, "Free love didn't work then and it won't work now."

I countered that I wasn't talking about "free love" as it had been previously defined and that, no, this wasn't what happened in the '60s. I explained my understanding that what did happen in the '60s was a sexual revolution *for men only*, giving men nearly unprecedented access to women's bodies and energy. For heterosexual women, however, this was new only in quantity, not in quality—just more of the same old exploitation of women, the same old objectification. Sex may have been "free" for men, but it wasn't free for us. We paid and paid and paid again for our unwitting collaboration in this gross misappropriation of our resources.

The ugly expectation that we were to spread our legs for men any time, any place, and were bad sports if we refused, was in large measure what catapulted thousands of us into our own crusade for freedom.

(I was not a Lesbian in the '60s and so do not know firsthand of Lesbian experiments in non-couple loving. But

I believe that almost all of us have more psychic and spiritual resources now and a more solid base of understanding so that whatever we try will be happier.)

Sometimes women argued with me, "You're just rationalizing your desire to sleep around," and I would hear later in some roundabout way that in my workshop I had been perceived by some to be urging everyone "to sleep with everybody they wanted to." Others contended, "You just don't want to take responsibility," or "This is how men do it," or "I'm sorry you've had such bad experiences, but you don't have to project your disillusionment onto the rest of us," or "I don't have enough energy for a relationship with one person, what would I do with more?" or "Having sex with lots of people isn't satisfying" or "I've tried promiscuity and it didn't work," or "I'm just not into group sex."

All these objections so missed the point that when women made them I hardly knew where to begin. Usually I had just given a speech or led a workshop where I had talked as cogently as I knew how—which was never cogent enough because I had no language for it—about an entirely new way of feeling and being with ourselves and any number of others. But patriarchy's Relationship Belief System is embedded with such incredible strength that despite my most articulate attempts, in many women the old mind stayed stuck fast. Their comments presupposed that we would continue indefinitely to relate on the basis of the dogma of the slave Ship, that we would remain trapped indefinitely in the sadomasochistic paradigm.

I never got over my surprise that anyone, even after my necessarily limited elucidation, could believe that I was

But We Did That Already!

recommending "multiple couplism."[1] I realized later that one
of the reasons for the misunderstanding lay in the way I had
described the scene where we all helped one another reach a
plateau of creativity and power that generated intimacy. I
realized that I was still believing in sexuality as a concept and
still perceiving it as stimulus/response: Sadomasochism.

But the new mode of being that I sensed we were moving
into, the one I longed for with all my heart, was so utterly
other than this that despite my inability to articulate it, such
responses from women confused me. To me they seemed to
be not only nonsense and gibberish, but anachro-
nisms—museum pieces. Since I could neither imagine nor
describe the new paradigm, I kept saying, "No, you don't
understand. That's not what I mean at all. None of that
applies to what I'm thinking and feeling. It's something else
altogether, but I haven't the words for it yet."

Trying not to feel frustrated at my inability either to
imagine or describe how we would interact outside PRBS, I
reminded myself that no one can see out of one paradigm into
another. Rooted deeply in sadism/hierarchy, I knew I could
no more envision peerness than I could guess what form any
aspect of our lives would take in an anarchic, women's world.

I also realized that trying to imagine new possibilities of
intimacy wasn't even desirable, that if I did I would
unavoidably take much of the old relationShip poem with
me—as I unwittingly had done in my vision of women
gathering among the stars. I remained aware that to the
degree that we take men's Relationship Belief System with us
into a new world, we will find that we have unavoidably

---

[1] From correspondence of Alex Allen, Mission Viejo, CA, May 14, 1990.

reproduced the old world. All the seeds of mensgame reside potently in this belief system.

But at least I had some idea what I *didn't* want the new world to look like. I didn't want any more sadomasochistic Ships: No "falling in love," no couples, no co-dependence, no breaking up—none of the poem of hierarchy and oppression.

I also knew basically what I *did* want: Women with me and with one another out of their free choice always, no coercion whatever, no matter how subtle or sweet, no one feeling compelled *in the slightest* to meet my needs or anyone else's. I had little idea how sex would function, but I knew that numbers—of partners, of times—would be irrelevant; maybe I would be sexual once a year, maybe three times a day, maybe never. Maybe with dozens of women, maybe with none. I had no idea.

My not being able to figure at least some of this out, and knowing that I wouldn't therefore have a chance to prepare myself emotionally beforehand, didn't trouble me unduly. I understood that, rather than bringing it into being by first envisioning it, women would have to walk step by step into our homeland.

PART V

JUMPING SHIP

28

The Bears and Anarchy

The basic feminist view that we should be true to ourselves had been very familiar to me for a long time.
But it had taken the trauma of confronting the Relationship
Belief System to get me to understand why and how our
knowing what we want to do and doing *only* that, knowing
who we are and being *always* that, might bring into being a
non-relational, non-hierarchical world, a world of
peers—women's world.

Groping toward an understanding of how society, not just
relation Ships, would change, I first turned for help to my left
brain, developing theory to justify the intuitive command that
I follow *absolutely and every moment* the desires of my heart.

Men responding to me on talk shows helped. Many of
them scornfully contended that if everyone did only what they
wanted to do, if there were no rules, no laws, no one in
charge, there would be an explosion of crime, there would be
total disorder, there would be—horror of horror—anarchy!

"Do you mean," I asked innocently, "that what we are
looking at in the world is *not* an explosion of crime? Are
you telling me that this is not *already* total disorder?" I

wanted to quote Emma Goldman to them, that wild and wonderful anarchist, on the subject of governments and crime:

The most absurd apology for authority and law is that they serve to diminish crime. Aside from the fact that the State is itself the greatest criminal, breaking every written and natural law, stealing in the form of taxes, killing in the form of war and capital punishment, it has come to an absolute standstill in coping with crime. It has failed utterly to destroy or even minimize the horrible scourge of its own creation.

Crime is naught but misdirected energy. So long as every institution of today, economic, political, social, and moral, conspires to misdirect human energy into wrong channels; so long as most people are out of place doing the things they hate to do, living a life they loathe to live, crime will be inevitable, and all the laws on the statutes can only increase, but never do away with, crime. What does society, as it exists today, know of the process of despair, the poverty, the horrors, the fearful struggle the human soul must pass on its way to crime and degradation?[1]

I agreed with these callers however that, yes, thank goodness, living as I was suggesting *would* mean anarchy. A very different kind of law-and-order than they recognized, but

[1] Emma Goldman, *Anarchism and Other Essays*, Dover Publications, Inc.: Mineola, NY, 1969, pp. 59-60.

order nevertheless, the order inherent in self-government—total and effortless, fluid, creative, and lusty.[2] I directed them to observe nature, the perfect anarchy. For billions of years, nature has gone blithely about her business of creating the most extraordinary life systems and forms with awe-inspiring brilliance and efficiency. The stunning fact is that through it all there has been *no one in charge*. No government agencies, no department chiefs, no bureaucrats making laws, demanding triplicates, forming committees to study proposals, holding endless meetings, or funding research. Not even a god.[3]

When left to itself—as unfortunately it has not been since patriarchy's debut—every part of nature simply does what it wants to do all the time, following with integrity its genuine desires, taking full responsibility for itself, and relying on all others to do the same—*needing* all others to do the same. In this way, nature's nearly indestructible ecological web is woven.

When, for example, the river runs where it wants to run and is neither dammed nor turned artificially out of its course, every strand of nature's web, including humankind, benefits. Even granting that rivers flood, floods, too, are necessary for the long-range well-being of the web.

But when rivers are forced to do something that is not in their nature to do, something they do not want to do, widespread disaster follows. For example, when men, who

---

[2] As Lucy Frey from Anchorage, AK, wrote in a January 1991 note: "In London at SisterWrite Bookstore, I bought a card that said, 'A woman without a man is like a country without a government.'"

[3] Sue Lampson from San Jose suggests that cats are among the best models of anarchy. Cats, she says, always know and do exactly what they want. They live totally in the moment.

are not rivers and therefore know nothing about *being* rivers, decided that they knew better than the River Nile how it should *be* and dammed it, they shredded the surrounding ecological web for hundreds of miles. Many species of plants and animals died out, disease ran rampant, desertification began its ravages, people who had farmed the rich lands along the Nile's banks, or had lived from its bounty as fisherpeople for thousands of years, were suddenly without means of survival and migrated in calamitous numbers to the cities.

Every living thing must be true to itself, must do what it wants to do, so that all other living things can be free to do the same. This is anarchy, this living in knowledge of total connectedness, and it is perfect order.

The patriarchs do not live in this knowledge and order, and haven't for thousands of years. Because they do not have the spiritual and emotional health that is a precondition for freedom and true power, when they do what they want to do, the rest of us suffer. But when I speak of the desirability of no one ruling anyone else—of no "archy"—I make the assumption that many women are moving, and moving rapidly, toward the soundness of thought and feeling that will make such freedom possible.

Emma Goldman defines anarchy as "the philosophy of a new social order based on liberty unrestricted by man-made law; the theory that all forms of government rest on violence, and are therefore wrong and harmful, as well as unnecessary."[4]

In nature's anarchic design, the denizens of the forest don't stand around watching the bears prepare to hibernate

---

[4] *Anarchism and Other Essays*, p. 50. For further quotations about anarchy from Goldman's essay, see Appendix II.

and mutter among themselves: "Look at those lazy louts! What makes them think they can lie around all winter while the rest of us have to work?" They do not then march back and forth in front of the Bureau of Hibernation with their picket signs, chanting, "What do we want? No hibernation! When do we want it? Now!" and demanding, "Wake those bears up and put them to work!"

They don't complain or riot, not only because there is no one in charge that they might influence with such behavior, but I think also because they live every moment in profound understanding of the absolutely crucial connections among us, a wisdom that mensgame has programmed out of us. They know that in order for the web of life to stay intact and healthy, every living thing must be every moment as much what it truly is as possible, must have the individual power that springs from wholeness, and must have the freedom—most wildly, most expansively, most ecstatically—to create from moment to moment an ever new and unique Self.[5]

I think they know that because all living things are intimately connected, when the bears are true to themselves, when they are being as bearful as they can possibly be,

---

[5] I am aware here both of partaking of men's arrogance in believing I know what animals *are* and of anthropomorphizing—and therefore falsifying—animals in order to make my point. I apologize, but I think the point is worth it. I want to make clear, however, that every day I gain more respect for animals, feel more humble in their presence, and am more willing to accept that, in my present gross psychic state, I cannot understand them. But I look forward eagerly to the rapidly-approaching time when we will again be able to communicate with them in direct ways. And the time when we will never kill them, never force them to do anything they do not choose to do. I long for our ancient unity and peerness with them.

everything that lives is more free to create fully its unique Self.

The bears' integrity is therefore not only good for everything else but *necessary* for the well-being of the whole. When bears are about their life's purpose of being every moment at the peak of ursinity, experimenting with the parameters of bearishness, *creating* bearness—and the more bearish the more joyful—all life rejoices. One filament of the web pulsing with creativity and power sends creativity and power zinging through the entire network.

In my past conventionally activist life, I acknowledged this fundamental connection in a negative way by agreeing that when any of us is oppressed, we are all oppressed. I know now that the positive of this is equally true: When any of us is free, we are all free.

But some argue that the case for doing only what we want to do—for anarchy—cannot be supported by analogy with the natural world. All is not cozy cooperation there, they say. Animals, for instance, are violent. They stalk, kill, and eat one another. Maybe the woodland folk are happy to see the bears hibernate, not because in this way the ecological balance necessary for life will be maintained, but rather because for a few merciful months the bears will be out of circulation, freeing the forest of their menace.

This argument ignores our growing understanding of the complex and complete interconnection among all living things. Since all of us are interdependent in life's web, and everything that affects any one of us affects us all, it is unthinkable that animals can have remained unchanged by the truly immeasurable male violence of the past 5,000 years on this planet. How can we presume to know their true natures when for millennia they have lived, as we have, in a reality of perpetual terror? We have no more seen a "free" or "natural" animal in the past few thousands years than we have seen a "free" or "natural" woman, or a "free" or "natural" anything.

The bible, however, as a history of the systematized genocide of the goddess people, inadvertently offers us a glimpse into their pre-patriarchal world, a world of other possibilities for animals as well as for ourselves. Courtesy of that eerily familiar world-mind comes the image of the lamb lying down with the lion. Totally alien to patriarchal thought, this remnant of goddess culture hints evocatively that all is not as it seems, that other ways of being are always open to us.

When we are all free, I will observe animals and say, "This is how they behave in anarchy, in perfect freedom, in total self-government, in absolute love. This is therefore how they truly are." Until then, I am reserving judgment about their nature, as I am reserving judgment about yours and mine.

Though the bear story is an analogy, not an argument, and can be taken only so far, a basic assumption about our experience as humans can be made from it. We are part of nature's mystical, magical latticework, totally interdependent.

When I am in a big city surrounded by enormous buildings, I often look up at the thousands of windows signifying thousands of offices and hundreds of thousands of workers and think, "What can they all possibly be *doing* in there?" I know that there is actually little that needs to be done, and that anything beyond that is destructive—to the human spirit and to the soul of the planet. So I know that most people working in those offices are doing work that is dangerous to them and others.

But I also know that the greatest danger is that most of them are not enjoying the work they're doing. Most of them don't want to be in those offices and many are absolutely wretched there, but they are enslaved by their belief that they have no economic alternative.

The consequences to every living being of this massive unhappiness, this vast spiritual and physical bondage, are incalculable. Because we are connected to one another on every level as if by shining silver cords, the strands of our lives woven inseparably together into the web, the suffering of any one of us vibrates through every filament and is felt by us all. When any one of us betrays our Selves, does what we don't want to do, what is not in our natures to do, what causes us to live less powerfully, less creatively, less joyfully, the quality of every life on the planet is damaged. When we are not true to ourselves, we seriously endanger the health not only of our own but of everyone else's spirit on Earth. There is no way for any of us to live as fully as we are capable as long as so many others are sending distress to our souls through the threads of life's tapestry.

Like the other animals, to the degree that each of us is whole and living in our power—that is, knows who and how valuable we are, how we feel, what we want, and, honoring and loving ourselves, acts totally out of the desires of our hearts every moment—no one can control us, neither can we nor would we wish to control anyone else. Tyranny cannot exist when self-loving beings act with integrity.

Anarchy is the name for this ecology of the spirit. A new social and economic order, it requires that we love and trust ourselves, and are totally accountable for our own feelings and behavior. It requires that we dare to believe that when we have done enough of our internal cleansing from patriarchy, when we are whole again for the most part and sane, then doing what we desire to do all the time will bless us and all other living things.

For obvious reasons, the men who control the world tremble at the word anarchy. If everyone valued themselves, if they took full responsibility for themselves, if they knew exactly how they felt and did what they wanted to do every moment, they would be ungovernable. None of them could be forced to work eight hours a day at mind-numbing, soul-destroying jobs. The system could not survive for five minutes without the capitulation of people who absolutely believe that human beings have no choice but to do many things in life that they don't want to do, people who surrender responsibility for their lives to mensmachine.

The fact that the word anarchy has so much power to terrify the tyrants should put us on alert, since we know that patriarchy reverses the truth. In this light, its insistence that violence and disorder are inherent to anarchy makes it safe for us to assume the opposite: That given a certain level of emotional and spiritual health among its practitioners, anarchy by its very nature generates peace and order.

Those of us intent upon designing, creating, and living in a literal new world right now want to understand not only the theory but also how in our lives to follow nature's anarchic model. We want to know how we can reestablish the ecology of the spirit among us, and what would happen if we were selftrue.

Although we know we can't envision a new paradigm standing in the thick smog of the old, we can't help but speculate about how we might remake the world by having the courage and insight to live free from manunkind's self-serving assumptions.

What we know is that everything around us would undergo drastic alteration if we adhered fiercely to our desires. Take, for instance, toilets.[6]

Every time I talk about my vision of self-government and freedom based on desire, some woman objects, "But who's going to clean the toilets?" she asks. Sometimes another woman will call out, "I love to clean toilets!"[7] Several others will jokingly urge her to come and live with them. But toilets, both as themselves and as symbols of unpleasant work, remain a problem.

Let us give the toilet problem to a small imaginary community of thirteen women who are experimenting earnestly with the principle of doing only what they want to do all the time. These women live together in one large house or have separate houses and a communal building or some other arrangement that gives them some shared space.

In this shared space is a conventional toilet, and one day one of the women says, "Hey, you gynes! Look at this dirty toilet. Do any of you want to clean it?" Each woman checks out her feelings—and shakes her head. No one wants to. They all stand looking at the toilet and waiting for enlightenment.

But because these women believe that their desires are perfect guides to behavior, none of them says, "It's got to be done. Someone's going to have to do it whether she wants to or not. Someone's got to sacrifice so that the rest of us

---

[6] Alternatives to conventional toilets exist only because our new value system has already begun imposing itself upon our environment.

[7] *She* may, but most of us don't. I know I like to *have cleaned* them, I enjoy having them clean. In the past I haven't minded doing the yucky jobs because I saw this work as the means to another end. I believe that all our wants have been deliberately obfuscated by this kind of linearity.

will be comfortable." Trusting their feelings and knowing that they spring directly from their values, they realize that since none of them wants to clean it, something is wrong with the *toilet,* not with *them.*
The theory upon which they are operating is that if the work that presents itself is in harmony with their values, they will want to do it. If it promotes a world of peace and abundance and joy and love and beauty and health, they will delight in doing it, it will be a pleasure, it will *fit* them. Obviously the converse is also true: If a job is somehow out of sync with their world view, they will find it repugnant *and will not be able to do it.*
Already the experience of thousands of women in the United States bears out this theory. Women are walking out of jobs everywhere, and walking out *before* they have any other economic crutch. The typical experience, as it has been told to me time and time again, goes something like this. One day a woman upon entering her office realizes that she can no longer be there. Though she is frightened, inside herself she feels an enormous rush of optimism and power that propels her through her resignation that day and beyond.
Everywhere, these women—many of whom have still not discovered what they want to do or found other ways to survive financially—tell me that they have never regretted acting on that impulse. They assure me that the instant they decided, despite their economic terror, to stop squandering their precious lives doing merely tolerable, or boring, or infuriating work was the best moment of their lives.
I have learned that living in this way may have benefits I couldn't have dreamed of at first. A friend told me, for instance, that she had seen a talk show—she *thought* it was Sally Jesse Raphael—where four people who had been

certified as having had AIDS, three men and a woman, speculated about why they currently showed no clinical trace of it at all. Though none of them could answer how they had been healed, the friend who watched it noticed that their stories all followed a similar pattern. When they had been told that they had AIDS, they had each resolved that, since they had so little time to live, they would live exactly as they pleased for as long as they were able. They had then proceeded to do only what they wanted to do and nothing else—in the best of health an incredibly radical, difficult, and transfiguring act.

Already we are beginning, many of us without knowing or even caring why, to stop being ruled by fear, refusing to let it persuade us to be relational, reactionary, stimulus-response-bound. Trusting our desires, we are becoming free from every form of dis-ease in patriarchy.

As soon, for instance, as the women with the dirty toilet realize from their feelings of distaste that something about toilets as they are presently designed does not mesh with women's values, they ask themselves what it is about this object and the way it functions that does not belong in their new world. The answers begin to come at once.

First, they notice that it is too high for most able-bodied women. Humans were meant anatomically to squat while they defecate. Our colons need this added assistance for best cleansing. Next, they realize that it takes marvelous, scientifically unreproductible organic matter, matter that has picked up miracle substances from every organ and gland of the body, and destroys it, losing it to the life cycle for which it is so necessary. Last, they are appalled at its waste of water, the earth's most necessary, most precious resource. Water, they agree, is liquid life, solid light, full of intelligence and wisdom. If there is a tangible goddess, she is water.

The women of this community reach the conclusion that other women have reached before them, that what they need are toilets that fit them—physically and ecologically. What they need are custom-made composting toilets. As they follow through on this decision, they notice with excitement how it alters their entire living space. Because they can build composters anywhere, inside or out, they don't have to put them in something called a "bathroom." This opens up their minds to possible rearrangements of tubs and wash basins as well. Do these need a separate room? Might the tub not be warmer and sunnier on the south side of the bedroom (if there is such a room!) or in the kitchen, or in the greenhouse or sunroom, or somewhere else? How many bathtubs and showers and composters does the community need, and what would be the best location to allow re-use of water and easy transport of compost? Would covered walkways from living quarters to a central bathhouse or several strategically placed composters cut down the numbers of tubs and toilets necessary, and would these arrangements be comfortable and convenient?

The entire conventional floor plan that has developed out of menstream values is then up for rethinking. As are energy sources, and placement of living areas in accord with natural heat and cool. As are rigidly square corners that abruptly stop the spiraling flow of energy in a room, giving the occupants dis-ease. And so on.

As they follow their desires, the very look of their world radically, marvelously changes to reflect the change in values. Because they are emotionally and intellectually healthy and largely deprogrammed from their conditioning, they can transform their abstract values into concrete reality by fulfilling their desires.

Their toilet experience reinforces these women's understanding of patriarchy as the reaction against, the reverse of, women's ways. Men, trapped in the illusory future by their own linear time deception, begin, for example, with projected goals. They then decide what jobs need to be done and when they must be finished in order for these goals to be reached on time. Their next step is to get other people to do these jobs whether they want to or not—genuine desire is not only irrelevant but actively discounted and discouraged.

The truth is, of course, that people most often don't want to do these jobs and sometimes even intensely dislike doing them. But they are coerced into them by their need for money. Hence the necessity to oppression of an exchange system. How else could men force people into spending most of their precious lives doing things they don't want to do?

However, living in the conscious value-rich present—and the present is all there ever is or will be—decisions about what needs to be done arise out of the desires of women who are in their power. If there is work that no one wants to do, the work itself is scrutinized for its anti-life, anti-freedom properties. The women do not look into themselves for the flaw. Pure desire, the fruit of integrity, can have no flaw.

Even when the women in the community cannot recognize at first why certain work is not desirable to any of them, they still refuse to do it. They refuse because they know that doing it despite their warning that it is not harmonious with their values is treacherous to themselves, subversive to the spiritual ecology of their community, and therefore disruptive to all communities, human and otherwise. They understand that ignoring or resisting their desires will tear this shimmering metaphysical web apart in ways both obvious at once and insidious over time. This keeps them firm in their resolve not to capitulate to old ways of being and thinking, never again to let guilt—the "shoulds" of the fathers—dictate their behavior.

Their belief in the validity of their desires gives them the courage not to do work that no one wants to do even when in the old world such work was believed to be absolutely necessary; the courage not to do it even when they cannot see how to achieve the same result in other ways; the courage to wait and see what happens when that work is not done; the courage to make decisions from that experience rather than from the post-hypnosis-like trance induced by brainwashing.

We are these hypothetical women. Shouldering the responsibility for becoming more fully who we are every moment by recognizing and honoring the desires of our souls, we help restore self-government, peerness, and freedom to all other living things in nature's gorgeous ecological tapestry.

More than this, in believing in our own internal voices we reinvent human nature, we create another, more expansive and inclusive, more interesting, more playful and at the same time more serious, myth of humanness. Guided by our desires, we live moment by moment in richest chaos—that is, at the summit of creativity where every possibility is present at once.

Out of this ripe and exuberant chaos, women are once again creating connections with all that is, animate and inanimate—the heart connections that have been lost for so long and so sadly missed.

29

Leaping Off Noah's Ark

One day as we two conspirators were talking on the phone, we almost simultaneously realized how the geographical distance between us, rather than facilitating freedom of choice as we had naively supposed, had in fact mandated coercion. Clearly, if we wanted to continue our experiment—the journey to freedom together—we would have to live near each other. Since I couldn't afford to live in her part of the country, we considered the possibility of her moving to Albuquerque. Fortunately, for many reasons she was excited by the idea.

And so in the late summer of 1989, she set up housekeeping in an apartment not far from mine in the North Valley, and we began the next stage of our research.

It proved to be a difficult time. Now we had, really for the first time, to make many conscious choices every day, and all our old relationShip patterns fought for their lives. Even though I had known that they were powerfully entrenched, I was astonished and shaken at how indomitable they suddenly appeared. I had forceably to prevent myself from doing a hundred automatic little acts, constantly checking with myself to see what they meant and if I really felt like doing them.

The situation was exacerbated by my knowledge that my co-experimenter was in a town that was strange to her, that she knew no one but me, and that if I didn't keep her company, she would be lonely.

So I struggled with myself over inviting her over to eat or to sleep or to talk, over telling her when I was going somewhere in case she wanted to come along. I struggled to feel *free* of the burden of her well-being. Almost every moment became fraught with significance, and since I still could not discriminate well between conditioned responses and real feelings—though I was getting better at it—the best I could do was to say no to the form and to nearly everything that smacked of the content.

I knew it all boiled down to being as honestly and clearly myself as possible all the time, refusing to take any responsibility other than this for her feelings, believing, in the teeth of my tremendous conditioning, that my being true to my own feelings and perceptions, my own wants and needs every moment was the greatest gift I could give her or anyone else.

Despite my intellectual understanding of the necessity for this, it was as close to impossible to do as anything I had ever tried in my life, and I often failed. But I persisted in trying, against every seemingly "instinctual" message to "be there" for her in the old ways. I struggled to "be there" in integrity, in honesty, in my power, fully and only answerable for myself and knowing that she was—*must be allowed to be*—fully responsible for herself.

It became clear that all our long theoretical discussions and clear intellectual understandings had not and could not have prepared us for the actual living of freer lives. When it came right down to connecting in different, mutually powerful ways, both of us floundered.

Nevertheless, as we hung in with the experiment, we both underwent enormous, soul-shaking changes. We began to take genuine accountability for our own feelings, detaching our ultimate happiness from dependence on the other's presence in our lives. We did hard and excellent work, and were justifiably proud of ourselves.

But even while my left brain congratulated me on seeing through and escaping from the RBS, dwelling smugly on the differences between this experiment and my "relation Ships," the feeling lingered that there was still something too familiar about it.

Not fully conscious either that I was searching for something or that my frustration at not finding it was mounting, I went over and over patriarchy's Relationship Belief System in my mind. I began to feel bogged down, as if all the exciting, rapid growth of the preceding years had come to a near standstill.

Feeling stymied, I went to Hawaii to speak that winter, having no idea that I was on the brink of discoveries that would be momentous in my life, catapulting me clear of my most adamant conditioning and changing everything.

It began as I sat talking with a group of extraordinarily vital, perceptive women at lunch in Honolulu. We were continuing the discussion that had begun that day in my workshop, marveling at how pervasive coercion was in relation Ships, how incredibly subtle. As I was again circling and examining the point of my workshop that relation Ships are by definition coercive and designed to subjugate us, trying to see it from different angles, suddenly I had a realization that took my breath away.

The central piece, the core of PRBS, the part I had missed every time I had scrutinized it in the past was the number two. *Two* was the prime imperative of patriarchy! *Two* was the perfect number for coercion. It was so obvious that the moment I recognized it, I couldn't believe I had so long and so consistently overlooked it. When I stood that fantasy starry-eyed couple before my desk that day so that I could get a glimpse of the form of the relationShip poem, the first fact I should have noticed was that there were two people standing there.

Of course, I knew that tyranny could exist with any number—we can even tyrannize ourselves—but in a dichotomous, binary system, two is the ideal number for inequality, for sadism, for the reproduction of patriarchy.

As soon as I recognized two as perfect for coercion, I remembered how I had been rejecting the binary, dichotomous male mind with all my strength for years, recognizing, as women do, that believing in only two alternatives is being caught in a mind vise, the very essence of non-freedom. I knew that women had always thought in three or more, that the triple goddess predated men's trinity by hundreds of thousands of years, and that though men perpetuated the trinity in order to subvert the goddess, they have been unutterably confused about it, and only comfortable when making it essentially a duo—-God and Jesus, or Allah and his prophet. I knew that men feared the number thirteen because it is the number of lunar months—hence, menstrual cycles—in a year, and that they therefore developed and now tolerate their exceedingly exasperating and cumbersome twelve-month calendar.

So though I knew that numbers were critical to phallocracy and that they therefore had to have something to do with the enslavement of women—which is what phallocracy is about—I had not been wary enough of men's number dogmas to doubt so basic a masculinist "fact" as two.

"Two" had so deeply invaded me that, like the air I breathed, it had seemed "natural," and what seems most natural is most taken for granted, most invisible. I realized sitting there with those women that "two" was my deepest conditioning, that recognizing it now as mind control, not "nature," I had come to the foundation of patriarchal thought in myself. I recognized this by the depth of its invisibility, as well as by the strong though momentary wave of fear that swept over me when I finally confronted it—both excellent clues.

But I knew that two was essential to tyranny also by the amount of propaganda that had been necessary to make me internalize it so deeply. It was evident to me that no other concept in our present world receives anywhere near as much attention. Nearly every magazine, book, movie, ad, song, myth—the animals marched into the ark by twos—every conversation, every living example promotes two as the inevitable, the only conceivable human romantic/love relation-Ship number.

Looking at this incalculable mass of brainwashing material and the constancy with which it is purveyed, I decided again that anything that *really* came naturally would not have to be so frantically insisted upon. Surely this was another case, methought, where they did protest too much. In thinking this, I followed my simple rule that manunkind does not spend money or effort putting out messages that will cause women to re-discover our power and be free, and that the most money and effort will be directed toward keeping us securely in the jail cells of our old minds.

In a matter of seconds, as we do, and while the conversation at the lunch table continued, I went through this internal process of validating as knowledge the intuitive message about two. I immediately began to confirm aloud the ways in which the concept of two had functioned in my own life as the powerful tool of oppression I had just discovered it to be. The generous gift of the attention of the women at the table helped me find clarity quickly.

I realized at once why as long as there are only two people, there will always be coercion, why there will always be a "relation Ship," no matter how strenuously the two are trying not to have one or what they are calling it instead. I knew that the reason I had been feeling uneasy about the "experiment" was that despite our refusing all the other dictates of PRBS, our continued bowing to the imperative of two kept us locked in the Ship's brig. That is, though we might be doing it less in both intensity and frequency than in our more conventional relation Ships, in our experiment we were still compelling and controlling each other. We were still keeping one another from freedom.

Understanding the dynamics of this subtle, loving coercion immediately, I gave the following hypothetical example:

May and Ruth love each other so deeply that they are unwilling to risk having a relation Ship. Since they know that there isn't any way to outsmart the officer on the bridge, they don't live together, they don't call themselves a couple, they don't assume they'll sleep together every night, they feel comfortable not always knowing where the other is, they have so many internal resources that they are secure without the other, and they try not to take unethical responsibility for making the other happy.

But they are human beings with needs and desires that cannot be gainsaid, and they know that their highest moral responsibility is to acknowledge and satisfy these. They also care deeply for each other and hope for each other's happiness. This being true, as long as there are only two of them, their needs and their love will cause them to coerce each other.

I explained how this worked by talking about their sex life, choosing sex because it is the one need that mensmachine states categorically is essential for a relation Ship to meet, so that what is going on with sex is almost always easiest to see. Society has trained our eyes upon it so fixedly that though we may not know what is going on in other areas of our lives, we almost always know where our sex life stands. Not that we always or even sometimes understand the multi-decked vessel beneath it, but that we know in a general way if it's going well or badly, comfortably or problematically.

If, I said to the group, I were to bring the subject of sex up to them, both May and Ruth would tell me at first that they have a wonderful sexual connection. But as I listen to them, I begin to hear behind the words a different scenario.

May calls Ruth on the phone and says she'd like to come over that evening. Ruth agrees, and so after supper May appears at Ruth's door glowing with good feeling and energy. She throws her arms around Ruth and dances her across the room, singing, "Oh what a beautiful evening, oh what a beautiful night!" "Ruthy," she laughs as she takes off her coat, "the moon loves me. All the way over here the moon sang me love songs. It got me ready, now I want to dance naked around the cauldron, I want to join arms with hundreds of wild women in the moonlight, chanting unimaginably ancient words, I want to beat drums for hours, all of us together, raising power. I want to fling myself all hot and steamy into the stream where the moon lies across it, and revel in the shock. I want to feel—skin and hair and grass, breeze and tongues and fingers—everything! I am so *alive!*" She pauses. "But barring this, I'll be content to bathe with you and rub you all over with warm oil afterwards and take you to my heart for the night. What do you say?"

Ruth has watched and listened with delight. She adores this vitality of May's, her passion, her sensuality, her lyrical vision. She also knows that May is transformed when she makes love in this mood and has long periods of high creative energy afterward. She wants May to feel like this, to have what seems for her a necessary integration of body and mind.

But the truth is that Ruth isn't feeling very peppy that night. Until May called her in the afternoon and asked to come over later, she had been looking forward to a quiet cup of tea and a book in bed for an hour or so before an early lights out. Now she realizes that she should have been true to her own needs earlier and not invited May over at all, to say nothing of being sexual and sleeping with her.

Ruth is now in the classic relationShip double-bind—one part of her damned if she does, another damned if she doesn't. If she decides to be true to one part of herself, she says, "Not tonight, May. In spite of that wonderful fantasy you spun, I just don't feel like it. Actually, I don't even feel like having company tonight. I would have told you earlier, but it took me until this moment to know it myself."

Part of being true to these feelings and needs is that though she has nearly to bite her tongue off to do it, Ruth carefully avoids apologizing, or showing any concern about what May is going to do with all her ardor. It is self-abasing to apologize for her feelings and both matronizing and dishonorable to try to take care of May's needs in any but the way May is asking her to meet them. If Ruth says, "I'm so sorry, May. I just can't tonight. But I feel terrible about your not being able to have what you want and need so much. I really wish I could give it to you," she is focusing attention upon her own need not to feel bad about doing what she has to do. In the guise of comforting May, Ruth is, in fact, compelling May to comfort *her*, pressuring May to say something like, "Hey, don't feel bad, Ruthy. It's okay, honest. There will be other times."

May might not say such a thing if Ruth did not apologize and in doing so re-focus the situation. Such sentiments probably do not express with any truth how she is feeling. But since she isn't being given the space or time to deal with her own feelings, she reverts to PRBS conditioning, and compromises her integrity.

But what about the part of Ruth that loves May and wants her to have what she needs? This is the point at which two is most tyrannical. Ruth knows that, whether they have promised to be monogamous or not, she, Ruth, is really the only person available now in May's life to meet this need. Because May has no one but her, she feels great pressure not to turn her away. She also knows that she can't refuse her very many times—especially in succession—and still have May in her life because May's business is to get her needs met. Ruth knows that if she can't meet them, May will ultimately find someone else who can, and Ruth will lose her.

This is incredibly powerful coercion, though often subtle and almost always denied. And it means that Ruth is going to be sexual with May sometimes whether she wants to be or not. In so losing her freedom, she loses her integrity, and without integrity, she has no access to her personal power. Stripped of her power, she will not be able to experience true intimacy.

But I decided to try a scenario in which May and Ruth recognize this syndrome before it gets too far advanced, and decide to reject the concept at its root by rejecting the dogma that two as the ideal number. (Using patriarchal reversal we can be sure that two is the very worst possible number there is for human freedom.) What might they do?

Assuming that they understand, feel, and act on the knowledge that "one" is ultimately the most whole, the most perfect number—only, that is, if they love and can rely on themselves totally—they can then choose to live in a community of other women they love. Nine, thirteen, perhaps twenty-one women they adore. They know numbers alone won't free them, that they could do PRBS stuff with any number of women simultaneously. But they also realize that as soon as they move out of the PRBS mind and into integrity, community opens up infinite possibilities for intimacy.

There's hardly any of us who hasn't said at one time or another, "Well, no one can be all things to anyone else." Presuming that one person could be all things to us or us to them grossly belittles our capacities and potential. Each of us is a universe in ourselves, immeasurably rich and various, utterly boundless. Depending primarily on any one outside person to quicken our desire, or spark our courage, or kindle our resolve to travel deeper and deeper into the unexplored territory of Self—the journey for which we were born—is hazardous in the extreme, producing that twilight life I call relationsleep or couplecoma.

I want to be awake and alive, to travel deep inside myself to the very stars of my firmament and beyond. I think I can do this most easily and completely while living daily in the midst of a hundred lovers whose ways of being excite and encourage me on this journey. None of them being everything or even "primary" to me or me to them, each of us being "primary" only to ourselves. Why haven't we paid attention when we said, "No one can be everything to anyone else?" I think we haven't because we didn't really believe we could have it all. The best we could do was to pick a partner who seemed to meet most of our needs and sacrifice getting the rest of them taken care of. Then, some months or years later, when we "broke up"—or should have broken up and didn't—we decided that we had either made a mistake in the first place, or that we had picked the person who was fine for a particular time in our lives but that we were in a different place now and needed somebody different.

The former is absurd—how could so many of us have so often picked the wrong person? Even with all our programming and abuse, it doesn't make sense that we could all have been so wrong so much of the time. The latter—needing a new partner for a new time in our lives—called serial monogamy, which supposes that at least for a short period of time one person can be everything to us, or that we can do without everything we need for awhile, is equally unacceptable and ridiculous.[1] What possible reason could there be for not having everything we want and need all the time? Why in the world does anyone need to sacrifice even for an instant? If we hadn't accepted this as a given, we would

---

[1] Annie Ocean from Roseburg, Oregon, at my spring 1990 workshop at Mother Kali's Bookstore in Eugene, suggested that if we were raised by many mothers, we would not cling so desperately to one person in a relation Ship.

never have accepted two. Two is based in sacrifice. Two is automatically disempowering. Part of why two is never enough is that no matter how well our two-Ships seem to be going, in them we simply cannot realize our full power. We are, I believe, capable of quickening one another's powers, of combining ours with others', of magnifying and amassing truly stupendous creative energy together. I believe we are capable of nearly unthinkably brilliant psychic technology, but that it requires our accumulated powers. Though two *unmerged* women's combined genius certainly surpasses that of one, every additional woman's does not merely add to it but increases it many, many times over. It is in larger groups that we are going to reach our stunning, our splendid, potential.[2]

I believe that the men who control the world understand very well this threat to their despotism. Tyrants always try to keep the oppressed from banding together, and in the case of women—who are the goddess in all her power—the effort has been colossal and continuous over thousands of years.

Another reason, therefore, that we haven't paid attention to our own knowledge that no one person can be everything—or even enough—for any other one person is because we have lost the knowledge of our power: What it is, how it feels, how to access it, its dimensions. We have forgotten that it has its source in freedom and integrity. But more than this, manunkind has stolen from us our knowledge of its amazingly cumulative nature. Witches have always known that women must come together to raise power. But

---

[2] It has never occurred to me to think that there is any way to get everyone in the world involved in this. I know that a new way has to be pioneered by a few, by those who long for and believe in it most passionately.

by coming together periodically, they were merely simulating women's ancient ways. Women in the archaic world of the goddess lived the whole of their lives together, every aspect, every day. It is not enough for us now as we set about creating a new world to come together now and then. It is time to be together in large numbers for the rest of our lives.

Let us imagine that May and Ruth—wanting to be together but at the same time loving each other so much that they can no longer bear to keep each other in bondage—had decided several years before to increase the potential for freedom and power by adding to their numbers. Let us imagine that they live now in a close community of twenty or thirty women, all of whom are in their power, part of which means that none of them is shackled internally or externally to the PRBS. Now let's replay the scene where May enters, exuberant and creatively passionate.

This time, instead of finding only Ruth when she bursts into the house, she finds a roomful of women she loves, a roomful of women who love and cherish themselves, who honor one another and do not take unethical charge of one another's feelings, who are free therefore to enjoy one another wholly. A roomful of women in their power.[3]

There are so many of them that among them there will probably be at least one and perhaps more who share May's sensual intensity at that moment and can honestly, in full arousal—with absolute integrity and therefore total creative power—choose to join with her and others in being or doing what none of them can be or do alone.

---

[3] By "women in their power," I mean women who are becoming whole, who have done much of the inner work of cleansing themselves of the emotional, spiritual, intellectual, and physical poisons of patriarchy.

These women do not misdirect such exquisite energy into closed-circuit excitation, or mistake its presence as a need for ownership. They know that arousal depends on freedom and that their own freedom depends upon everyone else's. There is, therefore, no jealousy among them. Ruth, who wants May's fullest joy, can now relax and enjoy experiencing May when she glows with the completion of her circle of power. Since she is no longer responsible for being all things that May needs, there is absolutely no pressure upon her to participate in anything she does not wholeheartedly want. Her true desires can now come clearly into focus, and she can act on them without compunction. Since no coercion is inherent in the situation, since participation is totally voluntary, arousal—creativity and power—is now possible.

But participation in *what?* What kinds of things might women do in our full creativity and power? Like many women trying to imagine such behavior, Tatnall and Balcerzak suggest that together we would work what is conventionally called magic—in a barren land, women dream a forest into being overnight, for instance.[4] This—and much more, much that I can't begin to envision—seems perfectly possible to me.

The women of May and Ruth's community have the freedom of choice necessary for arousal and power in all realms of their lives. If any one of these women is exhilarated by an idea, chances are very good that another of them is aching for a good talk. If someone fervently wishes

---

[4] 'Arousal,' from "The Woofer-Tweeter Theory of Sexual Stimulus-Response," unpublished paper read at the National Women's Studies Association conference, June 1990, pp. 2-3. Tatnall and Balcerzak's scenario of possible arousal behavior appears in Appendix 1B.

to pursue a particular project, someone else will probably feel creative and passionate about it, too.

Whatever any one of them needs, whatever any one of them wants to do, there is every possibility that among twenty or thirty women someone else will, totally without pressure, be in a matching spiritual, emotional, intellectual, and physical space. In this way, everyone gets her needs met and lives in her power without infringing on anyone else's freedom.

But if it happens that no one is in the same mood at the time that someone wants a companion, she will simply have to take responsibility for whatever feelings this leaves her with, and deal with them herself. Because this allows her control of her own life, she likes it this way. She has no wish to be at the mercy of anyone else's moods or desires.

Freedom is not only essential for abundance, it is the fecund *core* of it, its creator. Only when everyone is free to do exactly what she wants to do all the time is there plenty of everything for everybody—food and clothing and shelter and attention, companionship, and touching. Freedom is the foundation of women's world.

In non-coercive space such as Ruth and May's group share, love and power between and among women can only blossom. What it might become I think we can scarcely imagine. On this planet we haven't yet even approached our potential for intimacy and joy. Though I had known for a long time that it is women's privilege now to make this possible, I took it to mean that in time women would discover—among a multitude of other things—the rightful, natural place of sex in our lives, its authentic functions and ways.

I was mistaken.

PART VI

SWIMMING FOR THE SHORE OF THE NEW WORLD

Preface to Making Love, Not War

B y the time I came to the end of writing this book, I had despaired for a long weary time of learning how to love and touch outside the war zone. Then, during a weekend in the mountains, less than a week before the book was to go to press, I suddenly knew as if by magic how I could touch and be touched without sadomasochism, in power and peerness. I had had all the pieces—they were, in fact, already in this book—but I hadn't put them together. Then, miraculously, during countdown, they coalesced.[1]

Though obviously I can't now clarify and refine these impressions through experience before publication, I nevertheless want to put the gist of them, raw, in this book, bringing to a more formal conclusion my work of the last five years and opening the next era. In the book that will follow this one[2] I'm sure I will flesh out these ideas from my experience, deleting, adding, changing, and dressing them up with examples. But even though they are naked and vul-

---

[1] Jean Tait of Ojo Caliente made major contributions to the epiphanies of those days. But we were so aroused and in such another world that I have no idea which revelations were hers and which mine. The truth is that, truly sparking, we had most of them almost simultaneously.

[2] It will be about anarchy at Freedom in New Mexico.

nerable, I am offering my new-born thoughts here to bring this book, in its womanly way, full circle.

30

Making Love, Not War

Nearly four years since I began my rebellion against relation/sex/slave Ships, experience and my Wise Old Woman are telling me that sex as we know it is a patriarchal construct and *has* no rightful, natural place in our lives, no authentic function or ways. Synonymous with hierarchy/control, sex is engineered as part of the siege against our wholeness and power.

What I now call "touch," however, is another matter. Although I know people touch in a certain specific way in sex, I needed to use the word to designate another way, a kind of physical connection that truly makes love, not war. So touch, as I use it from here out, differentiates between powerful connections and sadomasochistic, no-power, sexual interactions.

Sex/excitation is exchange—with all the adversarialness of that mode. When I am having sex and stimulate my partner, she is required—if she wants to stay aboard Ship with me—to respond. Her excitation is part of my payoff. She also pays me back for my attention by giving me hers, by stimulating and exciting me. This is the contract, the deal, the excitation exchange.

As in any exchange economy, in the excitation economy neither person gets one hundred per cent of what they want, and often much less. Each must compromise and negotiate at least a little—must continue to pay attention even after her excitement has abated if her partner is still excited and requiring it, for instance. She knows that in order to get what she wants she has to make these—what she may consider—inconsequential sacrifices. But while she is acting as if she still wants to be sexual when she would really rather stop, she is not being honest with herself or her partner. She loses her Self in this way.

Since sex, quintessentially goal oriented, forces her into illusory future time, she also loses her power by staying the majority of the time out of the present moment, the only time that truly exists and therefore the only time she can have, feel, and exercise personal power. This is why linear time, a mensmachine invention—means-to-ends thinking and behavior—is a prerequisite for oppression, for sadomasochism, for sex.

Goals assume linear time—a future in which one presumably will reach them—even if that future is only seconds away. What we know as sex is always the means to some end other than itself, is always fundamentally cause-and-effectful. We have sex to feel loved, or to bind someone to us emotionally, or to get pleasure from their response, or to feel successful by being able to excite them to orgasm, or to dominate them, or to reinforce ownership, or to satisfy the Ship, or to have an orgasm, or for all of a combination of the above, or for a thousand other purposes. By its very nature sex is never in the moment. Always purposeful, always intended to elicit a response, always the means to some other end, always future bound, sex is never in the honesty or power of the moment. Sex without a goal is not sex. Because it takes us out of the moment of our power, sex is essentially about *non*-power; in fact, being sadomasochism, its purpose is to de-power us. Intimacy, deepest heart connection, requires that we be in our power. Taking us out of it, sex renders intimacy impossible.

In sex we are not present. All our behavior is geared toward causing whatever is happening at the moment to continue or to intensify in a non-existent future, or toward trying to get something *else* to happen then. Our enjoyment comes from evidences that we are being successful in reaching our goal—perhaps going into a delirious trance ourselves or feeling powerful because we are sending her into a delirious trance, and so on. Focused on that illusory future when we will both respond in a way deemed satisfactory to all concerned, including the officer on the bridge, in sex we are absent in any given moment. When we are totally out of the moment—our only realm of power—we are deeply involved in control, betraying and losing our Selves in stimulating and, amoeba-like, responding to stimulation, thoroughly sadomasochistic. Stimulus-response is not about connecting. It's about everything else *but*.

Since sadomasochism is control, it is ultimate power-lessness. Control and power are not merely different but antithetical, not able to exist in the same place at the same time. Sex can't be about power because it is based in linear time; sadomasochism/sex is impossible in the present moment.

Over the years I progressively mourned the dying of my hope that I could learn to love and touch women in some wonderfully satisfying but non-sexual way. I had recently begun trying to become reconciled to not touching at all except in the usual casual ways—quick hugs and kisses on the cheek, a little tentative stroking of an arm, a brief holding of a hand. But then my mountain weekend taught me that when I am in my power—present in the moment, free of the need to try to find self-worth through others—this kind of touching is possible. I also knew instantly how to go about it, as if it had always been my way with lovers. I realized, in fact, that I had been familiar with it all my life, but that I hadn't taken it seriously because it is more like friending and mothering behavior—both devalued activities in mensgame—than like highly valued romancing and relationShipping.

We all need to touch and to be touched. This is not a conditioned or false need but one we are born with. Babies who are not touched die, though all their other needs are met. Old people revivify, stay more alert, healthy, and active when they have an animal to touch and care for. Touch of the non-sexual variety keeps us well and buoyant.

I'm sure we are also born with the knowledge of how to satisfy our need to touch and be touched in truly connecting, non-exploitative ways. Unfortunately, this is programmed out of us at an early age, and so all too often touching doesn't satisfy us. We can only get what we need from touch that neither asks nor expects anything in return—unconditional touch.

In every sex survey I've seen, women admit that what they like best about sex is the affectionate, non-orgasm-directed touching and closeness. Even most of us who have ready and splendid orgasms prefer what precedes and follows the genital stuff. As for why I didn't notice sooner that this was women's most common theme and wonder at how it contradicted menstream propaganda—well, manunkind's brainwashing machine has been very thorough.

Touching a woman unconditionally, I am not seeking to satisfy some personal need by getting her to feel a certain way—orgasmic, impressed, in love with me—or to respond: Squeal in delight, express gratitude, ooh and aah or murmur "That feels so good"—responses that in their turn are designed to set up echoing responses in me: Pleasure that she likes it so much, for instance, or that I'm such a good lover.

Instead, touching her because I am filled with tenderness for her, wanting to let my body participate in the blessing of that, to give myself fully to the energy of love in my hands and arms, in my whole body, I communicate and commune with her. When I touch her for the joy that touch gives me at that very moment—wanting nothing more from it—then my touching is not sadomasochism/stimulus-response. I am not stimulating her, not trying to control her feelings or behavior. My touches are exactly what they seem. Honest, integrated, and totally in harmony with arousal and power, they can connect my heart with hers.

Like the woman who prepares food simply for the enjoyment of the act in the moment—not as means to some other end—I know now that when I touch for no ulterior reasons, when I refuse the linear-time lie, my touching is not a stimulus; it requires—it *desires*—no response. It is not in the reciprocal, exchange, adversarial, war paradigm at all, but is instead simply a gift, part of women's universal and beautiful non-exchange economy of abundance.

Because the skin is one large, very marvelous sensory organ that loves and needs touch—that is *for* touch—when I touch this woman she will probably enjoy it too, just as others will enjoy eating the cook's food. And this is fine. But it is not for this that I touch her. Touching becomes exploitation—sadomasochism, sex—when I used it as exchange, expecting, or desiring, or demanding something in return, some payment. Touch is meant to be loved for itself alone, not as a means to some end. When I think of the feeling behind this unconditional touching, an image comes to my mind of me kneeling beside my sleeping child. Overwhelmed with love, I stroke her face, feeling the beloved cheek with its warm baby down, the delicate bones of her skull as I smooth her hair back from her damp forehead, through my fingers reminding my entire body and all my senses and emotions how dear she is to me. Communing with my Self, experiencing love fully in the moment, I neither want nor expect anything from her or ask more from the experience. It is enough just as it is.

Jan Smiley told this story in my workshop at the Michigan Womyn's Music Festival in 1989: "I was sitting on the porch and the neighbor's cat came over. I was so glad to see her, and she was so glad to see me—we had a wonderful moment. I had the vision that I could be like this with other women. I'd just have to go against everything I've been taught."

What she's been taught, as we all have, is not just to make something of it, but to make something *else* of it, to change it into something other than itself. But her experience with the cat on the porch recalled her to herself, reminding her that that moment—being all there was anyway—was sufficient. She didn't need to prolong the cat's visit, or intensify the gladness of it, or get the cat to purr louder or rub against her knee harder or promise to come back again tomorrow for more. Everything was completely satisfactory just as it was.

But how does the act of comforting fit into this? When we touch someone to comfort them, we seem to be using touch for a purpose other than itself. We may not be expecting a response, but we *are* expecting an outcome. Having a goal—helping her feel better—aren't we out of the moment and our power?

It seems to me that comforting often *is* sadomasochistic, with the comforter in stimulator/sadist position, and the comfortee in masochist/responsive. One-up, the comforter is thinking perhaps that she has the capacity to make the comfortee feel better, which she uses to elevate herself at the comfortee's expense. She could also easily feel superior because she doesn't have the comfortee's troubles. If the comfortor is one-up, the comfortee has no other place to be but one-down.

But I want to think that stimulus-response/sadomasochism is not inherent in comforting, that perhaps it merely partakes of the general habit of oppression. Because touch comforts me, I want to be sure that when I am comforted or when I comfort someone with physical closeness I am not participating in sadomasochism. The following "comforting" story gives me food for thought.

An old Hopi woman a year before her death at 101 or thereabouts (she herself couldn't remember), befriended Jean Tait and taught her. On one occasion, the old woman took her along when she went to visit a woman of her tribe whose daughter had just been killed in a motorcycle accident. They found the woman sobbing in great retching, wrenching spasms, spasms so deep and shattering that they were seriously alarming her friends. Opening her blouse, Jean's old woman friend drew the bereaved mother's head to her breast and put the nipple in her mouth. Then she sat holding and rocking her while she nursed. Soon the terrible convulsions quieted. The woman continued to suck, crying but not dying—comforted.

When her friend took out her breast and gave the woman her nipple, Jean's first embarrassed thought was, "But this is sex!" That impression, however, soon gave way to wonderment at women's wisdom and sadness at the extent of patriarchy's warping of our true perceptions.

Though men have sexualized our breasts and other parts—buttocks, thighs, vulvas—we are not sexual beings by nature. My desire is to arrive at the place in my feelings and perceptions where no part of a woman's beautiful body can throw me back into my ugly conditioned excitation routine. I want to experience the freedom and power in looking at and touching another woman's breasts without a voice in my crying, "Oh oh! Now you're being sexual!" and without then going into my post-hypnotic sex dance. I want to know women as we truly are without men's spurious sexual projections upon us.

Though I haven't time to watch myself try this out before the book is printed, I can learn some things from looking back at my forays into sex, and imagining myself there again.

When a lover touches my vulva, I can't relax and enjoy the simple pleasure of it because, well trained as I am in stimulus-response, I knew what is required of me. I have a duty to perform: To make something *else* of it, to turn it into sex. So I deliberately begin to conjure up the feeling of excitation.

(At this point, many women have to take themselves right out of the situation and fantasize in order to obtain the required feeling and make the expected response. This is such a laborious, forced, and unnatural act, however, that

306

many give up trying for the feeling and make the response without it—the infamous "faking it.")

As I think about it, I realize that my excitement comes from within myself, not from her; it is my version of salivating when the bell rings. No matter how skillful and loving she is, she does not excite me. I make a choice to generate the excitation, and then I get to work and do it like the good puppet I am.

As I examine my experience I remember that I often lie in bed, just before sleep or while reading or talking, with my hand touching or lying over my vulva. I am not excited, I am not thinking of sex, I am not preparing to masturbate. I simply enjoy the feeling of touch there. Someday I am certain that I will understand how the touch-adoring vulva, kissing, and the rippling orgasm fit into freedom, intimacy, and power—if indeed they do. Obviously, with my epiphany about touch in general, my revelations to myself have just begun.

Though sadomasochism persists in some other aspects of my life, it is weakening in them all. The joy is that in the most difficult one—touching and being touched physically by others—I am no longer afraid of my old enemy. The escape route is clear and straight before me, and I know that I will soon be safely and permanently in no-man's land—home.

Part of my escape will be to dare to risk touching and being touched, dare to believe that I can do it without obligation, without the necessity of exciting someone else or becoming excited myself, and with none of the programmed false desire that constitutes the *habit* of response. Though to me this will be ecstasy, no matter what parts of the body I touch it won't be sex or even sexual. Touching that is not means to some end other than itself is not sex.

I am going to ask for this kind of touch directly from the very few women I know who, because they understand and feel this way too, can therefore do it, and who I know will participate only if they genuinely want to. When they touch me, I am going to practice experiencing the freely-given tenderness or comfort in it, refusing to trick myself into excitation.

I anticipate that touching in this way will allow me to *be with* other women in my true feelings and theirs at the moment, that through it I can know them. For a long time I have wanted to be as attuned to women—including their bodies—as if they were all longtime shipmates but without the sadism/co-dependency and sex. I believe that without all that cockamamie between us, I can discover intimacy.

I am inexpressibly relieved to know that there are other women like me, women who also won't need, or want, or finally even be able to stimulate or to respond; that though mensmachine's bell will keep ringing, we not only won't salivate, we won't even hear it. Phallocracy is in its death throes in our souls, and on that unforgettable day when we discover that we are peers, we will know it is dead.

Sitting here on Monday, thinking about the amazing cataract of understanding that rushed into me over the preceding weekend, nearly drowning me in the pleasure of arousal, I am flooded with relief, with waves of the most unaccustomed, sweetest freedom.

My knowledge during that mountain weekend that I was capable of this—without having to try it out, without having to touch anyone—kept me the entire time in a state of incalculable bliss. And I not only knew that I was capable of it but that I was no longer capable of anything else. I lived for those three days in women's free world. If I can be whole and free for three days, I can live the rest of my days in that joy and love and freedom, the world that, despite everything, I have believed in and longed for every moment of my life.

When we have escaped forever from the bondage of father Linear Time, his means-to-ends oppression, his cause-and-effect scam, when we always find touch itself totally satisfying at its very moment of happening, just as it is, without its having to *do* anything to or for us, when our touches have no other or future intent—are always in the no-sex mode—we will have discovered unimaginable power. It is the power in *this*—not in women's sexuality, as I have hitherto supposed—that men fear.

Like many of my feminist sisters, I have believed that the churches' hatred of the body and of sex, their instructing women to be sexual only for pro- not re-creation, their teaching both men and women that celibacy is the most godlike, holy way, sprang from their fear of women's truly formidable sexual power. It is true that men are afraid of our generativity, but I don't think they understand it well enough to concoct such a plot. Because they are sexual—not generative—beings, they perceive in sexual ways, in excitation, stimulus-response ways. In this mode, they thoroughly misunderstand women, equating our power and creativity with what they know of their own sexuality.

It is also true that, needing women's energy for survival, they hate and fear Lesbianism that withholds it from them. But if they understood, there would really be no reason for them to fear women's sexuality. They only need to look around them to see that even in communities that have large Lesbian populations and where women are most likely to be having frequent and passionate sex with one another, the status quo remains unchanged. If women's being sexual with women was the powder keg we thought it was, patriarchy would long ago have been blown right out of the Milky Way. But since women have been sexual with women as long as patriarchy has been around and the status quo has not been affected to any degree, it is clear that women's having sex with one another does not change anything. The reason for this is that sex de-powers us, that it is quintessentially *no-power*. What men are really afraid of in us is the power of arousal, but because they do not experience it, they don't perceive the incredibly important difference between it and excitation.

I think, therefore, that menstream religions that hold up celibacy as best, purest, and holiest, are misconstruing archaic women's non-sexual and therefore extremely powerful modes of being. I think men projected upon women their own self view. They saw what women *didn't* do, but they couldn't see what they *did* do. They understood and could therefore see sex but they couldn't understand and so couldn't see intimacy and power. Eastern and Western religions, including the "New Age" church—all are efforts to usurp by imitation women's creative power. But because our ways are alien and incomprehensible to men, the philosophies that have arisen from their imitation have always been blasted and ruinated echoes of women's truth.

Though phallocracy's sex doctrines now have nothing more to do with me, it took me a long time to find my way out of their swamp. The men who have controlled the world now for about five millennia used many ploys to keep me enmired. Besides confusing excitation (control) and arousal (power), one of their most cunning was to impose their shattered psyches upon me, encouraging me to forfeit my integrity—and hence my power—by thinking of myself in pieces: My intellect, my body, my spirit, my emotions, my feminine and masculine sides, my child or adult within, my sexuality. They taught me to disconnect each part, give it a discrete label, and store it separately in a box out of which I took it at "appropriate" times: Now I am thinking, now I am "in my body," now I am having emotions, now I am being spiritual, now my child is speaking, now I am being sexual. Sometimes I'd take more than one part at a time, have thoughts and feelings at the same time, for instance. Still, even doing parallel play, my pieces remained separate—at least I thought I knew which was thinking and which was feeling. In my mind they didn't become indistinguishable.

But as I picked through the pieces of my smashed Self, I didn't notice that, like an earthen pot that has been dashed to the ground and broken into thousands of pieces—many small as dust—I had been able to rescue only a few of the larger bits out of which to reconstruct myself. So when I tried, I couldn't put together a whole person: Most of *me* was missing. In other words, the parts of me that patriarchy urged me to notice and name didn't add up to a complete psyche.

That the pieces were named arbitrarily added to the confusion. How could I know, for instance, whether or not the word "body" in menstream culture described anything real to me? I began to suspect that what I experienced as "body," was infinitely different, infinitely more, infinitely other than the analytical male mind in my head could fathom.

When I began to explore this I realized that body is not a separate entity, that, in order to divide and conquer me, the masters had broken the fragment they then labeled "body" off from my Self. But this didn't mean that it ever fulfilled some separate function, that it was ever only a "part" of the whole.

It *was* the whole. Whole means no parts. Serving no function but being themselves, wholes cannot be labeled according to function. They simply and profoundly *are*, and are all, all at once, not reducible or separable over space or time. Indivisible, like rainbows. I realized along the way that because whole means and is "holy,"[1] I was not a composite of manunkind's phoney constructs, that none of them had any place in me. Separately or together they did not describe anything real about me. I am inestimably more and other than all of them put together.

So to be whole, to have integrity, ceased to mean to me any longer to unify all the spurious "parts" of myself. It came instead to mean to cease to think of my Self as composed of parts—or separate aspects—at all. It meant to recognize that none of what I perceive as parts really exist, that as purest illusion they serve only to confuse and scatter me.

The coercion that kills feeling and intimacy, for instance, is not just the coercion to *do* certain acts for whatever reason—such as sleep together because that is what lovers do—but perhaps even more the coercion to *be* a certain way. In this case, to be un-whole, to be boxed up in various small erroneous categories, erogenous zones, neighborhoods.

Sex is what the conquerors labeled one of the shards of my fractured Self. It has no meaning except as a role in patriarchy's analytical strategy to alienate me from my Self so—or so they hoped—that I can never experience me, never *be* her, never be free. Sex is central to menstream myth.

---

[1] Insight from Elizabeth Grindon at Mama Bears Bookstore in Oakland, California, February 2, 1990.

I am perfectly persuaded that women in archaic, pre-patriarchal times would not have been able to imagine sadomasochistic touch, or to conceptualize entities as fractured off as "sex," or "sexual energy," or "eroticism," or "sensuality." I am as certain as if advised by my own clear memory that there was no concept of "sexual," no delineations "friend" or "lover," and therefore no line thinkable or possible between friendship and loverhood. No sex, no doing "it" because there was no "it" to do.

This means that living in present time, and trusting and following their desires—to eat when hungry, caress when heart-full, sleep when tired—every act was simple, beautiful, true, and complete in itself.

I am reconstructing my wholeness, not out of phallically-broken fragments of myself, but by tossing out all the pieces altogether. I know I can do it because I have done it somewhat already. I have, for example, erased from my Self both the feelings attending the constructs "monogamy" and "non-monogamy" and their philosophical core. They mean nothing, are nothing, anymore. I know the day is coming when the word "sex" will also be meaningless to me, just so much blah, blah, blah.

I live now with several women in the mountains of New Mexico. We have only recently come together and are still in the first stages of learning. At our home in Freedom, though we are not going to live together in the same space, we plan eventually to build a common bathhouse—with hot tub, sweat house, cold plunge, showers, and, perhaps, swimming pool. Seeing one another naked every day, being together without clothing, massaging, stroking, holding one another when we haven't the false barrier of cloth between us, we will get lots of practice in non-sexual, non-stimulus-response, touching. In my vision of us, we will find out how to go beyond sex, where no touch is sexual or can be interpreted as sexual because we are in the moment, in our power, not using touching as a means to some other end. Like our wild archaic sisters, we will have no inclination to do "it" because there will be no "it" to do. Sex as a concept will become extinct among those of us who choose this way.

We will have equally ample opportunity in all other activities to connect in power and intimacy. My hope is that as many of us as wish will learn to live in perpetual arousal. I want heaven on earth, and to me that means living at last in the beauty and strength of women's ways.

I can't say how this will look or what it means we will be doing. But of course we will have stopped worrying about what to do, how to act with one another. We will do what we are. As our whole Selves, we will always simply *be.*

I also know that many women will have no desire to be part of this experiment, however it develops, that it is not the enterprise for which they feel they were born. I have great respect for women's way of listening to and following our hearts. I trust this mode completely, as I do the choices that come out of it.

But I was born for this, I and innumerable others. This shift in how I perceive my Self and my potential is what I most deeply desire. I know that in order for me to open up space in my thought and feeling for more whole, creative, and intimate ways of connecting with others, I have to clear my mind of preconceptions and assumptions that limit what is possible. I believe that if I can do this, if I can leap out of my mind bindings, I can discover how to get every one of my needs and wants met, and met abundantly and happily, as "sex"—designed to deprive and hurt—could never meet them.

I believe I can have all the touching, all the closeness, all the genuine intimacy I can desire and bear—and that I will continually desire and bear more until I discover that there is no end to my capacity to feel and to love. Before my recent momentous weekend, I was beginning to take a couple of small steps on this journey to my Self. For one, I began to study arousal, determined to learn from it what it had to teach. I decided that when I felt aroused, instead of focusing this feeling and energy upon some external person—thinking of a lover's warm, insistent lovemaking mouth, for instance, her eager breasts, the weight and movement of her body—or "grounding" it by touching myself (instead, that is, of interpreting it as a need to *do* something, in this case to be sexual and externalize my power as I have been trained to do), I would instead hold it close.

Deliberately and consciously keeping the energy of arousal inside myself, I would watch it, explore it, become acquainted and comfortable with it, and revel in *being* in my power without having to *do* something—anything, even creating forests—with it. I would let it teach me what it is, and what that means about me. I would let it lead me.

What it has thus far taught me is that believing that arousal has some purpose other than itself, that it is a means to some other end—creating communities, moving mountains, whatever—is stimulus/response, conditioned thinking. The stimulus (bell) is the wonderful feeling of creative power, the response (salivation) is the impulse to do something with it, to *use it actively* in some way.

Unlike Tatnall and Balcerzak, I believe that if we use arousal as the means to some end other than itself, we will be right back in linearity and hierarchy. Since there is truly no linear time in our universe and the means really *are* the ends, to center our attention on *being* instead of on doing keeps us in harmony with universal truth, connects us with our own and with universal power.

Another step I was beginning to take before the illumination of this last weekend was that whenever I was sexual—and even before the weekend the dance of excitation troubled me more and more—I vowed to be *conscious*, more conscious than ever before. I was determined to wake out of relationShip/sex coma enough to observe—at very least—why I *thought* I was choosing that behavior, at that time, with that person. I would watch myself in excitation just as in arousal, being aware of my honest feelings, my real reactions, not what I wished I were feeling, or what would be easier, more comfortable, more acceptable reactions. "Making love" or "having sex," I promised to study myself, like a rat, in patriarchy's most complex, potentially most illuminating, laboratory.

But even though I was less and less lured by excitation, I knew that I was still more able to deceive myself with and about sex than any other of phallocracy's strategies. So when I reminded myself—as I often did then—that if I chose to be sexual, I had to remain conscious, I told myself fiercely that I *meant* conscious: Conscious a hundred times over.

Since I am now able to love outside the war zone, I won't have to watch myself in excitation again. Having felt full arousal for long periods—the scope and freedom and power of my creative Self—I am no longer interested in my sexual experiment, or in sex at all. Why would any self-loving woman deliberately choose powerlessness and captivity?

Sometimes I try to imagine us when we have left mensgame far behind, when our metaphysical journey has brought us to the place where our hearts and heads are completely free of it. I think of us swimming gracefully and at ease in the sea of ambiguity and paradox between the old and new worlds; it is our element and matches our natural rhythm, just as chaos—every possibility present at once, total creativity—is our native land. I see that we wear no labels nor are interested in labeling others, any more than we have a concept of political correctness or of one path as the only true way. Best of all, I know that we are wild and free, capable of unspeakable joy, and able not only to bear but to bask in it for long, long periods of time—whole lifetimes.

It is possible that at first this unfamiliar terrain felt empty, flat, and unexciting to us. After all, stimulus/response (sadomasochism)—as presently constituting sex and all other human interaction—was absent, forcing us to realize that whereas we once believed that we were dependent upon others to excite us, in fact, our excitement had always been self-induced, that no one else *could have* excited us since it is our nature to be totally creative of every feeling we ever have regardless of where we perceive it as coming from.

In addition, ready-made, authorized feelings were not available here as they were in men's world; only embryonic seemingly-illicit, scary ones. As graduates of manunkind's Falsification of Feelings School, we were accustomed to being told all the time how to feel about everything. So because the parameters of feeling and thought were not carefully set and guarded by external authorities here, we may at first have had difficulty identifying how we felt.

Perhaps sometimes we may even have feared that we weren't feeling anything, the feelings were so novel. So we paid very close attention to ourselves, believing that something new was being born within us, so unfamiliar that it could hardly be felt yet. We trusted that freedom was teeming with feeling, rich, deep, and profoundly satisfying. And though we are still occasionally frustrated and frightened by the overwhelming ambiguity inherent in anarchy, we refuse to act on the worn-out lie that rules make us safe. Instead, we keep ourselves in the thorny, lawless way, having to make choices every minute on the basis of how we genuinely feel rather than relying on external structures and orders. We know that safety, as lauded by men, is spurious anyway. Among ourselves we say, "My freedom is your only safety; your freedom, mine."

On the other hand, we may not have suffered any such initial uncertainties. Women's world may have felt, as it did to me, utterly familiar and dear. Home, at last.

In being true to our Selves, in living in greater wholeness/holiness in these ways, I think we are receiving invaluable assistance from our "unconscious" minds. Hitherto we have accepted the "unconscious" as one of the parts—and in this case one of the off-limit parts—of our nature as humans. A sign that we are regaining our integrity and becoming whole again is that we are recovering conscious access to it, to that enormous underground reservoir of memory, knowledge, wisdom, and emotion of our deep, hidden selves.

What is happening in my own life, and must therefore be happening in others, is that my "unconscious" is beginning to connect strongly with my conscious. I am daily gaining greater and faster access to my inner Wise Woman.

A couple of years ago in the course of delivering a speech, I said, "What I want more than anything is to be able to hear my Wise Old Woman's voice clearly all the time." I paused, uncomfortable with that declaration. "No," I corrected myself after a moment's thought, "that's not what I want. I want to *be* her."

The theory of the "unconscious"—or "subconscious" as it was called in the '50's—has intrigued me since I first studied it in high school. (Freud positively *loomed* over American society in my youth.) It was the only explanation out there for why I was such a mystery to myself, why my motives were often transparent to others while opaque to me, why I was the hardest person in my coterie for me to get to know.

Though it was the only answer offered, it always made me feel helpless, unknowable to myself, out of my own direct governance, dangerous to myself and others, afraid and insecure. I believed it, as I believed a good deal of nonsense in those days, but I didn't like it.

Feminism rendered the concept of the unconscious even less agreeable to me. How could I deprogram and recreate myself if I was working so in the dark, not knowing what was really down there in my spooky depths. I had been warned that bugbears would leap out and grab me if I kept poking around in there—and occasionally they did.

But over the years, it made less and less sense to me to believe that my "natural" state was to be cut off from nine-tenths of my knowledge, to have conscious access only to the merest tip of the iceberg of myself. Finally it made so little sense that I asked myself the inevitable feminist question: What's in it for the men who control the world to make me believe that the "unconscious" is a given of human nature?

That was easy to answer. If I believed that I could have instant access to all my innumerable and mighty and hitherto hidden resources all the time, chances are that I *could*. And if I did, I would be impossible to deceive and enslave. Remembering everything—including all the post-hypnotic suggestions that have been put to me, knowing everything about who and why I am, seeing everything clearly and without projection, I would be prodigiously powerful. I believe, therefore, that the "unconscious" is another mensmachine construct and ploy, but one that is weakening under the assault of our individual awakenings. I expect in my lifetime to *be* my Wise Old Woman, to be fully reunited: Seeing with her/my real eyes, hearing with my long-lost ears, feeling with my long-estranged heart, speaking with her/my tongue, functioning with all my being—merged with her, one complete whole woman. No more "off-limits" signs, no more armed guardians of the gate sitting on my shoulders, their duty to cut me off at the neck from the rest of me, allowing only a carefully censored short message to pass between my inner Wise Woman and me now and then, preventing me from joining her, from becoming intact, virgin (belonging to myself alone)—my Self.

Initially, they may have split our psyches in two (and more) by violence. We know now that multiple personalities often arise out of violence. Perhaps those of us who developed only two personalities—our conscious and our *un*conscious—(and is there anyone with just two, I wonder? How many separate entities live in the average "unconscious"?) were simply so focused on the ever-present reality and potential of pain, so intent on hearing the voices of our torturers in order to survive by outguessing, manipulating, agreeing with, and placating them, that we neglected our own voice. Perhaps over time we stopped hearing it, then lost the capacity to hear it, and finally forgot we had ever heard it, forgot that we had ever had a complete Self, had ever been whole. People who are nine-tenths "unconscious" are easy to rule.

I am also being helped on my journey Selfward by a shift in my understanding of "organizing," having arrived at the understanding that this concept is inherently hierarchical and old-minded in every way. Looking back on my vision of us in our pre-patriarchal village, I recognize how strewn it is with artifacts of the current paradigm.

Sex is there, for instance, despite its camouflaging costume, because stimulus/response is there. Not just genital stimulus/response or excitation, but the assumption—up in the night sky—that we must *do* something with arousal, when the truth is that when we are in our power we will never need to worry or even to think about what to do. The most loving, generous, kind, powerful, pleasurable, delightful, useful, inspiring acts possible will simply flow from us.

Though understood rather than stated, organization is very present, also, and likely a dozen other phallacies.

Re-visioning that scenario, I see that we do not meet together "regularly," having decided where and when. We do not come together with a certain purpose. How it happens, more likely, is that I have a desire to go to the forest meadow and so I go, having no expectations or even hopes that anyone else will be there, or that anything will happen—these are irrelevant. I want simply to be there, and I act upon that desire. If others are there because they too feel like being there, that's fine. And if out of our combined arousal some activity arises, that's fine, too. But nothing is planned, ever. I have always thought that a planned ritual was a contradiction in terms.

Mary Ann Beall tells this story. One morning during the anti-war fervor of the Vietnam days, Mary Ann, who lives just outside Washington, D.C., felt a desire to go to the White House. So she caught the bus to the city. Though there were many people on the bus, her attention was drawn to one who she somehow seemed to know was also on his way to the White House. Sure enough, they got off at the same stop and headed in the same direction.

When they arrived, both bought tickets for the tour. Mary Ann noticed several other people on the tour with whom she felt an immediate and deep affinity. At the end of the tour, without knowing or having spoken to one another, those individuals—all of whom turned out to be Quakers—gathered on the lawn in prayer for peace and refused to move. They were arrested and served time in jail together.

What impresses me about this story is not the resistance or the fact that they suffered imprisonment for their beliefs. What impresses me is the absence of overt, hierarchical organization. I am awed that they listened to their own hearts, forming some psychic bond with one another, and that the "action" arose spontaneously, naturally, from their values and passion, from who they were.

Mensmachine has taken from us our knowledge that everything flows unobstructed and perfect when we are being whole and in our power. We have forgotten that actions arise organically out of who we are, and believe mistakenly that we must *make* them happen, we must organize people to do things. I don't think that anything important ever came from the control we call organization and that it has done incalculable harm. I, for one, am eager to discover how things might come together in all areas of life without it. I long to live in such power, in such a non-coercive, non-linear, women's world.

I long to live every moment in full knowledge that I am god.

When my daughter, Kari, was in her early teens, she delighted in trying to shock me, in seeing if she could get a rise out of her liberal but still Mormon mother. One of her favorite wiles was to say, "Mom, I'm god!"

Knowing full well what she was up to, I would act nonchalant and retort, "Well, then I guess you won't need your allowance this week, right?" But the truth was that such blasphemy *did* disconcert me.

Then feminism came along with the totally sensible notion that the goddess lived within every woman, that every woman was the goddess. Though this sounded very different to me from "I'm god!" I soon realized that of course it was exactly the same. Believing it, I believed, like my teen-aged daughter had purported to believe, that I *was* god.

So one day I called her and with immense satisfaction announced, "Kari, I'm god!" Though a little taken aback—was I mocking her?—she rallied gamely, "Right on, Sonia. Go for it!" So I went for it, my proclamation sweeping me right back into the bible of my youth which stated unequivocally, "God is love." Well, I thought, that's true, I am love. Love is not an act, not something I *do*. It's what I most fundamentally *am*. And not just love, but *unconditional* love. And not just unconditional love, but power and creativity and joy. These are not characteristics of me, but my essence.

Suddenly, the common menstream belief that this essence of me, this spirit, lived inside my body, felt suffocating. Examining it closer, I spied what seemed to be yet another patriarchal reversal. It made sense that phallocracy would teach that the spirit—this love that we are—is imprisoned within the body because of how small and powerless this makes us feel, how not like deity at all, how inaccessible to one another. Therefore, closer to the truth might be the concept that *the body lives inside and is permeated by the spirit,* since this leaves the spirit—us as love—totally free to expand to fill all space, to be in each others' presence all the time, to be Wild, to be divinely, perfectly powerful.

To live in consciousness of my Self as total, ever-expanding, all-inclusive love—this is what is possible for me and for us all in women's world. This, not some woman's body, is what I most unceasingly, passionately lust for.

No one knows how the world will look when those of us who want to have left behind "relation Ships," "sex," the "unconscious mind," "organization" and the hundreds of others of patriarchy's chains, when we are once again Wild Women. But what is absolutely clear to me is that for thousands of years we have been homesick for our Selves, hungry for the lost magic of existence. And that deep within us through all those frightening and lonely centuries we have guarded a treasure, a precious secret knowledge: Someday women, reuniting love and freedom, would transfigure the world.

I am one of those women, hoping with all my heart that you are, too. Because this is that day. Our work, our prodigious, dazzling work of life and love, has begun.

APPENDIX IA

Some Paired Woofer/Tweeter Behaviors Identified in the unpublished paper, "The Woofer-Tweeter Theory of Sexual Response: A Challenge to Power in the Patriarchy" by Sally Tatnall and Phyllis Balcerzak, July 1988.

The first of the pair they consider to be woofer/stimulus or dominant behavior, and the second they consider tweeter/responsive or submissive behavior.

1. Likes being on top: prefers the bottom
2. Makes the actual first overtly sexual move: sets the stage completely for the other's sexual move
3. Likes watching partner: enjoys being watched
4. Has orgasm last: has orgasm first
5. Is less self revealing: is more readily self revealing
6. Plays baseball: watches partner play baseball (on rare occasions will play)
7. Likes to be "doing": likes to "talk about it" more
8. In an argument, will withdraw: in an argument will scream, rant and rave
9. In game of "chase me" is the pursuer: is running away, teasing to be chased

10. When seeing someone they are interested in, will stare and observe: aware of being stared at, will talk to someone, laugh, throw head back, have jolly good time pretending no awareness of stare
11. Will take active role in mechanical physical things: will stand by and admire, occasionally will be taught
12. Will rub back of lover's hair in a caress: will smile sweetly in return
13. During sex, excitation and orgasm will be more quiet and still: during sex will move more, make noise, etc., lots of response
14. When first getting to know potential lover, will ask for date directly: when first getting to know, will find ways to connect—send book they might like or information of interest
15. Likes sex in the evening or when sense of personal power is lower: likes sex in the morning or when personal power seems higher
16. In an argument will prefer to be left alone: in argument will nag other to express themselves
17. When feeling troubled, will keep to self and solve problem: when troubled will seek help from best friend
18. Will engage with others of their kind around how to do X: will engage with others of their kind on how to be, how to express, and interpersonal relationships
19. Is more stimulated or aroused by partner's responses: is stimulated or aroused by what partner is actually doing to her
20. Always has lots of facts, details, and figures: always refers to experiences, feelings, and relating

21. Likes being admired for what they do: likes being admired for who they are
22. When admired for what they do are embarrassed and deny it: when admired for who they are don't believe it
23. Offers security: takes care of the ego
24. Runs to the store: organizes kitchen supplies
25. Leans back: leans forward

APPENDIX IB

'Arousal,' from "The Woofer-Tweeter Theory of Sexual Stimulus-Response" by Sally Tatnall and Phyllis Balcerzak, 1990, pp. 2-3.

She had been dreaming, or thought she had been dreaming, because there was nothing like it that she knew of—and yet it was so very clear. Like the crystals in the great cave of knowing. She could see this dream image/creation with pointed detail and color. And this was not the first time. It had first come to her when she was planting with the other women.

They had been chanting as they walked along the rows of overturned earth, spreading the seeds that would grow to nurture the community. Looking off in the distance, she saw a line of trees—tall, dark, leafy, branching out and giving shade. It was odd because she knew there were no trees there, though there was great desire for them. They had journeyed to barren country.

But why was she seeing them now? Was it time to bring trees to this land? The idea pleased her. Perhaps this was something they could focus the power on. She got up, feeling the energy of the idea moving through her. No question, no criticism, only a heightened sense of possibility, an experience of arousal.

She knew she was with her creative intention, her true desire, and she began to walk toward the cave. As she walked, she saw other women moving quietly yet purposefully toward this ancient ritual space of knowing.

Once the women had gathered, they began the chant that focused their vision. As the focus grew and became clearer, she could see an image of trees hovering just in front of her. Her sense of arousal increased as she realized they had all chosen a common thought and were applying their collective power.

The chanting grew to support the vision. She knew it was possible and that the forest was real. Soon the chant softened and in the same way they had gathered, they left the great cave of knowing, singing while they walked back to their sleeping areas.

The next morning she went outside to see, and there, growing out of this barren ground, were trees of all kinds in many stages of youth and maturity. She smiled and stood near a beautiful oak, experiencing their connection and honoring the sacred power of women.

APPENDIX IC

'The Orgasm,' or How Wildness Was Lost, from "The Woofer-Tweeter Theory of Sexual Stimulus Response" by Sally Tatnall and Phyllis Balcerzak, 1990, pp. 4-5.

She had been carefully taught by her grandmother how to ground her arousal when there was no focus for her creative desire. She had been shown the ritual movement with the earth as she released the energy and it flowed back to the mother. She knew how dangerous it could be for her aroused energy to go undirected and unfocused. Once she had fallen from a great boulder in firefly field because she had forgotten the ritual and had felt so scattered.

One year as the women gathered, there were strangers present. These strangers watched the women dance, chant, and focus their vision. They watched the power of creation and the returning of the energy to the earth. Frightened by the energy-focussing process, they learned the part that would end it, the part that returned the energy to the earth, the grounding part.

From then on, each time the women gathered, the strangers encouraged them to ground the energy they raised before they focussed on their vision. It wasn't long before the energy was grounded before the intention or vision had formed and the women began to lose sight of why they gathered at all.

Energy continued to rise inside them, but they learned from the strangers to fear it and sought to ground it so quickly that connection to the part of the process of creation and manifestation was lost finally to consciousness.

As soon as the power was linked to orgasm, the separation began, and soon the strangers were seen as the source of desire. Now, all that remains is the seed of power, the initial energy of arousal. When it begins to move deep inside, fear of power moves us to ground the energy.

APPENDIX II

Excerpts from *Anarchism and Other Essays*, by Emma Goldman, Dover Publications Inc: Mineola, NY, 1969.

Anarchism is the only philosophy which brings to man [sic throughout] the consciousness of himself; which maintains that God, the State, and society are non-existent, that their promises are null and void, since they can be fulfilled only through man's subordination. Anarchism is therefore the teacher of the unity of life; not merely in nature, but in man (p. 52).

Real wealth consists in things of utility and beauty, in things that help to create strong, beautiful bodies and surroundings inspiring to live in. But if man is doomed to wind cotton around a spool, or dig coal, or build roads for thirty years of his life, there can be no talk of wealth. What he gives to the world is only gray and hideous things, reflecting a dull and hideous existence,—too weak to live, too cowardly to die. Strange to say, there are people who extol this deadening method of centralized production as the proudest achievement of our age. They fail utterly to realize that if we are to continue in machine subserviency, our slavery is more complete than was our bondage to the King. They do not want to know that centralization is not only the death-knell of liberty, but also of health and beauty, of art and science, all these being impossible in a clock-like, mechanical atmosphere.

Anarchism cannot but repudiate such a method of production: Its goal is the freest possible expression of all the latent powers of the individual. Oscar Wilde defines a perfect personality as 'one who develops under perfect conditions, who is not wounded, maimed, or in danger.' A perfect personality, then, is only possible in a state of society where man is free to choose the mode of work, the conditions of work, and the freedom to work. One to whom the making of a table, the building of a house, or the tilling of the soil, is what the painting is to the artist and the discovery to the scientist,—the result of inspiration, of intense longing, and deep interest in work as a creative force.

Anarchism, however, also recognizes the right of the individual, or numbers of individuals, to arrange at all times for other forms of work, in harmony with their tastes and desires (pp. 55-56).

Indeed, the keynote of government is injustice. . . the annihilation of individual liberty. Government, organized authority, or the State, is necessary *only* to maintain or protect property and monopoly. It has proven efficient in that function only (pp. 57-588).

In destroying government and statutory laws, Anarchism proposes to rescue the self-respect and independence of the individual from all restraint and invasion by authority. Only in freedom can man grow to his full stature. Only in freedom will he learn to think and move, and give the very best in him. Only in freedom will he realize the true force of the social bonds which knit men together, and which are the true foundation of a normal social life.

But what about human nature? Can it be changed? And if not, will it endure under Anarchism? Poor human nature, what horrible crimes have been committed in thy name! Every fool, from king to policeman, from the flatheaded parson to the visionless dabbler in science, presumes to speak authoritatively of human nature. The greater the mental charlatan, the more definite his insistence on the wickedness and weaknesses of human nature. Yet, how can any one speak of it today, with every soul in a prison, with every heart fettered, wounded, and maimed?

John Burroughs has stated that experimental study of animals in captivity is absolutely useless. Their character, their habits, their appetites undergo a complete transformation when torn from their soil in field and forest. With human nature caged in a narrow space, whipped daily into submission, how can we speak of its potentialities?

Freedom, expansion, opportunity, and, above all, peace and repose, alone can teach us the real dominant factors of human nature and all its wonderful possibilities.

Anarchism, then, really stands for the liberation of the human mind from the dominion of religion; the liberation of the human body from the dominion of property; liberation from the shackles and restraint of government. Anarchism stands for a social order based on the free grouping of individuals for the purpose of producing real social wealth; an order that will guarantee to every human being free access to the earth and full enjoyment of the necessities of life, according to individual desires, tastes, and inclinations.

This is not a wild fancy or an aberration of the mind. . . (pp. 61-62).

INDEX

Index

Index

Index

Index

Index

soon caught up in 228
Sacrifice
  be willing to for me 91
  cannot save others 165
  denial of Self and life 163
  each partner must sacrifice 127
  faithlessness to Self 120
  someone's got to for the rest of us 272
  virulent form of control 165
Sadism
  consciously choosing and intensifying 213
  difficult to discern in myself 201
  effort had no effect on but kept me awake 209
  face up to my 191
  hard to spot 229
  heated sex direct to me from ovens of sadism 208
  in my bed 216
  inevitability of 201
  nearly inescapable 191
  tried to think my way out of the 186
Sadistic system
  thrill in of being "on top" 44
Sadomasochism
  a daily constant 190
  able to laugh about its presence was a relief 207
  conscious 188
  definition of 44
  information from women who consciously choose 187
  is patriarchy 44
  our present model of behavior 187
  we will have erased 314
  women dethroning patriarchy by eradicating 201
Scarcity

contrived of love, of touching 189
  panic caused by overcomes us 232
  patriarchal construct 115
Self
  boundaries of my 66
  fear of loss of 114
  had got to night sky by being true to Self 251
  not composed of parts 312
  travel deeper into unexplored territory of 288
Self-deception
  my capacity for still large 221
Self-denial
  nothing joyful can come from 130
Self-determination
  responsibilities of 43
  violating Susan's right to 46
Self-esteem
  need to rescue others to have 43
Self-government
  order inherent in 265
  restore by honoring desires 277
  vision of based on desire 272
Self-hatred
  propensity to project 102
  restimulates old feelings of 215
Self-love
  a basis of power 130
  increases my and power 255
Self-sacrifice
  life-time of 65
Selfish 44, 118, 131
Selftrue
  what would happen if we were 271
Sensuality

Index

About the Author

Dr. Johnson was excommunicated from the Mormon church in 1979 for uppityness, and she has been uppity ever since:

In 1981, she was presented with the *Playboy* First Amendment Award and refused the $5,000 prize; in 1982, she fasted for 37 days for passage of the ERA; in 1984, she ran for the presidency of the United States as the nominee of the Citizens Party, the Consumer Party, and the Peace and Freedom Party.

A nationally prominent speaker and author of three previous books, she is currently doing only what she wants to do in the mountains of New Mexico with other uppity women.

Inquiries about engaging Dr. Johnson for speeches and workshops should be directed to Wildfire Books, Star Route 1, Box 55, Estancia, NM, 87016 (505) 384-2500.

WILDFIRE BOOKS

—————————————— Book Titles ——————————————

☐ *The Ship That Sailed Into The Livingroom:*
Sex and Intimacy Reconsidered $12.95

☐ *Wildfire: Igniting the She/Volution,* 294 pages $10.95

☐ *Going Out of Our Minds: The Metaphysics*
of Liberation, 359 pages..............................$12.95

☐ *From Housewife to Heretic,* 416 pages $10.95

—————————————— Audio Cassettes ——————————————

☐ Living The Dream, 114 minutes........................$ 9.95

☐ Sonia Speaks: Going *Farther* Out of Our Minds,
90 minutes...$ 9.95

☐ Sonia Speaks: Telling the Truth, 60 minutes..............$ 9.95

☐ Sonia Speaks: From Housewife to Heretic, 80 minutes ......$ 9.95

—————————————— Video Cassettes ——————————————

☐ Living The Dream,
114 minutes..$19.95

☐ Sonia Speaks: Going *Farther* Out of Our Minds,
100 minutes..$19.95

ORDERING INSTRUCTIONS

Check off boxes to indicate selection. Order Amount: _____

Shipping and Handling: $2.00 per item: _____

Total enclosed: _____

Name _____

Address_____

City _____ State_____ Zip_____

Please forward your order to: Wildfire Books, Star Route 1, Box 55
Estancia, NM 87016, (505) 384-2500.
Call for credit card ordering.